CRAZY IN THE KITCHEN

BY THE SAME AUTHOR

Virginia Woolf's First Voyage: A Novel in the Making

Nathaniel Hawthorne (Feminist Reading Series)

Casting Off: A Novel

*Virginia Woolf: The Impact of Childhood
Sexual Abuse on Her Life and Work*

*Conceived with Malice: Literature as Revenge in the
Lives and Works of Virginia and Leonard Woolf, D. H. Lawrence,
Djuna Barnes, and Henry Miller*

Vertigo: A Memoir

Breathless: An Asthma Journal

*Writing as a Way of Healing: How Telling Our Stories
Transforms Our Lives*

Adultery: A Memoir

AS EDITOR

*Between Women: Biographers, Novelists, Critics, Teachers,
and Artists Write About Their Work on Women*
(coedited with Carol Ascher and Sara Ruddick)

The Letters of Vita Sackville-West to Virginia Woolf
(coedited with Mitchell A. Leaska)

A Green and Mortal Sound: Short Fiction by Irish Women Writers
(coedited with Kathleen Walsh D'Arcy and Catherine Hogan)

*The Milk of Almonds: Italian American Women Writers
on Food and Culture* (coedited with Edvige Giunta)

Melymbrosia: Virginia Woolf's First Novel

CRAZY IN THE KITCHEN

Food, Feuds, and Forgiveness in an Italian American Family

LOUISE DeSALVO

BLOOMSBURY

Published by Bloomsbury, New York and London
Distributed to the trade by Holtzbrinck Publishers

All papers used by Bloomsbury are natural, recyclable products
made from wood grown in sustainable, well-managed forests.
The manufacturing processes conform to the environmental
regulations of the country of origin.

Library of Congress Cataloging-in-Publication Data

DeSalvo, Louise A., 1942–
Crazy in the kitchen: food, feuds, and forgiveness in an Italian American family/Louise
DeSalvo.—1st U.S. ed.
p. cm.
ISBN 1-58234-298-9
1. DeSalvo, Louise A., 1942—Childhood and youth. 2. DeSalvo, Louise A., 1942—Family.
3. Italian Americans—New Jersey—Biography. 4. Italian Americans—New Jersey—Social life
and customs. 5. Italian American families—New Jersey. 6. Italian Americans—Ethnic identity.
7. Cookery, Italian—Social aspects. 8. Food—Social aspects. I. Title.

F145.I8D475 2004
974.9'00451'0092—dc22

2003015297

First U.S. Edition 2004

1 3 5 7 9 10 8 6 4 2

Typeset by Hewer Text Ltd, Edinburgh
Printed in the United States of America by
R.R. Donnelley & Sons, Harrisonburg

for Edi, for Ernie, for Craig, for my father,
and in memory of my grandparents

And might it not be . . . that we also have appointments to keep in the past, in what has gone before and is for the most part extinguished, and must go there in search of places and people who have some connection with us on the far side of time . . .?

W. G. Sebald, *Austerlitz*

CONTENTS

CONTENTS

PROLOGUE: WILD THINGS

There were wild things in my grandparents' stories about the Mezzogiorno, the South of Italy, the land that they came from so many years ago, always wild things. Wild jackasses that tossed you off their backs if you dared to mount them, that wouldn't let you ride them through the sun-scorched fields in the heat of day to get to the field where you had to work. Wild wolves that came into villages at night to carry babies away to eat them, which was one reason why it was necessary, always necessary, to close up a house at night, even in summertime, even here in America, even on the fourth floor of a tenement in Hoboken, New Jersey.

There were wild, raging seas that surrounded the land my grandparents came from, wild seas that drowned fishermen, that spun overloaded ferryboats around and around and then swamped them so that they sank to the bottom of the sea. There were rogue waves forty feet high that engulfed seaside villages, that left no trace of buildings or of people when the waters receded. Rainfalls so powerful they made the land slide away, down hillsides, or into the sea. Rainfalls so relentless in some years that they washed away all the good earth and made it impossible to grow anything to eat.

And even the earth was wild. There were earthquakes that came without warning, that opened deep gouges in the earth's crust, earthquakes that swallowed people, animals, houses, entire villages. Earthquakes that made buildings crack and crumble and come crashing down on families eating their suppers, praying together, tangled together on the floor in sleep. There were volcanoes that erupted, covering villages with lava, volcanoes spewing deadly gases that suffocated people as they were arguing, gathering food, working in the fields, sweeping steps, cleaning houses, cooking supper, baking bread.

There were wild sandy winds that came up from Africa that could rip the stubble off your face if you hadn't shaved in the morning, or, if you had, could leave your face as scratched and scarred as if you'd had a ferocious argument with a wild woman. There were bitterly cold winds that came down from the north in winter that could turn a person in a field into a frozen statue.

There was the sun in July and August, about which my grandfather always shook his head. The sun that baked the ground, that took every droplet of moisture from it, that raised blisters on your body, that made working in the fields in summer a purgatory, that turned people like my grandfather who worked the land as dark as the land they worked. And, my grandfather said, those who worked the fields in summer in the land where he came from would go straight to heaven no matter how many evils they had committed because, by doing this work, they had already atoned for their sins.

In my grandparents' stories, there were swarms of mosquitoes that could engulf you, give you a hundred mosquito bites, and malaria, which could kill you. Dangerous vipers that fell out of trees and wound themselves around your neck and choked you to death. Vipers that slithered out from under rocks and struck you and poisoned you. There were tarantulas that could bite you and drive you crazy. And the only cure, my grandfather said, was to dance and dance and dance until you fell to the ground, exhausted, and then you would be cured, because the dancing had used up all the poison.

There were feral cats that ate their babies, my grandmother said, which was all right, because the babies would die anyway—there wasn't even enough food for people in the land where my grandparents came from. There were bands of wild dogs, even more dangerous than wolves, my grandmother said, because wolves traveled at night, but dogs traveled during the day, and in packs, so you could encounter them while you were in the fields and this was why you needed a stout stick, when you worked outdoors, to beat off the dogs.

There were parents wild with grief because their babies had been taken away by wolves and eaten, or because their children had died of malaria, or of starvation, or for no reason at all. There were wild gangs of children without parents, roving the streets, living in alleyways, under bridges, in railroad tunnels, wild gangs of children, stealing money, stealing clothing, stealing newspapers for bedding, wood for fires to warm them, stealing food or garbage so they would not starve, and these gangs of wild children would crawl all over you if they caught you, and take the hat off your head, the boots off your feet, your overalls, your money if you had any, your long underwear even, my grandfather said. There were wild gangs of bandits hiding out in the countryside, living in caves, who would beat you and steal from you and maybe kill you if you were unlucky enough to encounter them.

There were men wild with rage at their wives or sisters who disgraced them, who dragged their women into the piazzas of villages to beat them so that all would see they were men who could keep them in line, my grandmother said. And there were men wild with rage at their children who had to be beaten to make them obedient, and children so wild that no amount of beating would make them behave. There were wild girls who would become wild women no decent man would marry, roaming the streets after dark, going with any man, for a coin, for a meal, for a place to sleep, disgracing their families, making it impossible for their sisters to marry, getting old, getting ugly, getting diseases, dying alone.

And there were ferocious invading armies as far back as anyone could remember—armies of Romans, Lombards, Greeks, Arabs, Germans, French, Spanish. Some would murder everyone in a village, burn the buildings to the ground, leave no evidence of life. Others would force the people to become slaves, would work them to death or move them to faraway places. And none of these invaders, my grandparents said, had ever helped the poor of the South. And the people from the North, my grandfather said, they were invaders, too.

And this was why there were men and women who joined wild bands of peasants and brigands and anarchists who fought the invaders, who rebelled against the conquerors (and I imagined my ancestors among them), and this had been going on for as long as anyone could remember. And, my grandparents said, many of our people—men, women—fought for their right to a crust of bread even though the government called up armies to fight our people when they rebelled.

But there were wild vegetables more delicious than any in America, and some you couldn't even get here. There were *lampascioni* (bulbs of the wild tassel hyacinth), *cicorielle* (wild chicory), *acetosella* (sorrel), *radicchielle* (dandelion) that you could find in the fields, and cook and dress with olive oil and a little salt, if you had any. But you needed permission from the landowners to scavenge, which wasn't often granted, or you could steal them, which is what my grandmother did when she was hungry, but stealing was dangerous.

And there were wild fish in the lakes and streams and in the sea, but you could not fish without permission because it was against the law. The rich, my grandfather said, owned everything. The poor, my grandfather said, owned nothing in the land where he came from, they did not even own their own shit, which was taken from them by the landlords for fertilizing the fields where the poor, like my grandfather, worked for almost nothing.

But there were wild flowers in spring everywhere—asphodel, mustard, orchids tiny as a fingertip, scarlet poppies—and these flowers were the earth's gift to the poor, my grandparents said, and they were so beautiful they could make you cry. The flowers, I liked to hear about, because there were very few in Hoboken, mostly pots of geraniums on fire escapes. But one summer, my grandfather showed me a flower growing between the cracks of the sidewalk on our block, and he told me that this flower, the cornflower, also grew in the land where they came from.

My grandfather said that except for the flowers, it was hard to live with all these wild things, but that it was hardest of all to live with the wild things—the fish and the vegetables—that could have appeased your hunger but that you couldn't have.

Then one day, my grandfather told me, there were wild gangs of people rushing up gangplanks to steamships in all the ports of the land where my grandparents came from, clutching suitcases and packages and babies, for their trip across the ocean to America. And one of these people was my grandfather, and then, later, one of these people was my grandmother. This was how my mother's parents had come to America, my grandfather said. And this was how my father's parents had come to America too, and their story was similar but not the same.

And, no, my grandparents said, they would never go back to that place, they spit on that place, they said, though not because of the wild things that were there. They spit on that place because there, no matter how hard you worked, you stayed poor. The place they came from, my grandfather said, was like a parent who wouldn't feed its hungry children, a parent who cast out its daughters and sons to scavenge for food in other places. Wherever you could earn your crust of bread, wherever you didn't go hungry, my grandparents said, is where you should call home.

After my grandparents died, I forgot what they had told me about the place my ancestors came from. Years later, I began to remember their stories. And then I learned that their stories, which I believed were fabrications when I was young, were true, all true.

Part One

CUTTING THE BREAD

THE BREAD

My grandmother is in the kitchen cutting the Italian bread that she has made. The bread that my grandmother has made is a big bread, a substantial bread, a bread that you can use for dunking, or for open-faced sandwiches, or for scraping the last bit of sauce from a bowl of pasta, or for toasting and eating with jam, or for breaking into soups and stews, or for eating with a little olive oil and a shake of coarse salt, or with a thick slice of slightly underripe tomato, or with the juices and seeds of a very ripe tomato and some very green olive oil (*pane e pomarole*).

My grandmother's bread is a good bread, not a fine bread. A bread that will stay fresh, cut side down, on the breadboard for three or four days, depending on the weather. A thick-crusted, coarse-crumbed Italian bread. A peasant bread. A bread that my mother disdains because it is everything that my grandmother is, and everything that my mother, in 1950s suburban New Jersey, is trying very hard not to be.

My grandmother's bread and the pizza she makes from her bread dough—tomato and cheese; garlic and olive oil; onion, sugar, and poppy seeds—are the foods that sustain me throughout my childhood. Without them, I know I would starve, because I hate everything my mother cooks. Hate it, because my mother burns the food that she cooks or puts too much salt in it or forgets to time the chicken and brings it to the table running with blood because she doesn't pay attention or because she is angry at my grandmother, at me, at the world, or because she is depressed and doesn't care about food, doesn't care about anything. Hate it because the ingredients themselves are terrible—gristly meat, bloated bratwurst, fatty sausage, slightly off hamburger gotten for a bargain that she tries to disguise with catsup and Worcestershire sauce. Or hate it (without realizing it then) because I can taste the rage in her food, can hear it in the slamming and banging of the pots and pans in her kitchen, in the clash of metal against metal in her stirring.

The kitchen, when my mother is cooking, is not a place I want to be. And so. No cookie-baking in the kitchen. No rolling out pie dough together. No lessons in how to make sauce.

And my mother's rage—at me for being selfish, at my grandmother for living with us since my grandfather died, at herself for her never-ending sorrow at not being able to create a life that can sustain her in spite of her loving my father, loving us (me and my sister), or so she says to my father, but never to me—scares me, makes me want to hide in a closet or rush from the house. It is a thick, scorching rage that I cannot predict, cannot control, cannot understand, a rage that I can feel against my skin. It is a rage that I do not want to catch from her. Though, of course, I do.

And so. I do not eat my mother's food if I can help it. Do not enter the kitchen when she cooks. Do not help her cook, for she will not let me, and prefers when I am not near her, when no one is near her. Do not help her clear the dishes, do not help her clean after we eat. And I leave the table, leave the kitchen, as soon and as fast as I can after what passes for supper in our house.

My eating my grandmother's bread and my not eating my mother's food is one reason my mother screams at me. (She has others: that I will not play with my sister and so keep her out of my mother's hair; that I sulk; that I answer back; that I have a mind of my own; that I am a burden; that I always have my nose in a book; that I do not love her; that I escape the house as often as I can; that I climb onto the roof from the upstairs bathroom window whenever there is a fight in our house, which is often, and so make a spectacle of myself, and let the neighbors know that despite my mother's superclean floors, her superladylike behavior, and her super-American ways, all is not well in our house.)

My eating my grandmother's bread and my not eating my mother's food is another reason my mother hates my grandmother, her stepmother, not her "real" mother, who died when my mother was a baby. A mother, she laments, who would have loved her, who would have taken care of her, and not resented her, as this woman does, this fake mother of hers, because they are not the same blood. My mother shouts this whenever they fight, which is often.

But I do not know what being the same blood means or why their not being the same blood should divide them. For, at times, when my mother talks to my father about what is happening in the world, she says that all people are created equal, and that the differences among people are only skin deep. But once, when I ask her if she and my grandmother were created equal, she said, no, because my grandmother never showed her any love, because my grandmother is a pain in the ass, because my grandmother drives her crazy. She says that some people, like my dead grandfather, deserve respect, and others don't. And that my grandmother is one of the ones who don't. And that if I don't shape up, I'll become one of the ones who don't, too.

THE OTHER BREAD

My mother does not eat the bread my grandmother bakes. My mother eats the bread that she buys a few times a week from the Dugan's man, who comes round in his truck to our suburban neighborhood in Ridgefield, New Jersey, where we move after my grandfather dies. This bread, unlike my grandmother's, has preservatives, a long shelf life, my mother says. You can keep this bread for a long, long time without it becoming green-molded. To my mother, this bread is everything that a good bread should be.

The bread my mother buys is white bread, sliced bread, American bread. A bread that my father, my sister, and I eat only under protest or when it is transformed into something else. A bread that my grandmother would never eat, even if she were starving, and she told my mother so the one time she tasted this bread, and she told my mother, too, that she knows what it is to starve, what it is not to have enough food, and that even if she did not have enough food, she would not eat this bread.

My mother thinks that eating this bread will change her, that eating this bread will erase this embarrassment of a stepmother—all black dresses and headscarves and scavenging for dandelions on the neighbors' lawns, and superstitions, and tentacled things stewing in pots, and flurries of flour that ruin my mother's spotless kitchen, and infrequently washed Old World long woolen undergarments—this embarrassment of a stepmother who, my mother swears, never bathes, who treats water as if it is something to pray to, not something to wash in. (When my grandmother sees the amount of water my mother puts into the bathtub when my sister and I bathe, she mutters "Mare Adriatico" in disgust, clucks her tongue, and walks into her darkened bedroom to say the rosary.)

Maybe my mother thinks that if she eats enough of this other bread, she will stop being Italian American and she will become American American. Maybe my mother thinks that if she eats enough of this other bread, people will stop thinking that a relative of my father's, who comes to visit us from Brooklyn once in a while, is a Mafioso, because he's Italian American and has New York license plates on his new black car, and sports a black tie and pointy shoes and a shiny suit and a Borsalino hat tipped way down over his forehead so you can hardly see his eyes. And if you can hardly see his eyes, my mother says, what kind of a man must the neighbors think he is? Maybe my mother remembers the incarcerations, deportations, and lynchings of Italians, the invasion of Italian neighborhoods in Hoboken, New Jersey, during the war when we lived there. Maybe my mother thinks eating this bread will keep us safe.

This bread that my mother buys from the Dugan's man is whiter than my grandmother's bread. It is as white, as soft and as spongy, as the cotton balls I use to take off my nail polish when I am a teenager, as white as the Kotex pads I shove into my underpants.

My mother eats this bread all the time, morning, noon, and night, and she uses it to make us toasted-cheese sandwiches. Two slices of American cheese pulled in shreds from their cellophane wrappers, slapped between two slices of buttered American bread (torn when buttered, because it is so soft) fried in a too hot frying pan while my mother, distracted, walks away to do something else until she smells the butter burning, says "Oh my goodness," returns to the stove, flips the sandwiches, gets distracted again, walks away again, smells the butter burning again, says "Oh my goodness" again, and serves the sandwich to us with lots of catsup on the side to disguise the filthy taste.

After Thanksgiving, my mother uses this bread to make turkey sandwiches with stuffing and gravy and cranberry sauce, the most acceptable use for this bread because then the bread is toasted, which hardens it, and, because the toaster we have is automatic, my mother can't fuck up the toast, unless she shoves it back in for a second round. My mother uses this bread to make French toast, too, what she calls her special Sunday night supper. But because she has never developed the knack of completely beating the egg that coats the bread, her French toast always has little pieces of coagulated egg white hanging off it, which I call snot strings.

Sometimes I pull the snot strings off the bread and hang them out of my nostrils. This I do, not to infuriate my parents, but for my own amusement, to distract myself from the funereal atmosphere of our supper table. But when I do it, my father reprimands me for my bad manners, tells me to respect the food my mother made, says all he wants at the end of a day's work, after taking guff from his bosses and hearing the rat-a-tat-tat of the machines all goddamned day long, is a nice meal, and some goddamned peace and quiet. I ignore him, look at the ceiling, pretend he's not there. He comes after me. I jump up, run away. He chases me around the table, out of the room, up the stairs.

But my sister and I like having this bread in our house because you can do many things with it. You can take a piece of this bread, pull off the crust, smash it down, roll it into a little ball. You can play marbles with this bread. You can pull the middle out of a slice of this bread and hang it over your nose or twirl it around your finger. You can pull the middle out of a slice of this bread and bring it up to your eye and pretend you're Nancy Drew looking for clues to a crime that was committed in your kitchen. You can take circles out of this bread and smash them down into Communion wafers and play "Holy Priest of God" dishing out the body of Christ. (This doesn't get my mother angry; this amuses her. She has no use for Holy Communion, for the Church or its priests, even though she sends us to Catholic grammar school.)

You can also eat this bread with your meal, and sometimes we do, if there is none of my grandmother's bread. But when you eat this bread, it sticks to the roof of your mouth and you have to pry it off with your fingers. Then you get yelled at for your horrible table manners, and are told to leave the table and go up to your room. Which is a good thing. If your father had a hard day at work and is in a lousy mood, or if he was out fighting fires as a volunteer and is exhausted, he'll chase you up the stairs to your room, but you can usually outrun him, slam your bedroom door shut, push your bureau against the door. Then you get blamed for ruining dinner.

My grandmother's bread doesn't stick to the roof of your mouth. Which is why I like it. Which is why my father likes it. That my father likes my grandmother's bread more than he likes my mother's bread makes my mother angry. That my father likes my grandmother's bread means that he's on my grandmother's side (the wrong side) in the ongoing bread war. That we like my grandmother's bread means that there's no hope for this family making it into the big time. It means that we're stuck in the rut of where we came from, that we're satisfied with who we are, and not striving for all that we can be. My mother is striving for all that we can be, here in suburban New Jersey. And she wants us to strive along with her.

CONVENIENCE FOODS

From the Dugan's man, my mother also buys apple pies, blueberry pies, lemon meringue pies, pumpkin pies (in season), seven-layer cake, pound cake, chocolate-covered donuts, and crullers, to satisfy my father's sweet tooth when she is too depressed to make a dessert of her own, and she is usually too depressed to make a dessert of her own. Italians, even rich ones, I know from my grandmother, don't eat much dessert—a piece of fruit, maybe, expertly peeled and sliced with a little knife—so my father's wanting dessert every night means that all is not lost, that he might become American American. And so my mother buys pies, donuts, crullers, and cakes a few boxes at a time and displays them on the counter, invitingly, and dishes out dessert after dinner to him, triumphant.

Me, I reject dessert. I am suspicious of things that come in boxes, things that get delivered to your door by a man who drives up to your house in a little white truck. I have learned this from my home ec teacher in junior high school, who teaches us that "fresh is best," who tells us that there should be no shortcuts in the kitchen.

But my mother just loves it when the Dugan's man comes cruising down our street. "The Dugan's man, the Dugan's man," she shouts as soon as she spies him, and she grabs her wallet and runs out of the house to be the first on line.

The Dugan's man knows that a warm smile can charm a woman into an extra box of sugar donuts, an extra pie, an extra box of English muffins, which "freeze well." My mother, usually frugal,

16

buys far more than she needs, far more than our family will ever eat.

After the purchase, there's always some small talk with the Dugan's man, some laughing, more laughing than there is in our house. The Dugan's man wears a uniform and a hat. He seems like a respectable gentleman. But I think he's a con man. So I rush out of the house after my mother to superintend the interaction. She carries on, ignoring me. With the Dugan's man, she becomes someone else. She smiles like she did in pictures of her taken during the war when my father was away in the Pacific, when she hung out with her friends in our tiny living room, or when she sang as she made a simple supper for the two of us.

"Merda," my grandmother calls everything that my mother buys from the Dugan's man.

From time to time, unsure that my grandmother's assessment is correct, I take a tentative bite of something and conclude that, yes, the stuff from the Dugan's man tastes like the cardboard box it comes in, that it is *merda*. And the canned stew my mother gives us is *merda*, too. And the canned vegetables she believes contain more vitamins than the real thing because they are canned "at the peak of freshness," and the canned spaghetti, the canned ravioli, and the canned soups. All these, my mother thinks, make great midday meals or really good quick dinners. All these, my grandmother thinks, are the devil's work.

But my mother is a convenience food junkie. I think she has things ass backwards. I'd rather have something wonderful to eat at the end of the day than have a spotless house, which I can never invite my friends to play in anyway. I'd even make something for myself if my mother would let me cook, which she won't, because she believes that the kitchen is her domain.

But when I tell her I want *real* food and not the fake food she thinks is food, she calls me spoiled and ungrateful, and she launches into a lecture about how good I have it, how I don't know anything about doing without, and how there are lots of kids in this world who would love the privilege of eating what she serves.

In our house, good food on the table probably wouldn't matter anyway. Because even if we had good food—a little eggplant Parmesan; tiny lobster tails grilled with a little olive oil, lemon juice, and parsley; a pasta with a simple tomato sauce—our mealtimes would still be the disasters they always are.

MAKING THE BREAD

My grandmother's bread (the bread that my mother will not eat) is a bread that my grandmother makes by hand in my mother's kitchen, much to my mother's disgust, at least twice a week, sometimes more, depending upon the season and upon the appetites of those who eat her bread—me, my sister, my father.

It takes a lot of time for my grandmother to make the bread—getting the fresh yeast, assembling the ingredients, mixing the bread, letting it rise, punching it down, letting it rise again, shaping it, letting the loaves rise, baking them, letting them cool, storing them properly. This is time that my mother thinks is wasted, time that my mother thinks my grandmother should spend helping her clean the house. "Your house, not my house," my grandmother says when my mother complains that nobody helps her. "Me, I have no house," my grandmother says.

To make the bread, my grandmother dumps a whole bunch of flour onto the Formica surface of the kitchen table. She mutters under her breath about how this flour is not "real" flour, nothing like the *semola* that rich people used in the old country. And she is outraged that the beautiful flour you could get there, you can't get here, a sure sign of her adoptive land's barbarism (though there she couldn't afford that flour, often couldn't even afford the adulterated maggot-infested flour sold to the poor). Still, she can't understand why what they grew there, they can't grow here. Why what her bread tastes like here, isn't what fine bread tasted like there (even though the bread she ate there wasn't fine bread).

19

Here, she says, the flour is whiter than there, more like talcum powder than a proper flour should be. And it is farmed on a land sprayed with poisons. It is bleached. It is bromated. It is packed in paper, not in cotton sacks. And by the time you buy it, it is stale and has taken on the taste of the packaging.

My grandmother takes a pinch of my mother's packaged flour between her fingers, tastes it, and says *merda*. *Merda* is one of my grandmother's favorite words. Her other favorite words are *sonnamabitch, sonnamagun, bastardo* (my father), *bastarda* (my mother), *stunod, bestia gramma* (evil beast—which she uses to refer to politicians, priests, movie stars, and anyone who parks their car in front of our house), and *sfaccim'*, my favorite, which, my father says, means sperm of the devil. (I find this out when he smacks me for calling him *sfaccim'*.) From my grandmother, I learn not only how to bake the bread, I learn how to curse and swear like a Southern Italian peasant woman.

The flour my grandmother uses, she takes from my mother's store, which is kept in a bin in the bottom of the kitchen pantry. My grandmother uses a lot of flour each week, pounds and pounds of flour, because she bakes so much bread. This is because she eats mostly bread, a great deal of bread, just like she did in the old country. For, she tells me, there, bread is the food of the poor, bread dipped in water or wine if you were lucky enough to have bread and water or wine. Here, though, she can eat soups that she dips her bread into. And she can eat other things made with flour—pizza, *zeppole*, calzone stuffed with onions, black olives, capers, tomatoes, cheese, anchovies, parsley. This she considers a boon, a bounty, a blessing. This outweighs all the evil of this new country that she has come to.

My mother doesn't let my grandmother have her own supply of flour. Even though my grandmother uses more flour than my mother. Even though letting my grandmother have her own flour would be the logical thing to do. Even though it would remove one of the causes of friction between them. That my grandmother uses so much of my mother's flour is a source of contention between them, because my mother often reaches into the pantry for a little flour to thicken a sauce or bake a piecrust (and although my mother is good at very little in the kitchen, she is good at baking pies), only to discover that my grandmother has used all of her flour.

"Jesus Christ," my mother says. "How much more of this can I take?"

When my mother discovers that there is no flour left, she searches the house to find my grandmother, who is down the basement tending her bread, or in the dining room sitting by the radiator knitting or crocheting, or in her bedroom near the window saying her rosary or staring out the window at the plumes of smoke from the Public Service electric plant. And when she finds her, my mother starts yelling.

"If you had any respect for me," my mother shouts, "you'd keep your hands off my flour. Or you'd have the decency to tell me when there wasn't any more."

My grandmother glances at my mother with disdain, shrugs, and continues doing whatever she was doing—tending, crocheting, knitting, staring, praying. This drives my mother crazy. This makes my mother shout even louder. Because what my mother wants at this moment is confrontation, drama, resolution, change (on the part of my grandmother). And my grandmother will never change.

Sometimes my grandmother wants to fight. Sometimes my grandmother spits back at my mother, "You're not my blood," to answer my mother's accusations. But usually when my mother comes ranting, my grandmother just waits for my mother to go away, to leave her alone. My grandmother has come from a land of the poor, of the despised, of the powerless, a land where she has learned that the most potent weapon you can wield against your adversary is an utter and complete indifference.

To compensate for the dreadful flour she is forced to use, my grandmother uses fresh yeast, a little barley flour, and some salt. The barley flour gives her loaf some character, some color, some heft. Yeast in foil packets my grandmother regards with as much disdain as the tomatoes in little cardboard boxes with cellophane windows my mother buys from the local supermarket. Both are *merda* as far as my grandmother is concerned. And so my grandmother gets her yeast from the baker who owns the local bakery where I work during the summer and after school, who agrees to let my grandmother buy some of his yeast.

At first, the baker wants to give my grandmother the yeast free. But she is too proud to accept his generosity, which she misperceives as charity, and a condemnation of her. Besides, she is far too wary to accept something from someone she doesn't know. This would put her in his debt. And so they have agreed (through me, for he speaks no Italian and she speaks little English) that she will pay him twenty-five cents a week for some of his yeast.

And so, every baking day, she walks down the big hill to the bakery, and back up the big hill to our house, carrying her fresh yeast. It is one of the few errands she undertakes that gives her any satisfaction.

When my grandmother makes her bread, she makes a well in the middle of the flour and into it pours bay-leaf-scented water she has warmed on the stove. In my grandmother's village, they used water from the sea to make their bread so you didn't have to add salt, which was too expensive. Besides, the water from the wells, if they contained any water at all, was often contaminated. So in my grandmother's village, you had to buy water from the water vendor, if you had money to buy water.

My grandmother flicks the flour into the yeasty water with her fingertips a little bit at a time and stirs the mixture round and round until it comes together into a shaggy mass.

Making the bread, a welcome ritual that redeems the difficulty of my grandmother's days, of my days. A time I share with her, sometimes wordlessly, sometimes accompanied by her stories; and her bread, her pizza, her *zeppole*, are food I like, food I can swallow, food that does not disgust me, food that instead sustains me and nourishes me.

The two of us, in the kitchen, ignoring my mother's annoyance and disapproval, her unnecessary clanging of pots and pans during this important time. The two of us, enveloped in a nimbus of flour, inhaling the yeasty, narcotic vapors that transport her to a little white village by the sea, where she returns in reverie. Though she would never return there, she said, because life was so difficult. No work to be had. No food to be had. And the land was poor though it had once yielded bounty beyond imagination, even for the poor. Melons round as a baby's bottom; tomatoes red as blood, artichokes the size of a man's fist or as small as a little snail; grapes, oranges, fennel, onions, olives—all so perfect, all so delicious, she was told. Until those *sfaccim'* (may they rot in hell through all eternity) took the land from the people, wouldn't let the land rest, wouldn't let the workers rest. They worked the land until it refused to yield; they worked the peasants until they dropped dead or left for America.

Throughout my childhood and adolescence, when I hear about Italy, it is this impoverished village she describes to me while she makes the bread, this little white stone village that tumbles down a hillside to an azure sea, that I imagine all of Italy to be. And when I travel to Italy after she dies, it is this bread, her bread, that I hope I will find there.

KNEADING THE DOUGH

When my grandmother kneads the bread, she takes off her shawl, her sweater, her apron, her dress, because she sweats a lot because kneading is such hard work, and she stands in the kitchen at the table in her underwear. Coarse unbleached white undershirt over a substitute for underpants that looks like a large diaper (these, she makes herself because you can't buy them here). Black stockings, rolled down around her ankles. Old black shoes, their backs cut off, with a hole cut into the front of the right shoe for her bunion.

When my grandmother strips down, my mother huffs and leaves the room. My grandmother acts as if nothing has happened. She has mastered the art of pretending that my mother isn't there unless she wants to argue with her. And because she is making the bread today, she has better things to do than argue with my mother.

We can hear my mother in the living room complaining about how, if she ever wanted to, she could never have a friend over for tea in the afternoon, what with my grandmother walking around the house in her underwear. "Dear God, what have I ever done to deserve this?" my mother asks. My mother has only one or two friends and would never invite them over to tea in the afternoon anyway, so what she says seems ridiculous. Still, I understand what my mother means, because I never invite my friends to my house. It's too risky, what with my mother and grandmother's constant arguments over my grandmother's strange ways.

*   *   *

When my grandmother kneads the dough, she gives me a little batch to knead too. She shows me how to lean into the dough, to push it away, to gather it back onto itself, to lean into it again. The two of us kneading the bread, rocking together.

After my grandmother kneads the dough, she gathers it into a ceramic bowl one of her relatives has sent to her from Italy to let it rise.

When she first came to live with us in Ridgefield, she would take the big bowl of dough, carry it up the stairs to her bedroom, and settle it into her bedclothes. This is where she would let the dough rise. To my grandmother, this was normal. This is what her mother had done, and her mother's mother, and her mother's mother's mother. But to my mother, this was barbarism incarnate. Dough belonged in kitchens, not in bedrooms. "Jesus Christ Almighty, how much more of this can I take?" my mother asks, as she slides past my grandmother on the stairs.

To keep peace in the family (even though he himself disrupts the peace), my father builds my grandmother a special little platform with little legs that sits on top of the radiator in the kitchen where she can place her dough to rise. The platform is made from plywood stained maple to match the Early American furniture in our kitchen.

My father tells my grandmother that it's warm here on top of the radiator, warmer than in her bed, and so better for rising. My grandmother is skeptical. Still, this is where she begins to rest her bread. (This annoys my mother. So after a while she starts using the platform to store her pots and pans so there is no room for my grandmother's bowl. So my grandmother again trudges her dough up the stairs to let it rise in her bed.)

After my grandmother sets the bowl of dough to rise on the platform, she dresses herself again. Pulls on her black dress (and, if it is wintertime, pulls on a second black dress over the first); pins the bib of her apron onto her bodice; ties the apron strings behind her; puts on her sweater; pulls on her shawl. Then she goes upstairs, pulls a multicolored crocheted blanket off her bed, takes it downstairs, tucks it around the breadbowl. Whether this is because she believes bedclothes make the dough rise higher, or because she is saving face by showing my mother that she will use her bedclothes even though she is no longer allowed to let the dough rise in her bed, I never learn. Still, this gesture, which seems part compromise, part self-assertion, shows my mother—and me—that although my grandmother may never win, neither will she ever lose.

When my grandmother arranges her blanket around the bread, she acts as if she is putting a child to sleep, that unborn ideal child against whom she compares my unfortunate mother. It is my grandmother's most tender gesture, this swaddling of the bread.

After the dough rises, my grandmother shapes her loaves into round puffy pillows, and she helps me shape mine into a little braided crown. These she puts onto a wooden board to carry up to her bedroom to rise again. While our breads rise, my grandmother takes some scraps and shapes them into little figure eights, which she fries in hot oil, then sprinkles with confectioner's sugar for my sister and me. *Zeppole*. These, we will eat when my sister comes home from playing with her best friend. This is our lunch on baking days. This is why I love the days when my grandmother bakes the bread.

My mother disapproves of me and my sister eating anything my grandmother cooks for us. "*Zeppole*," she sneers, "nothing but sugar and starch, sugar and starch," as if she were the queen of nutrition. But she lets us eat them anyway. As usual, she has been too busy fussing and complaining and cleaning our already clean house to make us lunch.

After the loaves have risen, my grandmother bakes them in the oven down in the basement. We have an oven in the kitchen but my mother won't use it, won't let my grandmother use it. She uses it to store pots and pans, so even though there are two ovens in our house, she fights with my grandmother over who gets to use the oven in the basement.

My grandmother doesn't mind going downstairs to bake her bread because in her village in Italy she had to bring her bread to a communal oven for baking when she had collected enough flour to make a loaf of bread. And although other women, scarves on heads, hands on hips, welcomed the opportunity to stand around the oven to socialize, and to gossip about the malefactions of anyone who wasn't there, my grandmother was never one for wasting time in idle talk.

When we moved to Ridgefield, my mother got a new stove for our kitchen, because she considered the old stove that came with the house unsightly. She had my father install the old stove in the basement, so she could use it during summers so the kitchen upstairs wouldn't get hot.

But my mother never uses the oven in the kitchen upstairs, even in winter, never lets my grandmother use the oven in the kitchen. My mother only uses the oven in the basement, only lets my grandmother use the oven in the basement. So even though there is an oven in the kitchen, my mother and my grandmother have to run up and down the stairs to and from the basement several times whenever they are baking.

My grandmother doesn't seem to mind. She doesn't have all that much to occupy her. Usually, when she's baking, she stays below ground in our dimly lit basement, sitting on a cast-off straight-backed chair near the furnace where it's warm, away from my mother, away from the commotion upstairs. This, I can't understand, though I do see why my grandmother puts as much space as she can between herself and my mother because I do the same thing. Still, the basement is dark, damp, unpleasant. (Years later, when I'm in the South of Italy, I learn that sitting on straight-backed chairs in dimly lit rooms where dust motes dance is what peasant women like my grandmother do when they're not working, which isn't often. In our basement, my grandmother must have felt at home.)

I think it's crazy that my mother won't use the oven in the kitchen. Especially since, when she bakes, my mother is always also cleaning out a drawer, tidying a closet, scrubbing the toilet. So she always loses track of time and often burns whatever she's baking.

My father can't understand this either. Whenever my mother runs up and down the stairs to and from the oven in the basement, my father asks, "Why are you always making things harder for yourself, Mil? Why can't you treat yourself right? Why do you make things harder for yourself than they need to be?"

Like how my mother washes clothes. In Hoboken, my mother used to heat water on the coal stove, wash clothes on a washboard in the sink, wring them by hand, and hang them outside on the clothesline to dry. It was hard work and it took a long time. Here, in Ridgefield, we have a washing machine and even a dryer in the basement; they came with the house. My father imagines that these appliances will save my mother time, will make her into a lady of leisure.

But although my mother washes our clothes in the washing machine, she won't let it complete the cycle. She wrings the clothes out by hand, because she wants to save water. She reuses the water in the washing machine for another load. This entails a lot of running up and down the stairs to interrupt the wash cycle. This entails a lot of rinsing of clothes in the basement sink. A lot of lugging heavy wet clothes out of the water, a lot of wringing, a lot of sweating, a lot of swabbing down the floor with the rag mop, a lot of swearing.

My mother refuses to use the dryer at all. "Uses too much electricity; it's too expensive," she says, and so she hangs the wash outside in summer, inside in winter on the lines that she has strung back and forth across the basement.

All this drives my father crazy. He calculates that my mother saves a dollar or so a month on water, five or so on electricity, which, he says, isn't worth it. "Think about your time, Mil; think about saving your energy for better things," he says to my mother, who doesn't listen. "A penny saved is a penny earned," my mother replies.

My mother won't wash my grandmother's clothing because it offends her. And my grandmother won't use the washing machine in the basement to wash her clothing because she is afraid of it, as she is afraid of all electrical appliances, but especially the washing machine because it combines water and electricity and she is certain that if she uses it, she will electrocute herself. So my grandmother washes her clothes in the second-floor bathroom we all share, in the basin or the tub, depending upon how many clothes she needs to wash.

"Jesus Christ," my mother says, when she wants to take a bath but encounters a tubful of my grandmother's clothes soaking, "how much more of this can I take?"

After my grandmother finishes baking the bread, she cleans up, but not the way my mother wants: clean enough so you can eat off the floor, even though we never eat off the floor.

My mother's face is red with rage. She rescrubs everything with Ajax. She curses. "Sporca, sporca, sporca," she says. "Dirty, dirty, dirty." She spills water on the floor because she's so angry, makes an even bigger mess, tries to clean that. She turns down the corners of her mouth.

It is impossible for my sister and me to ignore my mother while we sit at the table and eat our *zeppole*, for my mother is cleaning the table we sit at, she is scrubbing around our plates and under our glasses. "Sporca, sporca, sporca," she repeats.

My grandmother is standing on the threshold of the kitchen, watching us eat, watching my mother clean. She is serene, proud of the fat loaves of bread cooling on the counter. She is looking forward to eating the leftover *zeppole* all by herself after we have finished eating, after my mother has finished cleaning, after my mother finishes her snack of a crust of toast and a cup of cold black coffee.

I concentrate on the crunchiness of the outside of the *zeppole*, on the warm pillow softness of the inside, on the cloying sweetness of the maple syrup that I use for dipping. Yes, it is impossible for me to ignore my mother. But I try.

THE KNIFE

The knife that my grandmother uses to cut the bread is not a bread knife, not a serrated knife like every well-equipped American kitchen now has. No. The knife that my grandmother uses to cut the bread is a butcher knife, the kind of knife that figures in nightmares, in movies like *Psycho*. The same knife, incidentally, that my father will use when I am a teenager, when he threatens to kill me. (Years later, I bring up the subject of how he grabbed the knife, came at me, how I got away because my grandmother put her body between us. "I never meant to hurt you," he said. "I was just trying to make myself clear.")

My grandmother would take a gigantic loaf of the bread she had made, and she would pull the knife through the bread towards the center of her chest where her heart was located, as if she were trying to commit an Italian form of hara-kiri.

"Stop that," my mother would shout, half fearing, half hoping, I think, that this woman, this stepmother who didn't love her, would pull the knife towards her breast just a fraction of an inch too far, so that after all the screaming, all the threats of "If I get my hands on you I'll kill you," we would finally have bloodshed in our own kitchen, finally have a real mess on our hands that would take my mother a very long time to clean.

"Stop that, for Christ's sake!" my mother would shout. She would pull the bread away from my grandmother and often she would cut herself in the process, not much, but just enough to bleed onto the bread. And my mother would throw the bread down onto the counter, where it would land upside down (a grave sin, my grand-mother said, for bread should only be placed right side up; to do otherwise was to disrespect the bread; to do otherwise was to invite the forces of evil into your house). And she would say, "Why can't you cut that goddamned bread like a normal human being?"

My grandmother would bend over the bread that she had made, turn it right side up, and make the sign of the cross over it and kiss her fingertips, weeping. My grandmother would weep because to her the bread was sacred and to her the only way to cut the bread was to pull the knife through the bread toward your heart. And perhaps she was weeping, too, for all that she had lost, for all that she never had, and for all that she didn't have. For the insufferable life she was forced to live.

My mother was afraid of knives, and if she could avoid using one, she did. She'd tear the lettuce instead of slicing it, and not because she didn't want to destroy the tenderness of the leaves. She'd use kitchen shears to dismember a chicken. She'd put blunt knives at our places instead of steak knives, even if what we were eating was fibrous and tough.

Some things, though, she couldn't avoid cutting, like onions, like carrots. So when she cut them, she ordered everyone out of the kitchen.

"Knives are dangerous," she'd say. "You have to stay far away from someone who is using a knife."

Before she went to bed at night, my mother would gather up all the knives in our kitchen, and she would put them away in a drawer. "This way," she said, "if burglars come into the house in the middle of the night, they'll have to look for them and we'll hear them. This way," my mother said, "we'll have a fighting chance."

I never believed this burglar bullshit. I always thought the reason my mother put away all the knives was because she was afraid that one of us might creep down to the kitchen in the middle of the night, take the butcher knife my grandmother used to cut the bread, climb back up the stairs, and kill the rest of us.

SLICING ONIONS

It was when we moved to the suburbs from Hoboken that my mother abandoned cooking foods that required much preparation and began cooking things that were cooked already. Although she said she was happy to live in the suburbs, happy to be out of Hoboken, our new house was an old house that needed a lot of work—stripping old wallpaper, sanding, plastering, painting, rewiring—all of which was done by my parents because they didn't have the money to hire someone, hardly had the money for this house, which they bought with a GI mortgage. And so my mother, too exhausted to cook, gave us TV dinners (usually turkey, Swanson brand, although sometimes we'd have meatloaf) for supper. Canned ravioli or spaghetti (Chef Boyardee). Beef stew (Dinty Moore). Chow mein (Chun King, with Minute Rice and canned fried noodles on the side). Instant mashed potatoes and canned beef gravy (this was a meal). Canned chili (with Minute Rice). Canned ham (with Minute Rice). Canned Spam (she gave up on this one because even my father wouldn't eat it; said he'd seen enough of it for a lifetime while he was in the navy). Frozen pizza that came in little squares.

Often, a canned vegetable accompanied whatever my mother heated up. Peas were her favorite; but she liked asparagus, green beans, and beets, too. Always, there was a bag of Dugan's bread plopped in the center of the table, inside its sanitary plastic bag. And when she was making a special effort, there was salad (iceberg lettuce, of course) slathered with bottled salad dressing (Russian).

But on holidays and on special occasions—birthdays, Easter Sunday, Thanksgiving—my mother spent a lot of time in the kitchen and cooked Italian foods (glory, glory) or one of our favorites. (For his birthday, my father's was liver and bacon, which no one else ate. For mine, it was spaghetti and meatballs. My sister had no favorite food. My sister ate almost nothing at all.) For holidays or special occasions, my mother would make a really good lasagna. Or chicken soup with little meatballs. Or sausage and peppers.

Cooking these special foods, though, flustered and exhausted her, and often she didn't have the energy to eat what she had prepared and she would only pick at what was on her plate. So eating the foods I loved, which I didn't get often, was tainted. For I knew what cooking these foods had cost my mother to prepare, and I knew, too, that no matter how much I pleaded for them, I wouldn't be seeing them for a very long time.

Always, as my mother made these meals, she cried. When I was a girl, my mother would cry every time she sliced an onion, and the foods she made for holidays and special occasions always contained onions. But my mother didn't cry the way everyone cries when slicing an onion, the stinging, unbidden tears annoying the corners of the eyes. No. When my mother sliced an onion, she *really* cried. Her chest heaved, her head sagged, her eyes bled huge tears onto the scarred Formica countertop where she did her cutting and chopping.

My mother would rub her eyes with the backs of her hands to try to staunch the flow of tears, which only made the crying worse. And she had a lot to cry about—that her mother died when she was a baby; that she was abused by the people who were supposed to be taking care of her after her mother's death; that my stepgrandmother never loved her; that her husband came home from the war an angry man; that her beloved father died when she was a young mother; that I was a difficult, temperamental child who gave her no comfort, who wouldn't do as she asked; that my sister was as prone to depression as she was. Still, the only time I ever saw my mother cry ("having a good cry," she called it) was when she was slicing onions. And because she always sliced onions on holidays and special occasions, I often thought that my mother specialized in dishes containing sliced onions (liver smothered in onions; meatloaf served on a bed of sautéed onions; sausages, peppers, and onions) because making them gave her an opportunity to cry, which she needed, because any day that was out of the ordinary was difficult for my mother. (Any ordinary day was difficult for my mother.)

Not that my mother didn't express emotion when she wasn't slicing onions. She did. But her emotions were always unleashed by what seemed to me ridiculously inconsequential circumstances. A broken cup. A neighbor's casual remark. A relative's impending visit. A stack of folded laundry tumbling over. A leaking faucet. A snowstorm.

My mother's emotions were always extreme and unmodulated. There was rage, not anger. Fury, not ire. Withdrawal, not reflection. Bewilderment, not wonder. Perplexity, not uncertainty. Confusion, not ambivalence. Despair, not discouragement. Despondency, not sadness. Misery, not sorrow. Worry, not concern or solicitude. Obsession, not passion. Terror, not fear.

But unless she was cooking, my mother didn't cry. (Not even years later, when my sister killed herself. On that occasion, my mother didn't cry, she screamed. Just once. But *scream* isn't the right word. The sound she made was one I had never before, have never heard since—a long, wavering ululation. Then, after, no emotion. Then, a long slow diminishment. Of the psyche, the body. So that in life, she was already joining my sister in death, journeying to a dark underworld of the spirit where she regained her dead daughter but lost her capacity for living. And by the end of her life, my mother couldn't speak, couldn't see, couldn't hear, couldn't move, couldn't eat. Though whether she couldn't feel, I can't say.)

When I was a child, I didn't like my mother to cry. I worried that her crying would turn into something worse than crying, that she would become depressed again, as she so often did, and become inaccessible to us, inaccessible, it seemed, even to herself. Then, my sister and I would be taken to relatives to be cared for, or not cared for, depending upon which of our relatives were willing or available.

"Sit down," my father would say to my mother when he saw her crying into the food. "What's bothering you?" he would ask.

I'd linger on the threshold of the kitchen until I was chased away, wondering whether I would learn about why my mother was crying, learn something, anything, about her life, about which I knew almost nothing. I knew she'd once worked selling shoes. I knew she was a good writer in high school, wanted to go to college, but couldn't. Knew she hated her stepmother, but I didn't know why. I wanted to learn something that might explain my mother's crying, her inexplicable rages, her strange ways—why she sat in a chair and tore at her fingers for hours, why she rarely ate what was on her plate but picked leftover food off ours and ate it as she was clearing the table, why she never drank her coffee when it was good and hot but absentmindedly forgot it until it was cold. My mother's behavior was a puzzle I couldn't solve.

I did not know then that my mother's mother had died when she was a baby. Did not know that after her mother died, she'd stopped feeding and almost died. ("Failure to thrive," the doctor had called it.) Did not know that the people who cared for her abused her (as a relative who cared for us abused me).

Instead of answering my father's questions about what was bothering her (for she seemed not to know the reasons for her sorrow), my mother would ignore him, sit down at the kitchen table, heave a deep sigh, pick up her cup of cold coffee, and sip it to calm herself. When she was at her worst, she just held her head in her hands until she could resume her work.

"I give up," my father would say, as my mother resisted his attempts to comfort her. And he would leave the room, go down the basement, work on one of his renovation projects.

If my mother saw me watching her, she waved me away, told me to go play with my sister, told me to get busy, told me to leave her alone, that she would be all right. My mother never wanted me near her when she was crying, just as she never wanted me near her when she was cooking, so I never learned her secrets. Whatever few culinary tricks my mother knew—the secret ingredients in her pumpkin pie, her lasagna, her red sauce—died with her.

But no matter how bad my mother felt, she usually managed to pull herself together to help me do my homework. She'd sit next to me at the kitchen table, helping me sound out words to spell them. She'd make me write my homework over if it was sloppy. She'd help me with my math, even though she had to count on her fingers. She'd dig some rice, a few beans, out of her cupboard for "product maps" for geography. "You have to make a success of yourself," she'd say. "You have to go to college, become a teacher, do something worthwhile with your life."

When my mother didn't want me near her, I thought her despair was an invincible shield that protected her from me. I thought her depression kept her from responding to my wants and needs, which she could not summon up the energy to satisfy. My presence seemed to add an even greater burden to her already overwhelming measure of sorrow.

"Your mother had a hard life," my father said when, as a raging adolescent, I would tell him that I hated my mother, couldn't stand being in this house, couldn't wait until I was old enough to get married and leave (for in those days, in a family like mine, the only way you left your parents' house was to marry).

"Your mother had a hard life," my father always said. But he told me nothing that could help me understand why. And then he would say, "All your mother wants from you is a little love." I didn't know what love felt like. I hadn't learned the language of love from her, the gesture that might convey the meaning, and I had become convinced that she didn't want my love. Now I know that I held myself aloof because I feared that what my mother needed, I couldn't give her; that trying to figure out what she really wanted would consume me, would take over my life, as it took my sister's.

Yes, my mother had a lot to cry about. And her tears became an ingredient of the food she prepared. I knew that when I ate her food, I ate those tears and I was afraid that in eating them I would become as unhappy as she was, and as unsatisfied. And this, I didn't want to be.

BREAKING THE DISHES

The people in our house behaved like characters in an opera or a tragedy (Greek, not Shakespearean).

In our house, a dish broken by accident, an oversalted gravy, some spilled oil, a messy floor, an annoying child, a late library book, a dirty dress, a missed curfew was never a problem or a challenge. In our house, everything was a *very big deal*, an occasion for high drama. In our house, no one ever went with the flow. There was no flow. There were only dangerous rapids, huge whirlpools, gigantic water-falls. In our house, you had to be wary, vigilant. To stop paying attention, even for a moment, was dangerous.

In my house, we gesticulated wildly. We shouted. Threatened harm to others ("I'll kill you"), to ourselves ("I may as well kill myself").

We stood chest-to-chest, shouting, so close to one another that we swallowed each other's saliva. We hurled insults like spears ("you no-good motherfucker"; "you son of a bitch"; "you atrocious bastard"). We threw ourselves down onto our beds, pounding our fists at the mattress when we weren't using them on each other. We menaced each other with whatever we had in our hands (pens, rulers, protractors, forks, scissors, knives). We slammed windows shut, pulled shades down, so that no one could hear what was going on in our house, so that none of our neighbors could see us or hear us. We—my father and I, but never my mother or my sister or my grandmother (and this tells you much about the differences among us)—rushed out of rooms, stormed out of the house. We threw things. We broke things. We destroyed things that had been given to us as presents (framed pictures, portable radios, jewelry), things that we loved (teacups, records, books, dishes, knickknacks), things that we had created (a cake, a pie, a sweater, a beaded necklace, the pages of a story).

My parents fought with my grandmother every day. My father threatened to ship my grandmother back to Hoboken, ship her to her relatives on Long Island, ship her back to Italy. Ship her, as if she were a piece of furniture, as if calling a long distance mover to box her up and relocate her to some place far away would solve all our household problems. My mother fought with my grandmother all the time about foolish things. Flour on the floor. Laundry in the bathtub. Candles burning in my grandmother's room around her statue of Jesus Christ taken down from the cross that my mother insisted were a fire hazard. They fought about foolish things because they couldn't fight about what their fights were really about: how my grandmother depended upon my parents, who despised her; how my grandmother never loved my mother; how my mother had been mistreated by her from the start; how my grandfather preferred my mother to her; how my grandfather brought my grandmother from Italy to care for his daughter and in return gave her very little.

My mother rarely fought with me. Instead, she told my father what I'd done (always, in my mind, a minor infraction—a missed curfew, a lost library book, a curt word) and my father would discipline me, always at the supper table.

After my mother served the meal in silence, he would begin:

"I heard from your mother that you gave her a hard time, that you didn't do as you were told."

I'd fight back, present my case. He'd perceive this as insubordination and tell me to shut up. But I wouldn't shut up: I'd fight back even more. Then, he'd begin his litany of threats:

"I'll kill you if you don't shut up."

"I gave you life, I can take it away."

"I'll throw you against the wall/out the window/down the stairs if you don't shut up."

"I'll make you wish you were never born."

"I'll knock some sense into you."

"I'll break your head."

"I'll break your legs."

"I'll break your hands so you'll never be able to eat a decent meal again."

He'd work himself up into a frenzy. Get up from his place at the table. Come at me.

I'd throw whatever I could get my hands on—a knife, a fork, a dish, a glass filled with milk or water. Our table was always set with mismatched plates, with odds and ends, because we were always breaking glasses, smashing dishes to the floor. I'd claw at my father, draw blood, run away, out the door, down the block, to a neighbor's house, to the library. My body and my spirit bore the scars of his rage.

But sometimes, when it all got to be too much, instead of fighting, I fainted. Collapsed on the floor. Disappeared.

My parents rarely fought with my sister, though they carped at her: "Clean your room"; "Change your clothes"; "Do your home-work"; "Stop biting your nails"; "Stop sitting there; do something productive"; "Go outside and play." Whatever my parents said to my sister, she never fought back. She gave them no trouble. Made no demands. Never raised her voice to argue, to contradict. She tried to make everyone get along, or she sulked, or she tried to pretend that everything that went on in our house was normal, that what was happening wasn't happening.

But often she withdrew. Sat on the bed we shared and stared at the wall; sat in a chair on our back porch, silent, twirling her hair, for hours.

The cost to my sister of being the "good child" was death. In our household, it was fight back or die. Being the child my parents hated was better than being the child they loved. My parents' love erased my sister, erased who she was, who she might have been.

When I was a little girl and I played with my dolls, I made them cry. I reprimanded them, yelled at them, hit them, punished them. I shoved their faces into mattresses to stop their crying, rubbed their cheeks against brick walls to show them who was boss. And I never pretended I was feeding them.

I didn't understand the way my friends played with dolls. All that shoving of little plastic nipples into tiny fake mouths, all that dressing and undressing, burping and diapering, all that trundling dolls around in tiny baby carriages, all that huggy, kissy, googoo nonsense. I didn't let *my* dolls think the world was one big lovefest. I taught my dolls what the world was like.

When I was a teenager, and the fighting in our house was at its worst, my mother clipped something called "A Kitchen Prayer" from a women's magazine. She backed it, framed it, hung it up in the kitchen over the counter where she organized our meals.

"Dear God," it read, "teach me to worship you each day in the kitchen as I go about my work. With each meal that I make, I will remember that my work is a form of worship, that cutting and chopping the food that I prepare for my loving family can bring me ever closer to You.

"Bless this food, Dear Lord. Bless this family. Keep them from harm so that they may live in your love and in your care.

"In the name of the Father, of the Son, and of the Holy Ghost. "Amen."

HOME EC

My father tells me that when I am about four, just after he comes home from the war, we are sitting at the kitchen table in Hoboken, and I decide I don't like what my mother's made us for supper.

Before my father's return, my mother or one of my grandparents would have gotten me some bread and jam. Now, things are different. Now, when I don't like what my mother has cooked, my father says, "Eat what's put in front of you."

I climb out of my chair, go to the icebox, pull out some chopped meat, some margarine (there's no butter because of the war). Grab a pan and a spoon from the cupboard. Push my chair over to the stove.

I shape a tiny hamburger. Turn on the burner. Start to cook.

My parents laugh. Tonight they've had some wine. They're happy their little family is together. The war is over. My father's safe. At other meals they've told me to eat my mother's cooking. But tonight they think that what I'm doing is adorable.

My father gets the camera. Focuses. Shoots a picture of me cooking.

"She'll be a good cook someday. Make somebody a good wife," he says to my mother, smiling.

My father and I haven't had our first big fight. The one that starts when he tries to take me to the park so we can get reacquainted. That starts because I want to dilly-dally as I did when I went with my mother during the war. That starts because I want to jump on and off every stoop we encounter. That starts because I won't soldier on to the park so we can have a good time.

Halfway there, I want to return home for a glass of water. A snack. To pee. To see my mother. To see my grandparents. Anything to get away from this man who carries me when I balk at walking, who insists that we do what he wants, not what I want.

We haven't yet had the fight that starts because he knows I'm not happy he's home, that I don't want him here, that I want my mother all to myself again. My father hasn't yet concluded that I am spoiled, selfish, incorrigible, ungrateful.

After my father takes his picture of me at the stove, he stops my cooking. Takes away the pan, the spoon. Takes away my hamburger. I'm too little, he says. It's dangerous.

He carries me back to the table. Pushes my supper towards me. "Children are supposed to eat what's put in front of them without complaining," he says. "And aren't we lucky we have all this good food?"

The kitchen is my mother's. But after we move to Ridgefield, when my grandmother moves in with us, she needs to cook, for she will not eat my mother's food.

My mother regards this as an attempted coup, a potential usurpation. (But what else was my grandmother to do? Go hungry?)

My mother retaliates by refusing to give my mother any space in her cupboards, in her refrigerator, in her pantry. So my grandmother lines up her pots and pans on the stairs going down into the basement. Shops every day and leaves her leftovers on her window ledge in winter, in the coal cellar in summer. Stores her beans, her olive oil, her orecchiette, which catch the sauce like little pools of sorrow, in her clothes closet. All this proves to my mother that my grandmother is crazy.

"Two women in the same kitchen," my mother says. "Dear God, why have you done this to me?"

*   *   *

When we first move to Ridgefield, before my grandmother comes, there is not another Italian in sight, which pleases my mother. She is moving up in the world. Away from the coal stove, the icebox, the four flights of stairs, the shared toilet, the washing of clothes in the kitchen sink, her stepmother's relatives, whom she detests for their coarseness.

Now my mother is away from the old ways, away from the dimly lit, cold-water tenement where she struggled up the stairs with two children and a stroller and groceries. She is away from the smell of other people's cooking, away from the old men playing pinochle on the folding table on the sidewalk. For a while, until my grandmother comes, my mother seems happy enough, though the loss of her father still propels her into a wordless, noiseless grief that takes her to some other place.

But now my mother has a new gas stove in the kitchen that she doesn't have to load with coal, or stoke, or wait for as it heats. She runs her fingers over her stove like a woman teasing a lover. She can't believe the magic of this stove. She walks into the kitchen. Turns the burners on and off. On and off. She is mesmerized by the flame and by her good fortune, though she will never use the oven in this stove.

Now my mother has an electric refrigerator that doesn't need huge blocks of ice that melt onto the floor. This one has a freezer compartment and shelves and bins for fruits and vegetables. Now my mother has cupboards so she doesn't have to shop every day like she did in Hoboken. Now my father can drive her to the supermarket at the bottom of the hill so she can stock up on the canned goods that will free her from the drudgery of making meals.

My father, with his passion for gadgets and for fixing things, buys, secondhand, a toaster, a waffle iron, and a little electric griddle for my mother's kitchen. He takes them to his basement workshop, tinkers with them evenings after supper. While he works, we hear, "Shit," "God damn it to hell," "Jesus Christ Almighty." We know the work isn't going well. We know the broken machine is not yielding its secrets.

So the pop-up toaster never pops up. The waffle iron browns on only one side. The red light on the griddle comes on when it chooses to, not when the griddle is ready. And because my parents are frugal, these renegade appliances are never replaced: they are on my mother's countertops when she dies.

My parents buy a run-down Victorian. But in it, they want to create a "modern" home. What the old house, with its wood moldings, parquet floors, arched doorways, and sleeping porches wanted, I suspect, was to be understood, respected, rehabilitated. But my parents have other plans.

They rip moldings off walls and throw them into the furnace. Cover wooden floors with rose wall-to-wall carpeting. Refit the wood stairway with sensible linoleum. Straighten the arched doorways. Rip doors with glass panes off their hinges—"Too hard to keep clean," my mother says. Paint the green glass tile surround of the fireplace with white semigloss. Enclose the upstairs sleeping porch for a study for me. Enclose the porch downstairs to make a room (it later houses a television) where my father spends much of his free time.

Instead of huge windows swinging out to invite the air, my father installs picture windows that don't open. The room pays my parents back for their desecration: it's asphyxiating in summer, bone-chilling in winter. Still, my father sits in it. But alone. No one else can stand it.

My grandmother moves to Ridgefield to live with us, reluctantly, a short time after my grandfather dies. She wears only black. She has entered a widowhood that lasts until her death, mourning a man she didn't love, a man who never loved her.

Her relatives don't want her. She has no place to go, and she can't afford to keep herself in Hoboken. She doesn't have much money. My grandfather's pension has gone to my mother. And my mother doesn't give any of it to my grandmother. Which makes my grandmother dependent upon my parents' generosity.

It never occurs to my mother to turn over the money to my

grandmother so she can live alone. She believes that she is entitled to the money and my grandmother is not, though because my mother has it and my grandmother does not, the stepmother my mother hates lives with her.

The life my grandmother desires is among her people in Hoboken, close to the shops where she can buy the foods she loves.

Once, several years after she moves in with us, at my father's urging, my mother relents. Gives my grandmother a small allowance for rent and food. But the place my grandmother can afford in Hoboken terrifies her. It is at the edge of town, in the projects. Police sirens blare; searchlights rake the windows. Gangs of teenage thugs scuttle up and down the stairs all night, shouting obscenities, banging on walls. She is ridiculed, taunted, threatened.

My grandmother sleeps with a knife under her pillow, a tower of pots and pans stacked against the front door, which is secured with two deadbolts. She lasts less than a month. Even Ridgefield, and life in my mother's house is better than this. My mother never lets her forget that she once tried to live alone. And that she failed.

My grandmother has always had very little, for she and my grandfather were very poor. And of the little she has, she hasn't taken much with her. A rolling pin, fashioned by my grandfather from a broom handle. A colander for draining pasta, and a handmade fluted wheel to cut ravioli—both bought with money sent her by my grandfather and brought to America when she came as a mail-order bride. Her bedroom set, bought by my grandfather when he married his first wife. A kitchen chair she positions next to the window in her bedroom to mourn in, to knit in. A gigantic cross with a crucified Jesus dripping blood to hang over her bed. A reclining statue of Jesus taken down from the cross, oozing blood from open wounds. A standing Virgin covered by a glass bell. Two sets of rosary beads: one for every day; the other, fashioned from crystal, a wedding gift from my grandfather, for special occasions. (For her wake, my mother has the undertaker twine the crystal beads through my grandmother's fingers. Before she's buried, my mother orders them removed. She keeps them all her life. And bequeaths them to me.)

My grandmother gets the smallest, the least desirable bedroom. She is in this house on sufferance and because my mother feels a filial obligation to her stepmother although she has no filial feelings.

The room looks north and west, over the swamps where the power plant and the New Jersey Turnpike will soon be built. And the room isn't completely hers because it has no lock on the door and because my mother keeps her clothes in my grandmother's closet. My grandmother doesn't have many clothes, my mother says, so she can spare the room.

After supper, in summertime, my grandmother sits in her chair, pulls back the curtain so she can see the setting sun, and says her rosary.

Sometimes I stand next to her and lean on the windowsill and watch, too. Doing nothing with my grandmother is preferable to doing anything with my parents. And watching the sun set is something only my grandmother does. At the end of the day, my mother is too busy clattering pans in the sink to take time to look out the window. Nor does she know when the sun is setting, for she keeps the curtains drawn.

To escape my mother, my grandmother goes to visit relatives in Long Island for a few weeks each summer. She would be glad to live on Long Island, but her relatives will only accommodate her for a little while each year.

On Long Island, my grandmother helps her cousin farm a small plot of land. They grow tomatoes, corn, beans, peas, zucchini, eggplant, basil. During these times, my grandmother eats lustily each day.

She and her sister rise at dawn, collect eggs from the chicken house, weed and till the soil before the heat of day. Some mornings they walk miles to pick wild blueberries and raspberries. These are made into pancakes, cobblers, muffins, and pies by my grandmother's cousin's niece, who lives with them. Other mornings, they hitch rides to the sea to collect mussels or periwinkles.

In Long Island, my grandmother is happy, living a life she might have lived in Italy had she not been so poor. Even when we visit, she is happy, and doesn't argue with my mother. These were my grandmother's relatives, not my mother's. And my mother could visit because my grandmother invited her, not because my mother was entitled to visit. In Long Island, I saw what might have been between them but wasn't.

I remember my grandmother sitting outside before supper, in the warm light of late afternoon, shelling peas into her apron. Stripping the husks off just-picked corn. Setting aside worm-eaten ears for chicken feed.

As she worked, my grandmother sang Pugliese songs that sounded Greek or North African. She sang to herself, beating the insistent rhythms with her foot. She sang songs that told of the Passion of Christ, of how Mary searched for her son Jesus; that told how farm laborers lost their love to the lust of overseers; that insulted in-habitants of neighboring villagers. Songs that praised the gifts of the land—figs, melons, wheat, herbs, wine (especially wine). Songs that blessed the cooking pot, the bowl, the spoon.

These songs my grandmother sang only in Long Island, never in Ridgefield.

When I am a teenager, although I dream about boys, and I dream about having sex with boys, I also dream about food. I imagine the food I will make someday when I have my own kitchen. Sautéed garlic, a tiny bit of lemon juice, a few twigs of steamed asparagus sliced on the bias, a bit of heavy cream, some salt and pepper, twirled through some fresh pasta like the one my grandmother cuts on her "guitar." Fennel and anise seeds mixed together, crushed, sprinkled on top of a nice pork chop, pan-seared on the top of the stove, finished in the oven, served with a sauce made from the drippings laced with red vermouth, served on a bed of caramelized fennel.

Where these ideas come from, I don't know. I don't read cook-books; we don't get magazines. I think about these foods as I wander the aisles of the local food market before I cross the street to join my friends at our hangout. And even though I have my own money, can afford to buy whatever I want, I know my mother would never yield her kitchen to my efforts. I know I must wait until I marry to eat beautiful food with startling tastes.

Occasionally, even though I know it's hopeless, I ask my mother if I can cook. She looks at me like I have a strange disease. Reaches into the cupboard for a can of ravioli to heat for supper. Chases me from the kitchen.

I want to marry as soon as I can. Not to have my own husband, but to have my own kitchen. One with a four-burner gas stove, an oven. Where I can cook and bake and roast whenever I want without anyone bothering me. Where I will have absolute control over what I make, over what I eat.

When I go to junior high, I have to take home economics, which I take every year until I graduate from high school.

The boys, of course, take shop, which I also would have taken if girls were allowed. I liked the thought of using dangerous machinery, of wearing goggles to protect your eyes, of cutting into wood, of working on cars, of welding metal to metal.

Girls were too fragile for shop. But I knew, from experience, that kitchens could be dangerous. There were knives, of course, and vegetable peelers, and hot burners, and scalding water and puffs of steam. These did not qualify as dangers for girls. It is the 1950s, when girls cook, and boys weld. So it's home ec, and only home ec, for me.

For part of the year, we learn to sew. This, I do disastrously (though as a young woman, I learn to sew very well from my mother, who insists sewing is important). In home ec, our first project is an apron trimmed with rickrack. Sewing this will teach us necessary skills.

It is the rickrack that undoes me. Instead of neatly trimming the edges of my apron, my rickrack wanders wherever it chooses. It even hangs off the edges.

I fail sewing. So I am very motivated to succeed in cooking.

Everyone in my class but me hates home ec. They make fun of our teacher, all round and soft and net- and apron-wearing and full of enthusiasm. She has very red cheeks because she's always thrusting her face into pots and pans and ovens. And she wears sneakers instead of shoes so she can race around the class to check oven temperatures, simmering sauces, sautéing pieces of chicken. She wears her hair in a crown of tiny spitcurls tucked hygienically into a net so that not a strand of her hair will fall into the food.

We have to wear hairnets, too. Most of the girls balk and complain. But I like it because the hairnets ruin the fancy girls' teased hair.

My hair, like everything else about my outward appearance, is sensible and can't be ruined. My clothing, which I buy with my mother on our infrequent angst-ridden shopping trips, is always the cheapest, the most serviceable, the least stylish, and I'm mocked for it by the fancy girls with teased hair, and so it pleases me to see their elaborate coiffures ruined. Unlike the fancy girls with the teased hair, I had no "look" to speak of, unless looking like you're fifty when you're a teenager is a "look." I have more important things on my mind than clothes and looking in a mirror—sex and books, to be exact. And I'm not "collegiate," either. I'm too dark and foreign looking. Besides, I'm not altogether sure I can go to college, even though I'm smart, even though I want to go to college and study hard things—philosophy, literature. There is the money, of course. My parents don't have much, certainly not enough to afford tuition, room, board. And a guidance counselor tells me that a person with my background (Italian? Working class?) will make very poor college material, that there were very few of us in college, actually, and those who entered didn't do well and usually dropped out, and so I should sign up for Secretarial.

But I sign up for College Prep anyway because, though my clothes are sensible, my spirit is far from sensible. It is, dreamy, artistic, and, at times, cantankerous and cynical. I'm different, I've convinced myself, from everyone else. At pep rallies, I can be found trying to read *And Quiet Flows the Don* while waiting for the festivities to begin, or scribbling in my diary about the idiocy of running back and forth to throw a large ball into a hoop several feet off the ground, or mocking the school cheers. When my boy pal Eddie asks me why, if I hate these events so much, I bother to attend them, I tell him that they get me out of the house, and besides, I *love* hating them.

I am very happy in the kitchen at school because I see our teacher as a soul mate. She acts as if she doesn't care what people think of her.

I love the long line of clean ranges in the center of the classroom. The cupboards filled with packages of spaghetti, jars of spices and herbs, tins of chicken broth, bottles of olives. The refrigerators that ring the room, which cool a substantial quantity of food: thick pieces of beef for stews; whole chickens; racks of spareribs; fresh vegetables; curly parsley.

I discover that there is ceremony in cooking. In the donning of aprons. In the tying of apron strings. In the sharpening of blades. In the rituals of the preparation of ingredients.

I don my very ugly rickrack apron, tuck my short hair into my hairnet, pull a knife out of the woodblock like King Arthur, sharpen it on the stone expertly, prepare to make magic.

I begin my education in the pleasures of the kitchen, in the pleasures of the flesh. I learn how little effort it takes to produce something that—unlike so many of the other things I must do in my life—can always be counted upon to provide pleasure. If you select fine ingredients, prepare them well, and cook them exactly right according to a set of rules, our teacher says, you can never fail in the kitchen. Your meal will always turn out perfectly.

I like this. Here, there is order, discipline. Here, I feel safe.

Of course, there is abundant drama, too, in cooking. And the transformation of the raw into the cooked becomes as compelling to me as the Russian novels I am forever reading.

What I learn about cooking appeals to the diva in me. And my teacher is a diva, too. She insists on perfection, scolds delivery boys if they bring inferior merchandise, gushes if what is brought is fresh and wonderful. The kitchen is her stage, and she swoops and twirls and stirs and beats and slices her way through our class in a dance for the ages.

One of the reasons I'm very happy in the school kitchen is that we get to eat what we cook at the end of class. These are our "tastings." And they are very serious affairs.

We have them at very neatly appointed tables set with serviceable matching placemats, dishes, glassware, and cutlery. We have sparkling water because our school, of course, does not permit wine. We have cloth napkins because our teacher believes that a beautiful table is essential to dining well.

Before we sit down to eat, our teacher insists we clear away all the dirty pots and pans. These are organized behind a screen.

"Only barbarians eat with dirty pots and pans in view," our teacher says. "When you get older, girls, you'll know you're in a fine restaurant if they whisk the dirty dishes off the table, take them into the kitchen. If they don't, if they make piles of filth on trays and leave them there for all to see, don't stand for it. Summon the captain. Insist that they be removed. One can never dine well surrounded by garbage."

And the food we make is, of course, better than the food my mother makes at home. Oh, it *is* 1950s food. And, yes, there *are* tuna fish casseroles, and chicken salad made with homemade mayonnaise.

But our teacher has been "abroad," and she is, she tells us, forever changed. So there is also sautéed sole with browned butter and slivers of roasted almonds, served with rice tarted up with little bits of sautéed celery, onion, and red and green pepper. A stewed beef, exquisitely tender, with carrots and tiny onions melting into the sauce. (She sneaks wine into the sauce, defying school regulations.) A roasted chicken stuffed with whole pierced lemons and fresh parsley (the only fresh herb she can find in the United States, she complains).

Our teacher shows us how we should take our food. Slowly.

Seriously. Sensuously. Pleasurably. With eyes closed to intensify the sensation.

"Close your eyes, girls," she says. "No peeking. No gulping. Tiny tastes. Tiny sips. Appreciate, appreciate."

It is a bacchanal, this class of ours. And I sometimes think that if our very sensible principal had known what was going on in this room, he would have canceled the class.

He thought we were learning how to be good housewives. But I was learning, under the tutelage of this unlikely guru, the wanton pleasure of the sybaritic life.

Part Two

WOUNDS

KEEPSAKES

After my grandfather dies, all his possessions fit into one large cardboard carton. His labor was of the manual, bone-crunching, muscle-aching kind. And though he worked hard from boyhood, these belongings are all he left when he died.

Birth certificate. (Commune di Vieste, Provincia di Foggia. Dated 4 settèmbre 1881, though when he arrived in America, officials gave him a birthdate in April, because they couldn't understand his reply to the question "When were you born?")

Passport. (Italian.)

Naturalization papers. (Dated 4 March 1944. The handwriting shows he doesn't often sign his name.)

Identification papers, bearing his photograph, for his work on the Lackawanna Railroad. (For the photo, he was docked pay.)

Identification papers, bearing his photograph, for his work on the piers. Occupation: *Laborer*. Height: *5 feet 3 inches*. Weight: *165 pounds* (he was a stocky man). Color: *White*. Hair: *Gray Black*. Complexion: *Ruddy*. (For the photo on the papers, he was docked pay.)

Cheap metal pocket watch, neither gold nor silver. (Worn on special occasions. But not to work. Not needed there, for the bosses told him when to begin work, when to eat, when to stop. He was not in control of how he spent his time, so he had no need to know what time it was. The watch, broken, is now in my possession.)

Nightshirts. (Two. Rough material.)

Nightcap. (One. The tenement was unheated.)

Long underwear. (Two sets. One heavy, for winter; one light, for summer. Worn day and night. Removed on Saturday, bathing day. Though there was no bathtub and he washed at the sink, standing on an old towel to catch the drips. The day to switch from the winter set to the summer, determined by a particular saint's holiday—which saint, I do not recall.)

Socks. (Five pairs, worn, darned.)

Workclothes. (Two sets.)

Workboots. (One pair, cracked, worn.)

Workgloves. (One pair, grime-encrusted.)

Gold signet ring. Initials "S" and "C" intertwined. (A rare self-indulgence. Now in my possession, worn every day, in memory.)

A slingshot. (Homemade.)

Lunch pail. (Metal. He ate only food prepared at home or by a relative; the only time he didn't was at his daughter's wedding reception.)

Pinochle cards. (Worn; used nightly in games played during the summer, outside on the sidewalk in front of the tenement, with neighbors, on a collapsible card table, lighted from above by a streetlamp.)

There were, of course, no books, no magazines (he could read neither Italian nor English); no recordings (he had no phonograph); no paintings. Nothing but a very large crucifix and two large photographs adorned their walls.

The photographs. The first, a wedding photograph of my grandfather and my mother's birth mother, the one who died, for whom my mother languished. The second, a wedding photograph of my grandfather and my stepgrandmother, the woman my grandfather brought to the United States for my mother's care, the stepmother my mother detested.

They are gigantic, the photos. As large as movie posters. Backed with cardboard. Crumbling, now. Far too large to display in any modest room (though they were displayed in such a room), or even in a large room, for that matter. I do not understand the reason for their size. Except to indicate the seriousness of marriage.

Today, almost a century after they were taken, they rest on his granddaughter's desk. After his death, they went to my mother. After her death, to my father. After my mother's death, when my father marries a second time, he wants to discard them and he tells me so, tells me to come right away to his house or they'll be gone.

"He wants to put the past behind him," my husband says. "Wants to start a new life."

Can my mother's family, my family, I ask myself, *mean so little to him now?*

I imagine the wedding pictures in a garbage bag at the town dump, soiled by coffee grounds, yesterday's leftovers. "I'm coming right away," I tell my father, hating him, thinking he is a mean, cold-hearted prick.

When I get them, I clutch at them, as if, in having them, I have resurrected my grandparents. As if, in having them, I have known my grandmother. I think that if I gaze at them long enough, they will yield secrets that will help me become more myself.

On the left of each photo, there is a bride, exhibiting a lavish bouquet of roses, two dozen roses, a bouquet far more sumptuous than my wedding bouquet, far more impressive than any I've seen. My grandmother's flowers are in a formal arrangement, fresh and alive. In a few years, she will be dead from influenza. My step-grandmother's flowers are arranged more loosely. Her name was Libera, and she was a renegade, a breaker of rules, and so it would be like her to ask for an informal arrangement. But her roses are wilted. Was she married on a hot day? Or as an economy did she and my grandfather arrange to have a bouquet made from flowers past their prime? This would be very like them.

My grandfather wears the same suit in each photo (his one good suit), and the same shirt, same tie, same lily-of-the-valley bouton-nière, same handkerchief (folded differently—into a large white oblong when he marries my grandmother; into a tiny saillike triangle when he marries my stepgrandmother). His shoes are not new, but polished: the first set, with buttons; the second, with laces.

In each, he strikes a gallant pose: head cocked, dark hair neatly slicked back. The hint of a rakish pompadour when he married my grandmother has disappeared by the time he marries my stepgrandmother.

In each, he seems proud of his bride and of his position as groom. In each, he smiles. In the first, however, you can see the pride in his smile, can feel the sexual tension between this woman and this man, can tell that this was a love match. In the second, his smile seems born of relief that he will no longer have to worry about his daughter's care. In the portrait with my stepgrandmother, he is not wearing a wedding ring. In his heart, he married only once; the second marriage was undertaken from necessity, not choice.

And the backgrounds. In one, my grandfather and his first wife stand in front of a screen portraying the colonnaded great hall of a palazzo; in the other, my grandfather and stepgrandmother stand near one depicting a stone wall and the trellised window of a country estate.

The stone wall of such a place, though was built to keep him out. Yes, he might have worked its land. But he could not walk on its lawns, lounge under its trees, swim in its brooks, eat at its table.

The photographers have done their best to make these folk look accepted, acceptable, well regarded, well respected. The poorer they are, the more recently they have arrived, the photographers have learned, the more elaborate and elegant they want the backdrops in their photographs.

But the dresses. Oh, the dresses.

My grandmother's, adorned with tulle rosettes, decorated with a scalloped border trimmed with beads atop an organza underskirt. My stepgrandmother's, layer upon layer of embroidered lace. The neckline of each, proper, decorous. The headdresses, closefitting, with spikes of pearls. The veils, floor-length, embroidered.

My grandmother stands with her feet firmly planted, and she looks bold and sure and proud and determined and purposeful. (My granddaughter Julia's face is very like hers.) And she was, I have been told, willful, like I am. But my grandfather didn't complain, just shook his head and laughed when she stood firm against him, for he loved her and was happy that he was in America, and not in the Old Country, for there, a man who could not control his wife was not a man at all.

My stepgrandmother stands in tiny pointed shoes fastened with satin ribbons, poised daintily. No sign, here, of the hardworking capable woman she was. She looks vexed, uncertain of her future with this man and his child.

If you saw these photographs of these women in these dresses, you would not believe that my grandmother sold vegetables door-to-door and took in washing; that my stepgrandmother would become the superintendent of our tenement, that she would collect rent for the landlord, and shovel snow, and fix things. In their bridal attire (bought? rented?), these women look wealthy, as wealthy as the wives of the *latifundisti*, the great landholders in Puglia.

On this one day, these poor women can pretend they are wealthy, privileged. Which is why, I think, these portraits are so large—these images are meant to obliterate that they're immigrants, obliterate the poverty of their lives.

Still, each woman seems uncomfortable wearing these clothes. Neither will ever wear finery like this again. But the three-piece suit is my grandfather's, and he wears it throughout his life. A man who works with his hands needs only one suit. To wear to weddings, christenings, funerals (those of others, and his own). More than one suit would be an extravagance.

And this man, who leads a hardscrabble life in this richest of countries (whose streets, he was told, were paved with gold, who tallies at day's end how little he's earned, how much he owes), has no need of more than one suit, carefully purchased, so that it does not look like a wedding suit but like a good suit. A suit a man can wear with pride, though in wearing it, he feels like an imposter. Feels like the bosses he despises, not like the laborer he is and the workers he respects.

My grandfather wears this suit eight times in his lifetime. At his first wedding. My mother's christening. His first wife's funeral. His second wedding. My mother's wedding, when he walks her down the aisle with pride, with joy, for he likes the man she is marrying; he gets drunk at her reception, he is so happy. (Drunk as he is, he is careful of his suit. He is always careful of his suit.) And he wears this suit on the day when he becomes a citizen of the United States.

When his daughter marries, my grandfather tells her that he will wear this suit, though it now looks old-fashioned, when her children are christened, when they graduate from college, when they marry— his grandchildren who will go to college, distinguish themselves, fulfill his dreams, marry well, make his work worthwhile. (He wears his suit to their christenings. But he is dead long before they graduate, long before they marry.)

He wears his suit, too, for his wake and his burial. But this time, it smells of mothballs, for his wife has not had the time to air it.

Because he was buried in his suit, there was no good suit in the box of my grandfather's belongings. No good shirt, good socks, good tie, for he was buried in them as well. Just one pair of everyday trousers. No everyday shirt (he wore the top of his long underwear in the house).

Toward the end of his life, my grandfather would try the suit on to make sure that it still fit (he was not getting fat, but was becoming bloated, retaining water for a reason he never discovered, for he never went to a doctor, not once). He tried the suit on because he didn't want his wife or daughter to waste money on a burial suit, and he didn't want the undertaker to slit the jacket of his suit up the back, slit the trousers to accommodate his girth, the way the undertaker had to for a friend. My grandfather didn't want to imagine himself going to the other side in a damaged suit. That would have made a bad impression, would have brought disgrace to his family. Even in death, *la bella figura.*

And yes, the suit still fit, he would discover whenever he tried it on, though it was a bit tight, especially in the thighs. And, as he pulled in his stomach and fastened the buttons of his trousers, he relaxed, knowing that this suit could still be put to good use.

If my grandfather had been a nostalgic man, there would have been a small bag of soil in the box, Pugliese soil, stowed in his luggage and brought with him to America so that he could be buried with it. But there was no bag of soil. No nostalgia for the old country. Yes, he missed his parents (dead), his relatives (most of them dead), his friends (because he couldn't write, he had never been in touch with them). But he did not miss the place he left. "I spit on that place," he said. He was better off, he knew, in America.

In that cardboard box of my grandfather's possessions, there was this, too:

One pass, No. E 9155, good for riding any Lackawanna train between all stations, good from January 1st, 1948 through December 31st, 1949 (except for trains 3 and 6), in the name of Mr. S. Calabrese, Retired Laborer, signed on the back, in the hand that showed he did not write his name often.

The pass was useless. By the time this perquisite was issued to him, he was too sick to travel. And by the end of 1949, he was dead.

SLINGSHOT

I am sitting at my grandparents' kitchen table in Hoboken. My grandfather and I are drinking our wine (mine diluted with water) and eating lupini beans for a snack. I love peeling the covering from the bean, love popping the bean into my mouth. I love its salty softness. Love that my grandfather lets me eat as many as I want, as messily as I want; love that he lets me pile my lupini beans in front of me on the oilcloth-covered table without telling me to put them on my plate.

The time is during World War II. My father is in the Pacific. My grandparents take care of me often. They live right next door to my mother and me, our apartments connected by a toilet.

Whenever my grandfather takes care of me, he gives me wine mixed with water. He drinks his wine; I drink mine. (In high school, I will be the girl who drinks too much at parties. The girl who drinks so much that I can't remember who took me home. The girl who drinks so much that I often pass out on the way home—once, in the middle of a four-lane highway.)

My grandfather tells me stories, in dialect. Sometimes he tells me what I think are stories about where he used to live. Sometimes he tells me stories about my mother when she was a child. Sometimes he tells me about what is happening in the world right now. Some of what he says, I understand. Some I don't. Words, phrases, sentences get through to me; then, suddenly, and always when the story gets interesting, I'm lost. But because I can't speak dialect, and he can't understand English, I can't tell him to repeat what he says, to slow down. So I can't be sure, now, if my memories of what he told me are pure, or if they are riddled with my own interpolations, and so part fabrication. I nod to keep him talking, nod as if I understand. I am sleepy from the wine, but not yet sleeping, and I fill in the blanks in my grandfather's stories. Soon, I will want to sleep. And will sleep, until my mother comes back. In the middle of my grandparents' feather bed. Under a giant cross with Jesus bleeding.

During the war, my mother welcomes my grandparents' help raising me. Whatever my stepgrandmother wasn't—warm, tender, congenial—she made up for by her brusque competence in caring for children.

I remember my grandmother's no-nonsense way of washing me, remember how she sang Italian songs as she cared for me, though she was not singing to me. I remember wandering into my grandparents' apartment, where I would be given small treats—a few almonds to nibble, a crust of homemade bread with honey, a hard biscuit. When my grandmother watched me, she sometimes played with me, though never when my mother was around. A game of patty-cake, cat's cradle, peekaboo.

While my father was away, I don't remember my grandmother and my mother fighting. My mother was happy to be near her father, whom she adored. And with my father gone, my mother had less to do, so she tolerated my grandmother's ways—how she ate cockles with a safety pin; how she rarely changed her clothes or washed; how she never combed her hair; how she didn't love my mother (though she seemed to love me).

If my mother came home, and found me drunk, she'd be angry. But my grandfather never stopped giving me watered-down wine. And my mother never stopped leaving me with him.

On this day, my grandfather tells me that I will go to school when I'm older. And that, when I go to school, I should be a good girl.

He looks out the window as he talks. Stops talking. Gestures for me to be quiet. Takes the slingshot he keeps on the windowsill, a stone from the assortment he keeps in a small dish. Slowly, carefully, he leans out the window.

There is a pigeon perched on our neighbor's clothesline, not far from the open window. Many of our neighbors keep pigeons in pigeon coops. My mother thinks they're a nuisance and disease-ridden—flying rats, she calls them—and can't understand this old-world practice.

My grandfather pulls back the elastic on the slingshot. Takes aim. Lets go.

The pigeon drops to the ground. In my alcohol-induced haze, this happens in slow motion.

My grandfather tells me to stay where I am. He runs downstairs, out the back door, into the courtyard. And though I know I'm not supposed to, because it's dangerous, I lean way out the window to see what happens next.

My grandfather picks up the pigeon, inspects it. The bird doesn't look dead. It looks startled. I think I see it move its wings.

Satisfied, my grandfather tucks the pigeon under his shirt. Back in the kitchen, he wrings its neck. The pigeon's head dangles, like the head of my abused and broken doll.

I have, in my young life, seen many animals brought home live from the market and slaughtered in my grandparents' kitchen. Also, on my grandmother's relatives' farm when we visit. My grandparents won't eat anything that doesn't come into their home alive.

I am curious about, horrified by, how my grandparents wring birds' necks, pluck their feathers, kill eels with sharp blows to the head, kill fish by plunging a knife between their eyes. I watch them strip the skin off animals with pliers, remove entrails, drain animals' blood. I am beginning to wonder when life becomes nonlife; beginning to think about death, beginning to have nightmares in which I, too, am dressed for cooking.

I watch my grandfather's work with the pigeon. He dangles the head before me, teasing me. This, he won't discard, for in this household nothing is wasted. Later, he'll dress it, impale it on a metal skewer, thrust it into the coals of the stove to roast, share it with my grandmother.

The entrails, though, are his alone. These, he chops and fries, dousing them with wine. He toasts a piece of my grandmother's bread, smears it with pigeon guts, pours the juices over, serves himself a little more wine. He is, at this moment, a very happy man.

After my grandfather eats the entrails, he puts the pigeon in a pot and stews it with a few tomatoes, garlic, parsley, and wine. Though it smells delicious, when mealtime comes I won't eat it. Won't say where it comes from when my mother pressures me to tell her where my grandfather got the pigeon.

Because it's wartime, there is much talk of death in our household. My mother and grandparents discuss the carnage of the war at the supper table and I have heard it. I have seen the pages of newspapers filled with pictures of GIs victorious, of GIs slain, though my mother tries to hide them from me. Images of the war, though, are every-where and can't be hidden—on the newsprint the vegetable man uses to wrap my mother's purchases; on the front pages of the newspapers for sale at Albini's, our corner drugstore.

Italy is at war against the United States, and my grandparents wonder how their relatives in Italy are faring. Throughout the war, they send them packages of clothing, of dried beans, dry biscuits. My grandparents want the Allies to win. Still, they don't want anyone from their villages to die.

And whether my father will come back from the war alive, we don't know. My mother knows he's in the Pacific, near some heavy fighting. She knows this because of coded messages in my father's letters.

During the war, my mother eats whatever is put in front of her (and it is almost always cooked by my grandfather). She is happy to have someone else attending to the business of food, happy to be with her father, happy to have help managing me. She enjoys what he cooks. She has not yet developed her revulsion for the peasant fare he and my grandmother eat. This comes later, when she moves to the suburbs and tries to put her Italian past behind her.

My grandfather was a farm boy, born into a family of farm laborers. As a small child, he worked the wheat fields with his parents.

My father tells me about one difficult day, when my grandfather's small hands were covered with cuts from the stalks he was binding after his parents cut the wheat, and he looked up to the road above the field. He saw a small boy, about his age, walking along the road, alone, carrying a bookbag.

This was during the 1890s, when workers in the South were poorer than they had been before. They borrowed money to live, couldn't pay their debts, lived like indentured servants. There was never food enough or money enough, though they worked from long before dawn until after dusk, and had to walk to and from the fields to the villages where they lived.

"Papa, where is that boy going?" my grandfather asked.

His father looked up at the boy walking alone on a road, for a boy walking alone on a road was an unusual thing.

"That boy," his father said, "is going to school."

"Papa," my grandfather said, "I would like to do that. I would like to go to school." For surely my grandfather must have thought that walking alone on a road in the morning was preferable to what he was doing, even if he was doing it with his parents.

"*Figlio mio*," his father said, "you cannot do that, you cannot go to school."

"But why can't I go to school, Papa?" my grandfather asked.

"You cannot go to school," his father answered, "because you are a laborer and your lot in life is to work in the fields."

"But Papa," my grandfather said, "what about my children?"

"Your children," his father answered, "cannot go to school, for their lot in life is to be peasants to work in the fields, like you."

When my father tells the story, he says that my grandfather paused a moment, looked at the boy on the road, and said, "But Papa, my children's children. Surely they will go to school."

According to my father, one of the reasons my grandfather came to America was so that his children, and his children's children, could go to school.

When my grandfather first came to America, he worked on the Lackawanna Railroad. In 1908, the year he left Italy, the income of farm workers in the South had plummeted; workers could not buy enough food to sustain life. My grandfather once told my father that, in Italy, he had always gone to bed hungry. Whenever I had a meal with my grandfather, he would pat his belly and smile. I would pat my belly and smile. Here, he always ate enough. And for this he was grateful. But it was not always so, not when he first worked on the railroad.

I don't know how my grandfather paid for his steamship passage to America. But, as with other Southern Italians, it was probably paid for by a *padrone* or a recruiter who went to the South to find laborers. He talked about the man who brought him here to work on the railroad. He always said this man was not a good man. My grandfather would have received instructions to lie about why he was coming to America, because recruiting workers in Italy, though a common practice, was illegal. He would have been told to say to the officials that, no, he had no promise of work, but that yes, he intended to work. Please God he answered correctly, or he would be shipped back to Italy.

Family lore has it that his passage was paid for, that its cost was deducted from his pay, that he paid far, far more than his passage cost, and that it took him many years to pay off the debt. This was why his young wife worked.

A dream of America was sold to laborers to lure them to America, where they provided the cheap labor needed for building railways, subways, buildings. During my grandfather's first years here, the dream faded. Though he never would trade life in this country for life in the Old World.

"Here," he said, "you work hard, you get paid little, you eat, maybe not too much, but you eat. There, you work, you work, you work, you don't get paid, you don't eat."

For years I believed (as I was taught in school) that the men who built America, made it great, were men like Henry Ford, John D. Rockefeller, Andrew Carnegie. But the people who built America were people like my grandfather.

The men who worked on railroad gangs awakened at three in the morning and walked to the line they were building, as they had walked to the fields in Italy. They worked from five until twelve without rest.

They had hard bread for lunch. Water, if it was available, was usually fetid. But always, there was wine.

After lunch, they worked again until four. Then they walked back to the boxcars where they lived, ate whatever supper they could manage, fell into a comalike sleep.

They slept, eight men to a windowless boxcar, on bags of straw crawling with vermin. They covered themselves with discarded horse blankets and they slept in their filthy work clothes, for there was no place to wash them, there was no place to wash themselves. Their bodies were lice-ridden, encrusted with dirt, covered with oozing sores.

People who saw them along the line made fun of them. Called them dagos, wops, filthy guineas. People who saw them working were afraid of them, of their filth, of their foreignness, and mothers pushed their children behind their backs, for they believed these men were dangerous.

If the men complained that they had no fresh water, the *padrone* would say they were never satisfied, they should starve to death, they didn't belong here. But they were here. And it was a *padrone* who brought them, who profited from their labor.

Their work was difficult and dangerous. They worked hunched over, in pain. They were too hot or too cold. They picked their way across the gashes the railroads made in the land, laying track, repairing track.

They were gone from their new homes in America for months, sometimes longer. Because many of them couldn't write, their families didn't hear from them, didn't know where they were.

When they returned, looking older, more beaten than when they left, they said little, for there was little to say. They wanted to sleep. They wanted to wash. They were filthy. Filthy with the soil of America.

Here, the unexpected happens: my grandfather becomes a cook on the railroad. The gang boss has decided that the men will work better if someone cooks for them, if they eat good food. So my grandfather trades pickax and shovel for frying pans, pots, and knives.

My grandfather knew how to cook—knew how to cook outside, for that's where you cooked, if you had something to cook, when you worked the fields. On the railroad gang, my grandfather wanted a hot meal at the end of a hard day's work, not just the bread and cheese rationed to the men for supper.

He began by cooking meals for himself along the railroad line, using what he scavenged. Then he cooked for himself and a few friends who scavenged with him. In time, my father told me, he persuaded the *padrone* to let him cook for all the men in his gang, with provisions provided by the railroad. By then, muckrakers were writing about workers' living conditions and the railroad owners were forced to improve them.

How he persuaded the *padrone*, I can only imagine.

Before the railroad provides him with equipment to cook for the men, he gathers twigs, pieces of wood, pieces of charcoal by the side of the railbed, marveling that there are such things to be had for the taking. If things had been this easy in the old country, if you weren't punished for taking what you found, he thinks, there would have been no reason to leave.

I see my grandfather trudging back down the line after his day's work, collecting twigs, putting them into the sack he carries on his back. I see him digging a hole, surrounding it with rocks, lining it with kindling, placing the wood carefully, paying attention to the direction of the wind, and lighting the fire with a match from the metal matchbox he carries.

He fans the fire, coaxes it to life. Takes a grate he's taken from over a drainage pipe, places it over the fire.

But what will he cook?

My grandfather was a country boy. He knows how to study the land. How to hunt animals, how to forage. This, he learned from his parents.

He knows how to find land snails after a heavy rain. How to scout for edible wild herbs and greens—bay laurel, savory, thyme, sorrel, dandelions, spinach, chicory, nettle tops—and for onion shoots, wild leeks, berries. How to make a trap, make and use a slingshot. How to rig a net so he can wade into a shallow stream and catch fish, river crab, river eel.

While the fire burns, I see him dressing what he's hunted. A squirrel, perhaps, killed with his slingshot. He puts on a pair of gloves, pulls the skin over the head, the legs. Cuts off the head and feet. Removes the glands and the internal organs. Cuts the squirrel into pieces. Rubs the meat with the pork fat he carries in his backpack, then rubs it with the wild thyme that he's found.

He puts the squirrel on the grill over the fire. After a while, the wild onions he's gathered. Then the bread he's given.

I see him eating his meal, slowly. Sharing his food (for he was always generous). I see him drinking from his flask of wine. A laborer, in filthy clothes, sitting on a rock by the side of a fire near a railroad track somewhere in New York State, eating food that satisfies him, not just food that fills his belly.

HANDWORK

Most days, as I was growing into young womanhood, my old Italian grandmother used to sit, silently, all day long, very close to the radiator in the corner of the dining room of our house in Ridgefield, New Jersey, her old black shawl covering her shoulders, her feet supported by an old painted stool, as she crocheted white tablecloths, or knitted sweaters or afghans with wool unraveled from old sweaters we had outgrown, had outworn, or despised.

Before leaving the house, I would stop by where my grandmother was sitting, to see what she was working on, to get a coin from her to buy a treat. Though she had very little money, she was generous, giving me surprise gifts of silver dollars, a paper bill she had safety-pinned to the underside of her skirt so my mother wouldn't find it and steal it. Her love for me defied explanation; she detested my mother, and I did little to deserve her love, nothing to invite it, except bake with her on occasion, or bring her a cool glass of water now and then so she would not have to interrupt her work, or let her teach me how to knit.

I spoke to her in English (for I spoke very little dialect); she answered in dialect (for she spoke very little English). My mother discouraged us from speaking dialect, from speaking Italian. I think my mother didn't want us to know our grandmother, and through knowing her, come to love her, as my mother did not love her. (I did love my grandmother. But as one might a forbidden, graven image. For my mother, I felt no love, but rage, and, yes, a deep and bitter yearning.)

My grandmother cared for me as she could not care for my mother. *Mia figlia*, she called me: my child. Something she never called my mother. For my mother wasn't her child but some other woman's child. The child of a woman more beautiful than she, a woman my grandfather loved until he died. A woman my mother mourned until she died, though she had experienced that mother's love only briefly.

"Mia figlia," my grandmother would say, a finger to her lips, when she thought it was a day that would be dangerous for me, a day I should stay out of my father's way.

"Mia figlia," as she pushed me behind her body when my father came at me, behind the body no one embraced.

"Mia figlia," when I graduated from grammar school, high school, college, though my education would separate us. "Mia figlia," when I married, when I became a mother, though she held no regard for maternity.

"Mia figlia," in a whisper, when she was dying.

As she worked throughout the day, my grandmother nibbled on almonds that she kept in her apron pocket. When I asked her why, in English, she would respond, in dialect, "For strength and for remembrance."

For strength and for remembrance.

I thought that it was my dead grandfather my grandmother was remembering. But that she had left family behind when she came here, I didn't realize. In the myopia of my childhood, this woman existed as my grandmother only, baker of bread, maker of pizza, knitter of garments I didn't often wear, crocheter of white lace tablecloths my mother used on our dining room table on holidays. I did not understand that she was a woman with a past.

Maybe it was not my grandfather my grandmother was remembering. But a father who loved her gruffly or not at all. A sister she slept with, or worked with in the fields or in the orange groves behind her village. A brother who tormented her or who looked after her when the boys of the village chased her and made fun of her, for she was no beauty, and long past the age when women marry.

Maybe it was a mother, too. A mother who sent her daughter to be married in America. A mother anguished in the knowledge that she would never see her child again, perhaps never hear from her. But happy, too, that her daughter would have a better life.

Was my grandmother remembering the mother who took her broom and swept the steps to her dwelling the day after her daughter left for America? Remembering the mother who wept as she wiped away the footprints her daughter had left in the red dust that blew up with the winds from the Sahara, footprints that had remained on the threshold through that mournful, windless night?

But sweep she must, for this was the work of women, and her duty, this sweeping, like working in the fields when there was work to be had, and fetching water when there was water to be had, and gathering herbs and vegetables—chicory, cardoons, fennel—on damp and misty days when it was possible. Yes, sweep and work and fetch and gather and weep she must, for her daughter, and for all those who left this small and ghostlike place. And weep, too, for those who remained behind.

During the winter, the radiator hissed and clanked, creating more noise than heat, though its corner was nevertheless one of the warmest places in our drafty old house. But sitting there had a price: it meant that my grandmother never sat in sunlight, and that she could barely see her work, for her corner of the dining room was forever in shadow, and the economies of our household forbade the use of artificial light during the day.

I knew that my grandmother was there, for she had nowhere else to go, nothing else to do after she did her small bit of shopping and her baking, but crochet and knit. She had no friends and no employment in Ridgefield. She was far from Hoboken, far from a meaningful life earning her keep as a building superintendent and complaining with her cronies on the stoop of our building.

I knew nothing of the South of Italy where all my grandparents came from. Knew nothing of my grandmother's village in Puglia, though I thought it was a barbarous place, for she sang me a song about a wolf coming through a window to steal a baby. This song scared me, but it was a song about something that happened only in that faraway place where my grandmother used to live.

All I knew of my grandmother's village was that she had left it behind. She never described where she came from, never told me its name, never said she missed it, never said she wanted to go back. So my grandmother's Italy became an Italy I created, a little white village with cubical houses tumbling down a rocky hillside to a crystalline sea. Imagined flowers blooming, trees fruiting. I saw black-clad women in headscarves walking through narrow alleyways, balancing huge bundles on their heads. I saw these women cooking in tiny kitchens with tiny windows.

When I thought about my grandmother's Italy, I did not imagine invasion, conquest, war, hunger, thirst, fatigue, resignation, despair. I did not see a waterless, sunbaked, grief-stricken, apocalyptic land bleeding its people to America.

My grandfather's first wife, his girlish wife, sold vegetables door to door from the handcart she pushed through the streets of Hoboken; she took in washing during her pregnancy and after, wearing herself down.

She died of influenza, like so many others, when her baby, my mother, was only three months old. Undertakers were so busy during this time they could not take the dead away, could not bury them quickly enough. My mother's mother was buried in an unmarked grave without ceremony, for during this time it was against the law for people to gather to mourn the dead.

Years later, my mother would wander that cemetery, looking for her mother. My mother would make a cross from pieces of wood she found, to mark a place that might have been her mother's grave, to stop her mother's soul from wandering.

Soon after his first wife died, my grandfather worked out an arrangement through people he knew with a woman from his province who was looking for a situation. He needed someone to care for his child, for the people who cared for his child did not take good care of her. He was desperate and had very little time, and he settled for Libera because she was known by people he knew and she came from his province, Puglia. She was desperate and had very little hope and needed him so she could come to America, and so she settled for him.

It was 1919. Because of the war, life was harder and more dangerous in Puglia than it had ever been. The poor were poorer; the rich, richer. And it was more difficult to leave.

A peasant army had fought the war. "They took our men, and gave them sticks to fight with, and marched them to the machine guns, let the Austrians kill them," my grandmother said.

On the boat, on the way over, my stepgrandmother knit the man who would become her husband a sweater from finely spun wool she had bought with money he sent her. She knew that it was sometimes cold in this new land, even cold indoors, and very cold where he worked outdoors on the railroad for many months of the year near a lake, far bigger than the one near her small village. She knit this man a sweater to show concern for him, to please him. She did not yet know that she would never please him, that no one could please him now but the tiny daughter she was to attend.

She crocheted herself a shawl, too, on the voyage over, for she was quick with her needles. The wool was thick, and the work went fast; she had nothing else to do, and was unused to inactivity. The shawl was black, and she was happy at her knitting, though she was crowded below deck with so many others, and permitted on deck for fresh air for just a little while each day. The black shawl was something she would wear around her shoulders to keep herself warm in this strange new place where, at least, she had some relatives.

She had enough to eat on her journey, and she was grateful for this. He had sent her much more than the 435 lire for her passage (he was a generous man, and this was good, her mother said). So she fed herself well, fed herself food that could be bought for a price, food she did not have to cook herself, more food than she had ever eaten—*pasta asciuta alla conserva di pomodoro*; *pasta asciuta al sugo*; *minestrone di pasta e ceci*. Although others complained about the food, she did not complain. She knew what it was like to have nothing to eat, to fill your belly with dirt and air.

But generous as the man was, she decided that she would not knit the child a thing, not now, perhaps not ever. For, although she would care for her, the child was his. Not hers. Not theirs. The child was not her blood.

My grandmother did not begin crocheting tablecloths until my grandfather died. When he was alive, she was inclined neither to finery nor extravagance and through all the years she lived with him, the tables she set were functional and austere.

Why she began crocheting her tablecloths, I cannot say. Perhaps to pass the time. Perhaps to leave something of herself behind, for there would be no children, no namesake, no one of her blood to tend her grave when she died.

If her stepdaughter wanted to use these tablecloths, all well and good, though Libera would never sit at the table with her. But if her stepdaughter didn't want to use these tablecloths, that too was all well and good. She would give them to the child who suffered, as she had, in this house filled with rage and sorrow.

Why my grandmother sat close to the radiator during the winter, I could well understand. Her body had never gotten used to the cold.

But I think, too, that the radiator became my grandmother's companion. It didn't yell at her, like my parents. Nor mock her. It didn't tell her what to do, what to wear. It didn't condemn her for who she was: a peasant from the South of Italy.

The radiator didn't betray her. In winter, it was warm; in summer, it radiated the idea of coolness, so that, for a woman used to so little,

78

it might have seemed little enough. The radiator, her needlework, her food, her mornings at church, our few moments together, her only comforts.

My grandmother took all her meals alone, even on holidays, when she'd bring a loaf of her bread into the dining room, place it directly on the tablecloth, and return to her place at the kitchen table, as if to protest how she was treated, or perhaps because my mother was not her blood, and so she would not break bread with her. (My mother would take the bread off the tablecloth, take it back into the kitchen to slice it, and place it in a bread basket, lined with a napkin.)

She ate, often, in her chair by the radiator, from the chipped bowl that was companion to my grandfather's. She fed herself with a large metal spoon she had brought from Italy, adjusting her shawl around her shoulders as she ate. It was larger than my mother's soup spoons, and bent and worn. My mother said it was dangerous to eat from such a spoon because who knew what it was made from, and whatever it was made from might react with the food my grandmother ate, and poison her.

My father said not to worry, my grandmother was too mean to die.

My grandmother held the bowl up close to her face, clutched her spoon in her fist (this annoyed my mother), and sucked her food into her mouth, satisfied that she was eating. Sometimes she'd offer me some of her food, but I'd refuse. I liked her bread, her pizza, her zeppole, but not those viscous greenish liquids she preferred for supper.

Sometimes she'd tease me, try to shove her spoon into my mouth to force me to taste what she was eating. I'd recoil. And she'd laugh. When she laughed (which wasn't often), you could see her gums, and her single pointed tooth in the front of her mouth, and then I thought that she looked like the witch in my book of Grimm's fairy tales, thought that my friends had good reason to fear her.

By the end of November each year, my grandmother would be wearing her long underwear; two or three dresses (one atop the other);

two or three hand-knit sweaters (one atop the other) in fanciful lace patterns out of keeping with her otherwise austere appearance; and her old black shawl. Everything except her long underwear was black, everything was frayed and worn, everything was poorly mended, for she had no patience with the needle.

Whenever she wandered into the kitchen to cook something warm for herself—a bean soup with whatever greens she could find at the market down the hill, a *minestra* made with a few winter vegetables, a bread soup with a handful of dried herbs from her cousin's garden, my mother would complain about her appearance. "You look like the wrath of God, dressed like that," my mother would complain, leaving the kitchen to go upstairs to organize an already tidy drawer. "Can't you dress like a civilized person?"

My grandmother would continue to buy nothing new, nothing American, nothing warm enough for winter, even though wearing more than one dress and all those sweaters and that shawl around her shoulders when she went to Mass or did her shopping on frigid winter mornings marked her as a peasant, disgraced my parents, and embarrassed me. Embarrassed me so much that I betrayed her by laughing with my friends rather than silencing them when they called her the old witch, or the garlic eater, when they held their noses and said "Pew, pew," when they claimed she ate babies for breakfast and people's brains for supper. (She did eat brains, though not people's; but this, I never conceded my friends.)

My father rarely communicated with my grandmother directly. He resented her intrusion into their lives, thought she was the reason why my mother was depressed, though he often ate her food, for he missed his mother's peasant fare. What could he do? Turn the old woman out of his house, into the street? Her relatives didn't want her all year round; she had nowhere to go; she couldn't afford to support herself. She was his cross to bear.

"Tell her to buy some new clothes, some warm clothes, goddamn it," he'd yell to my mother within earshot of my grandmother. "Tell her she's a disgrace. Tell her people will think we don't take care of her. Tell her to take a bath. Tell her she stinks."

My grandmother would manipulate another complicated stitch on the white tablecloth that rested on her lap, and she would ignore his yelling, ignore his words, and defeat him, as always. For this, if for nothing else, I loved her. I cannot count the times she threw her needlework to the ground, stitches slipping off crochet hook, ball of cotton unwinding across the floor, to put her body between his and mine. I cannot count the times she took a blow that was meant for me.

On rare occasions, my mother came home with a new dress for my grandmother (black, but with a pattern of tiny flowers), or a heavy cardigan (black, of course), or an overcoat (black, again). My grandmother, knowing that it was better to yield than to resist, and knowing that yielding was the most potent form of resistance, would take the item, hold it at arm's length, inspect it, take it upstairs, and put it in her bureau drawer or closet, where it stayed, unused, until she died.

Once only, she wore something new. A black silk scarf I bought her for Christmas with butterflies embroidered in black. It was expensive, but I bought it, because it was the only black scarf in the store.

When she unwrapped it, she wound it around her neck. "Seta," she said to me. Silk. I knew I had pleased her, and though she was unused to silk, and resented finery, she did wear the scarf, and I was glad.

There, by the radiator, my grandmother sat, ignored and despised, through the years, in that darkened room, on the straight-backed chair, in a space that was not Italy but that was not America either, crocheting tablecloths, knitting sweaters, making afghans.

There she sat, this woman at her needlework, through the late 1940s, the 1950s, the 1960s, into the early 1970s, until 1974. In that year, she became ill, couldn't get out of bed, and was taken to a nursing home run by the state, because my mother said she could afford no other. And there she died.

The sweaters are gone, and the afghans too. They were collected, thrown into giant plastic bags, and dropped into a Goodwill box after she died, together with all that unused clothing my mother had bought her. The worn underwear, dresses, sweaters, the old black shawl, tattered and motheaten, my mother threw into a garbage bag and put into the trash.

But the tablecloths I still have. They are now treasured heirlooms, which adorn our family's festive tables. I have many tablecloths to give, presents for my sons and their wives; gifts for my grandchildren, for you can crochet many tablecloths through the years when you have little else to do. And I will pass on, too, stories about the woman who made them.

My grandmother must have known how little we valued what she made. Yes, we used the tablecloths on Thanksgiving, Christmas, New Year's, Easter. But we never wore her sweaters, used her afghans. When my grandmother finished an afghan, we would throw it into the bottom of a closet; so garish and ugly were their colors that no one with any self-respect—this is my mother talking—would use them or display them.

But still, my grandmother kept knitting, kept crocheting. As if to crochet and to knit was what mattered. As if what she made was not important. As if the admiration of others did not matter. When she died, there were twenty or more sweaters, fifteen or more afghans, thirty or more tablecloths with patterns that looked like constellations of stars or gatherings of snowflakes or clutches of flowers or spiderwebs or motifs in Moorish temples, stuffed in bureau drawers all over the house, in boxes under her bed, and in the bottoms of closets.

Once, I saw my grandmother finish a tablecloth and begin a new one on the same day without stopping to take some refreshment, without holding the completed work up to the light of the window, without stopping to admire what she had accomplished. To crochet and to knit in the absence of anyone's desire but your own. To crochet and to knit because the very act of knitting, of crocheting gives you what others do not, what others cannot give you, what the country you left, what the country you came to does not give you: a sense of worth and some small scrap of human dignity.

My grandmother's hands, all dry and cracked and sere like the land she fled, making beauty. My grandmother at her needlework, affirming her right to exist in a world that did not want her.

DARK WHITE

In the photograph of my grandmother on her Certificate of Naturalization, she is dressed in black, as she always was: her life was one of perpetual mourning even before my grandfather died, for the family she had left in Puglia that she never saw again.

In the photograph, she is double-chinned, although she was not corpulent. Since arriving in America, though, she was well nourished. And for this, she was grateful, always blessing her food, blessing herself, and saying a prayer of appreciation before eating.

My grandmother never ate excessively. She considered gluttony unpardonable; and if you committed this very great sin, she believed you would burn in hell. She said that to eat just enough was a very good thing, and this is why she was happy she lived in America. But to eat too much was a very bad thing.

She condemned those of her relatives and my father's relatives who put too much food on the table, who ate too much, who threw food away when they could have transformed leftovers into another meal—a beautiful pasta, a nourishing soup, a simple frittata. My grandmother believed that eating too much, or throwing food away, meant that you were eating or discarding what could have been eaten by someone who was not eating enough. And when you were fat, according to my grandmother, you were showing those who could not eat enough that you could eat whatever you wanted, waste food even. This was the sin of pride: showing that you were rich enough to eat too much.

After we visited relatives, whenever my grandmother talked about the people who had eaten too much, she derided them, and walked around in imitation of them, and puffed out her cheeks as theirs were puffed out. She cursed and swore at them. She said that they were no better than the rich people where she came from, who ate too much while the poor ate too little. That they were no better than the Romans, who ate and puked while their undernourished slaves looked on. No better than the popes, cardinals, bishops, and priests who dined lavishly, who, if they were true Christians, should have been giving food to the people. (They took money from the collection boxes, my grandmother said, and used it for themselves. This was why she never donated money during Mass. She told me never to put the money my parents gave me into the collection box at church— better I should use it for myself or give it to the poor.)

Once my grandmother, when she was very angry about this, told me they should suck the fat out of all the people who ate too much, and fashion it into candles. (You can do this, she told me; you can make candles from fat.) And with these candles, she said, you could light the darkness of the world for a hundred hundred years.

In the photograph, my grandmother is light-skinned, although her skin burned when she stayed in the sun too long. But by late summer, she was well tanned because of her outdoor work on the farm of her relatives in Long Island. She was dark-haired, though graying at the temples, and her hair was pulled back away from her face, though not austerely, so that one wave dipped over each temple, its lustrous length braided and fashioned into a neat circlet at the nape of the neck. This does not show in the naturalization photograph, and, although her hair was beautiful and long, I could never imagine her wearing it down, for women who wore their hair around their shoulders, she said, were *puttane*, whores.

At the corners of my grandmother's mouth in the photograph,

there is a smile playing, and it might have been because she was happy that she was becoming a citizen of the United States. But I don't think so. For she was always suspicious and contemptuous of the ways of bureaucrats and government officials, and also of rules and regulations, taxes and fees and stamped documents and official ceremonies. But I think the hint of a smile on her face is one of disdain for the proceedings.

That her name was Libera suggests she probably came from an anarchist family, like my grandfather. His father's name was Libero, and these names—Libera, Libero—were ones that only Italian anarchists gave their children. Which is how their families might have known one another, through anarchist circles, for many Italian anarchists settled in Hoboken, where my grandparents lived.

It is during World War II. It has taken a long time—over twenty years—for my grandmother to decide to become a citizen. But now the United States is at war with Italy—Sicily has been invaded—and being Italian in the United States is dangerous.

When the United States first declares war on Italy, thousands of Italian Americans are arrested; more than two hundred are interned. The news sends shock waves through the country's Little Italys. And here, in Hoboken, police have raided Italian neighborhoods.

Many of my grandmother's relatives living in the United States are fighting in the war, both in the Pacific and in Europe, demonstrating their loyalty to the United States, their new land. In Italy, they are perhaps even fighting against family and *paesani*. Still, Italians and even Italian Americans are suspect. So she and my grandfather decide to become citizens.

Until the United States declared war on Italy, my grandparents had sent nonperishable food, money, and clothing to relatives there. And until Mussolini's abuses became known, they had defended him because he supported the South. After the United States joined the war, they were anguished and torn: they wanted to know the fate of their people—parents, brothers, sisters, uncles, aunts, cousins; they didn't want the land of their people destroyed; they feared that relatives in the United States would wind up on battlefields in Italy fighting against *paesani*; yet they wanted the United States to win the war.

Renouncing their Italian citizenship was fraught with difficulty. Though they knew they had opportunities here that they hadn't had in Italy, that they lived better here than they ever could have lived there, changing their citizenship meant admitting that they never would go back. And though they were deeply suspicious of governments, this constituted a betrayal of what they valued most highly: loyalty to their families.

Becoming United States citizens was the single most difficult act of their lives in this country.

My grandmother is eligible for naturalization because Italians are legally considered Caucasian, and only Caucasians, at this time, can become citizens. (In the 1890s, Italians hadn't been considered white, but by World War II, they were; until 1952, people not considered white were not eligible for naturalization.)

Naturalization granted my grandmother some of the rights and privileges of native-born Americans, but she was not completely accepted nor absorbed into the mainstream of life in the United States. Still, her naturalization papers remained precious to her always, for she kept them in the locked box that held her visa, her steamship ticket to the United States, her birth certificate, a lock of my grandfather's hair (cut after his death), the set of crystal rosary beads he bought her when they married.

She showed her papers to me once. When I brought home a certificate of my own: my grammar school diploma. Now each of us had important papers.

I am a toddler when my grandmother is naturalized, and my father is fighting somewhere in the Pacific. My mother and I live next door to my grandparents in Hoboken. And though I don't remember the event, I know that I attended the ceremony, for there is a picture in our family album commemorating the occasion, and the simple celebration of coffee and Italian pastries (cannoli, my favorite) that followed in my grandparents' apartment.

I am in my good tweed winter coat, leggings, and hat, and I stand next to my grandparents, who are soberly attired in their black winter coats. We stand on the steps of the courthouse; my grandfather holds my hand.

Though I am not aware of it, this is a defining moment in my life. For who I am (not quite Italian, not quite American), and who I will become (a person aware of inequities faced by Italian Americans in a country that has not yet fully equated the Italian American experience with the human experience) begins here.

Naturalization

1. *The act of admitting an alien to the position and privileges of a native-born subject or citizen.* Well, not really.

2. *The act of introducing plants or animals or humans to places where they are not indigenous, but where they can thrive freely under ordinary conditions.* This is Charles Darwin's meaning of the term. He said, "I would as soon be descended from that heroic little monkey . . . as from a savage . . . who knows no decency."

But what are "ordinary conditions"? And what does it mean to "thrive freely"? According to this definition, everyone in the United States, except Native Americans, is not "native" but "naturalized." But in the United States nonindigenous people are the ones deciding what other categories of nonindigenous people should have a legal right to be "naturalized."

3. *The action of making natural.* Which means that what you were—Italian—was unnatural.

4. *The act of becoming settled or established in a new place.* All those Italian Americans who feel settled, established, accepted, and com-

pletely at home, kindly raise your hands. Or have you ever, like me, been told that you were "an embarrassment," "irrational," "too emotional," "too noisy," "too shiny"—these last words, those of a former employer of mine, and on that day I wasn't even wearing my plaid taffeta blouse, pink stockings, and patent leather shoes.

Once, potential business associates of my husband wanted him to sign a clause permitting them to break the contract if he went crazy or was put in jail. This was the first time they were doing business with an Italian; they had to protect themselves, they said.

5. *The act of becoming naturalized, of settling down in a natural manner.* If, by "settling down in a natural manner" is meant doing things the way things are supposed to be done in the United States, then neither I nor my parents nor my grandparents ever became naturalized.

I remember reading Emerson's essay "Self-Reliance" in high school, and not understanding why self-reliance was considered a virtue. I remember arguing in college that not wanting to move away from your family was not necessarily neurotic, and neither was calling your family daily. I remember arguing against a twenty-three-minute lunch period when I taught high school.

Recently, in Liguria, my husband and I saw the students of a rural school having a leisurely three-course lunch in a celebrated local restaurant. We learned they ate there three times a week at the government's expense. I am sure this doesn't occur anywhere in the United States. "Now that," I thought, looking at the children eating their pasta, "is civilized."

"Libera Maria Calabrese." My grandmother has signed her name beneath her picture and on the line of the document calling for the "complete and true signature of the holder." She has signed slowly, carefully, for writing her name, I know, took much effort and concentration.

Years later, she watched *Sesame Street* with my children. She was trying to learn how to write, trying to learn to read English, after years of speaking only dialect. And I remember her signing the back of her Social Security check; this was the only time I saw her write her name.

I wonder, now, what it's like to live a life where you almost never write, almost never sign your name; what it means not to be able to use the act of writing to keep a record—of your feelings and thoughts and who you were and where you came from. Wonder what it means not to be able to participate in the creation of your identity through writing.

I can imagine the clerks waiting impatiently for this small and soberly dressed foreign woman to finish signing her name before they scrawled theirs (illegibly) at the bottom. (Who were these people? And why did they write their names so that I can't read them? But I have noticed this. Poor people, foreign people, people without power, often sign their names carefully, so that we will know who they are.)

No matter how much my grandmother cherished it, this is a strange and terrible document.

The clerk has recorded the petition number. Then typed a "personal description of the holder as of date of naturalization." A verbal portrait of my grandmother by a paid functionary who took my grandmother's testimony (about how much she weighed), but who also wrote down an observation. Much like the secretary who worked in the hospital where my husband was an intern: after listening to discussions among doctors about a potential diagnosis, she preempted their decision by writing hers—"paranoid schizorphrenic," say—on the form. They who have the power to fill in forms have the power to define us. And so it was with my grandmother.

I make my living reading books, mulling over the nuances of words, teasing out innuendoes, wondering why something is phrased one way and not another. And when I study this document, I realize there is something fishy here. There is what Virginia Woolf would call "an aroma" about the page.

The physical appearance the clerk has recorded reads: "Age 57 years; sex Female; color White; complexion Dark; color of eyes Brown; color of hair Gr. Black; height 5 feet 0 inches [she was short, my grandmother], weight 120 pounds; visible distinctive marks Mole on forehead; marital status Married; former nationality Italian."

Of course, some of what is recorded is significant—age, color of eyes, hair, height, weight, distinctive marks—so that no one else can use this document. And calling my grandmother's "color" "White" at this time in history meant that she was deemed Caucasian, hence eligible for naturalization. I can understand this, though I do not agree with what it signifies: that race exists; that it can be determined; that those deemed members of certain races should be afforded privileges, while others should not; and so on.

But why was it important to record my grandmother's "complexion" as "Dark"? What was so significant about her complexion that it had to be recorded?

There was, after all, a picture, appended to the document, which clearly showed what she looked like. And, as anyone could see, her complexion was "fair." My grandmother had to sign her name to attest that "The description above given" was accurate. Now what, exactly does "The description above given" mean? "The description given above"? "The description given to the clerk"? Or "The description above given to the person by the clerk"?

I have learned that when things are unclear, they are unclear for a reason. Especially in official pronouncements and on government documents. There is, you see, an advantage in being sixty years old.

That my grandmother testified that she was fifty-seven years old, and a female, and that she was 5' 0" tall, and that she weighed 120 pounds and that she had a mole on her forehead, I can imagine. Although I can also hear her mocking voice later telling my grandfather that this clerk, surely he was a *cretino* to make her say she had a mole on her forehead, or that she was a woman, when anyone with eyes to see could see these things for themselves.

But that the clerk asked my grandmother the hue of her complexion and that she answered that her "complexion" was "dark" I am absolutely certain never happened.

In March, in the dead of winter, it is not possible that my grandmother would have been considered dark by anyone who looked at her. In March, as her photograph attests, my grandmother was fair.

Whatever else my grandmother was—a peasant, poor, irreverent, Pugliese—she was not stupid and she was no liar. My grandmother either spoke the truth or, when the truth could not be told because it was dangerous, she remained silent and shrugged her shoulders. And although she disrespected and distrusted authority, my grandmother would have been scrupulously honest about the answer to any question put to her, for she was wary of the consequences of misrepresenting herself on official sheets of paper with official seals. This was during war, after all.

Had she been asked the question "What is your complexion?" my grandmother would have said, "Sometimes fair; sometimes tanned," and then she would have told a story. She would have told the clerk how she had to tie her scarf in a special way to protect her face from the sun; how she had to cover her arms when she worked in the vegetable garden so her skin wouldn't burn; then she would have digressed and talked about the beauty of vegetables at harvest, but also, of the wrenching pain in the back at day's end; she would have described how, by autumn, if she was careful, she would be a nice shade of *bruno*, the color of a toasted pignoli.

But my grandmother was not asked. It was the clerk who decided that my grandmother was "dark." My grandmother was Italian, from the South, a peasant, a *terrone*, a creature of the earth—and so, the color of the earth. "Dark," not fair.

Here on a document that my grandmother kept until she died, that my mother kept until she died, that I will keep until I die, that I will pass on to my granddaughter, is evidence that my people's whiteness was provisional, that government clerks used their power to create rather than record difference in physical appearance.

*   *   *

If my grandmother wanted to become a United States citizen, she had no choice but to sign her name on the line. There was not one white race; there were several, and some not as white as others.

Because my grandmother was not quite white, she was also thought to be not quite smart, not quite reliable, not quite capable of self-government, not quite capable of self-control, not quite capable of manifesting the traits of duty and obligation, not quite capable of adapting to organized and civilized society, not quite clean enough, not quite (or not at all) law-abiding (remember the Mafia).

Still, her people, my people, at this time were thought fit enough to build the nation's railroads, its subways, its buildings; fight its war; mill its fabric; sew its garments; mine its coal; stow its cargo; farm its fruits and vegetables; sell its foods; organize its crime; play its baseball; sing in operas; and, of course, make its pizza, its ravioli, its spaghetti and meatballs.

Notice, please, that the clerk did not write "wretched refuse," "human flotsam." The words "wop," "dago," "greaser," "guinea," "Mafioso" do not appear on the form, either, and for this, I should, perhaps, be grateful, though this is what the clerk might have thought.

There was a woman living in our tenement, my father said, a woman from Scandinavia, who did not believe that any Italian should be superintendent, that any Italian should act as if the building was "hers" to manage. She tried to get my grandmother fired. Started smearing shit on my grandparents' door. My grandmother took her to court. In court, the woman called her names. Argued that no Italian had the right to tell her what to do or to collect rent money from her, because Italians were "below her."

Journalist to construction boss, 1890s: "Is an Italian a white man?"
Construction boss: "No sir, an Italian is a Dago."

On the naturalization form, there is a picture of a man's hand pointing to the line where my grandmother had to sign her name, testifying that what had been written about her was true.

The picture of the hand was completely unnecessary; the blank line would have sufficed. But the hand is there. And it is the hand of authority, and it has dressed itself formally for the occasion, in white shirt and dark suit, and there can be no mistaking that it is a white hand, and that the white hand is a man's hand, and that the complexion of the white man's hand is not dark, like my grand-mother's, but fair. It is the fairest hand of all.

PASSING THE SAINT

In all the home movies where my grandfather appears, he is drinking wine. In one image, he stands behind the oilcloth-covered table in his tenement kitchen in Hoboken, and hams it up for my father's motion picture camera.

The food on the table—a huge loaf of my grandmother's home-made bread, the provolone, the mozzarella, the prosciutto, the mortadella, the olives—must be an antipasto for a special occasion. Someone's birthday. Anniversary. Christmas. New Year's. Because otherwise, my grandparents' table bears just enough food to provide nourishment, just enough so that either there are no leftovers, or only leftovers my grandmother plans to use for another meal, in a pasta sauce or in a frittata or in a soup.

In my grandparents' home, as in ours, there is no waste, almost nothing to throw away, for everything is reused. String from packages. Boxes. Grocery bags. Butcher paper. Rubber bands. On garbage day, my grandmother and my mother take down one very small bag each to the bins at the curb.

This is the way it is in my grandparents' household, and this is the way it is in mine, through all the years of my childhood. The legendary abundance of the Italian American table—the antipasto, the pasta, the roasted meats and the side dishes of vegetables and salad, the pastries for dessert—is in evidence, in greatly diminished form, on our table just a few times a year. In our relatives' households, eating much and eating well is the norm. It seems to be a way to put the privations of the past to rest. I am always startled by the excesses of these meals, and the waste. In our family, peasant habits die hard. And making do with less, so necessary in the Old Country, has become a thread that links my family to what was left behind.

In the film my father takes, my grandfather picks up a jug of wine, tilts his head back, pretends to swallow. It is his wine. He makes it in the basement, with my father's help; they stomp the grapes in a barrel to release their juices (only men can tread the grapes, he tells me); he ages the wine in oak until drinking time, then bottles it.

He's doing such a good job of simulation that you can see his Adam's apple moving. *Glug, glug, glug. Swallow, swallow, swallow.*

He looks at the camera, smiles. Then he puts the jug back on the table next to the bread. Very satisfied with his performance. He seems to expect applause, congratulations.

My grandfather, in his life of servitude, first as a *contadino* in the South of Italy, then as a laborer on the railroad in America, has always worked hard for someone else, under the control of bosses. He has never been in the spotlight, never been singled out for special attention or favor, never praised for his work.

He has lived his life as a worker. My grandfather has watched someone richer, someone of far higher stature than he, strutting in the piazza of his village, wearing a new set of clothes, as he staggered home from the fields. Watched the owner of the railroad cruising by the gang of workers in a private car as he bent his back to the sun to dig a trench. Watched the well-to-do in Hoboken walking past him on his way home from the docks to their elegant brownstones on the Heights; they made sure they did not come near him, for he was filthy, and he would have soiled their clothes.

My grandfather has been the center of attention so infrequently— at his Confirmation; his coming to America; his weddings; his naturalization—that he wants to repeat the performance. So he begins his playacting again. Picks up the jug again. Sidles into the camera's gaze. Repeats his routine.

My grandmother isn't laughing. She doesn't think my grandfather is funny. She walks back and forth behind him in that jitter walk that you see in old films and home movies. She moves behind him, swipes at the jug of wine, tries to take it away. Tries to stop him from pretending to pour the wine into his mouth. She grabs my grandfather's arm. Says something to my father. Puts a hand out to block the camera's view.

But he evades her.

My grandmother gives up. Takes her handkerchief from under her sleeve, wipes her brow, puts her handkerchief back, puts her hands on her hips. Frowns.

My mother doesn't think this is funny either. Though she adores her father, forgives him much, while he's pretending to chug the wine she looks away, pretends he's not doing this, pretends he's not there. He turns his back to her.

Glug, glug, glug. Swallow, swallow, swallow.

This time, there is no bravura in the performance. This time, my grandfather looks tired. This time, he looks like what he is: an old man, a tired man, a downtrodden man. A man who drinks too much, too often.

I am old enough to be sitting at the table in a regular chair, not a high chair. My mother is very pregnant with my sister. So this must be Christmas, or New Year's, 1946, a month or so before my sister is born. I am almost four and a half. My grandfather, whom I adore, will be dead in three years.

I look at my grandfather and laugh. I think that what he's doing is funny. He's happy he's making me laugh. He looks down at me, ruffles my hair. We have a special bond. His good humor has been an antidote to my mother's gloom, to my grandmother's brusque love, to my father's absence during the war.

My father has been home from the Pacific for about eight months when he takes these pictures. The motion picture camera is an unaccustomed extravagance my father has permitted himself. During the war, he sent home almost all of his salary, never wasting any money on carousing, as many of his friends did. He usually buys himself nothing, not even clothing when he needs it. My mother also buys very little, but what she buys is good. "I'm too poor to buy cheap clothes," she says. But there was one extravagant moment in my father's life, when he outfitted himself with a new suit, a new hat, new shoes, a new bathing suit, new pajamas, and a new bathrobe for his honeymoon with my mother. In general, like my grandfather and grandmother, he makes do with very little.

My father has allowed himself this camera because he wants to memorialize the family he has returned to. The family he yearned for while he was away. The wife he loves, whom he feared he'd never see again. The daughter who was just a baby when he left. The father-in-law who was more father to him than his own father. The mother-in-law who helped his wife take care of his child when he was gone.

So many people in my father's life have slipped away from him—his Italian grandparents, whom he loved as a boy, then never saw again; his Italian friends; the friends he saw killed. And he lost himself to war, too. He is not the man he was, and he knows it, and there is no way to explain what happened. No way to tell what burning bodies jumping from torpedoed ships look like; no way to speak of the men who killed themselves in gruesome ways rather than face battle; no way to describe the sound of bombardment; the sound of airplanes strafing a beach, the sight of men's backs ripped open; no way to say what it felt like to pry a wounded man from a plane that crashed into the deck of an aircraft carrier; no way to tell what it was like to pick up the remains of the dead after a battle (one bucket of remains equaled one body).

He is unused to small children, to a wife, and to civilian life. A man whose life now runs in slow motion, or in quickstep, but never in ordinary time. A man who wants to run for cover when trucks backfire; who wants to attack and kill anyone who disagrees with him, even his daughter; who wants to make love to his sometimes unwilling wife whenever he can, for making love helps as nothing else does; who wants to weep for what he has seen and what he has lost, but who cannot weep.

And so, he takes motion pictures of his family. For by taking pictures, he can be with his family, yet apart.

His father-in-law he loves, as he never loved his own, that reprobate, who escaped to Italy whenever he could (to a *comare* and to another family in Italy, my father sometimes thought), leaving his wife and five children to fend for themselves. He doesn't think that there is anything wrong with his father-in-law's antics. He doesn't turn the camera away; he even eggs the old man on, although he sees his wife's and his mother-in-law's disapproval. But they are women, after all, and their job is to criticize. There's not enough pleasure in this world, he thinks. Let the old man have his fun.

"They gave them wine to drink," my father tells me. "All the wine they could drink. Not water. Not very much food. But a lot of wine."

My father is telling me about my grandfather's life. About his work on the railroad.

"Why did they do that?" I ask, though I think I know the answer. Alcohol: antidote to rebellion.

"To keep them quiet," my father says. "To keep them working."

But he tells me that in the South of Italy, it wasn't always that simple. There, water was scarce, and safe water, scarcer still. He was lucky, he said. There was a good well in Scafati, where he lived when he was a little boy, a communal well close to the church in his neighborhood. Contaminated water could kill you. And one of the lessons your mother taught you as a child was not to drink any water, no matter how thirsty you were, unless she gave it to you.

Water was scarce. Water was dangerous. Wine was plentiful and safe. It wouldn't kill you, at least not right away.

When my father lived in Scafati, he watched workers in the fields stop to eat their small meals—a piece of bread and a slice of onion— always washing their food down with wine. Between meals, they drank wine when they were thirsty. "Passing the saint," they called it.

I imagine what it must have been like for my grandfather to work in scorching fields in summer with no water to drink, only wine. Now, there is an aqueduct that brings water into Puglia. But when he lived there, there was no aqueduct. Always, the people of the South were promised water. And they knew that, for centuries, aqueducts brought water into Rome. Why water for Rome? And no water for them?

When my grandfather retired from the railroad, he was an alcoholic. But that clinical word cannot describe the man he had become.

By the time I was born, the man who had stood so tall and proud beside two wives in his wedding photographs had lost his pride, his strength, his steely-eyed determination. Wine, antidote to his pain, his sorrow, his loss, his rage.

Anger was an extravagance. An emotion a peasant couldn't afford. Anger wasted energy. Anger changed nothing. Anger singled you out, anger made you a target.

Unless you used that anger, channeled it into political action. As the anarchists in his family had; as the labor organizers had; as the farm laborers who demanded a living wage had. But by the time my grandfather left Puglia, whatever his people had gained through work stoppages, strikes, land seizures had been taken away from them. They fought; many people were killed; they lost. Nothing changed until after the Great War.

So it was inside the house where anger appeared. Anger against the *padrone* who held you captive. Against the landowner who didn't pay you enough money to feed yourself. Anger that, no matter how hard you worked, you had little or nothing to show for it. Anger that you couldn't feed your family. Anger that you weren't treated like a man. Since you couldn't show your anger to the *padrone*, the landowner, it was your wife and children who saw the rage, who felt it.

My grandfather never hit his wives, never hit his daughter in anger. But you could see the rage. In his eyes when he talked about his days on the railroad. See it, when he pounded his fist on the table as he talked about how a man he worked with died because of a worn cable. Hear it, when he raised his voice about how you could expect nothing from politicians, how they were all corrupt.

He'd take a glass, pour himself some wine, and then some more. After his third glass, he couldn't remember why he was angry. After his fourth glass, he'd become sentimental, teary-eyed. That's when he missed his mother, his father, his *paisani,* his dead wife.

My grandfather dies at home, in his kitchen. On the day he dies, my mother, my sister, and I come home from shopping. We don't buy much; we buy every day. Still, wrestling two children, a stroller, and a bag of groceries up the steep tenement stairs is difficult. By the time we get to the fourth floor, my mother is sweating, she's dropped a few things on the stairs, and she's yelled at us to move along.

My mother knocks on my grandparents' door to tell her father we're home, to get some help. She'll settle my sister and me in his apartment for a snack while she unpacks, tidies up her kitchen. But there's no answer. My grandfather is supposed to be home. My mother knocks again. Still no answer.

"Maybe," my mother says, "he's in the toilet. Maybe he's gone out."

But my mother sounds worried. No one in our family goes anywhere without telling everyone where they're going, when they'll come back. Everyone always knows where everyone else is.

My mother bangs on the door. She yells, "Papa!" Still no answer. Something is wrong.

We go into our apartment. My mother drops her package on the kitchen table, puts my sister in her high chair. She tells me to crawl out the kitchen window, across the fire escape, through my grandparents' kitchen window, into their apartment. The window should be open; it's a warm September day. I've done this before, my mother watching. It's safe; still, it's a great adventure.

When my grandfather is taking care of me, he lets me sit outside, on the fire escape. He ties a rope around my waist, ties the other end to a chair. He lets me have a treat there—some bread brushed with olive oil. Lets me water my grandmother's plants. This is another of our secrets.

I look into the open window. See my grandfather on the floor. I crawl over the table, onto the chair, onto the floor. Rush to my grandfather.

He's on his side; his eyes are open; his mouth is open. In his hand, he holds a pencil. On the floor, there is a piece of paper.

I unlatch the door for my mother. She pushes past me, begins to scream. My sister hears my mother screaming and starts crying. I go back into our apartment, help my sister out of her high chair, bring her into our grandparents' kitchen.

I'm not crying. I don't know why my mother is crying. I'm wondering why my grandfather is sleeping on the floor. I don't know that he's dead. That he's had a massive heart attack. (My father blames the wine, the hard work my grandfather's done all his life. "He was like a father to me," my father says. "They killed him.")

"That doesn't look like Grandpa," I say at the wake. "And that doesn't smell like Grandpa, either."

I've gone up to the casket to see my grandfather's body. I'm a curious child. There is the smell of flowers, and the smell of mothballs, too, wafting from his suit.

"What did your grandpa smell like?" a neighbor asks.

"Like wine," I say. I remember my grandfather crushing grapes in the basement. Remember him drinking wine with me. Remember him drinking it, sometimes, right out of the bottle.

Our neighbor laughs when I say my grandfather smelled like wine. It's good to have something to laugh at during a wake. " 'Mbriago," our neighbor says. It's what they called my grandfather in the neighborhood. 'Mbriago, the drunk.

After my grandfather dies, everything changes. My grandmother starts wearing only black, wears it until she dies. My mother stops paying attention to me and my sister, forgets to feed us. After my grandfather dies, my mother stops smiling, and she rarely smiles again.

Soon after my grandfather's death, we leave Hoboken. Without him, my mother says, there's no reason to stay. My father thinks it will be a good move for all of us.

When we move to Ridgefield, and my grandmother comes to live with us, all the trouble between my mother and grandmother starts. My grandfather is not around to broker the peace between them. The hatred they've felt for each other all these years explodes.

After my grandfather dies, no one asks me if I miss him. No one asks me if I'm sorry he's dead. No one wonders why I don't cry. My father is too worried about my mother. My grandmother is always quiet. My mother is in a fog. Everyone thinks I'm not crying because I'm a good little girl.

Soon after my grandfather dies, I start forcing myself to look at the dead bodies of animals—pigeons, squirrels, the occasional rat—in the streets and in the park around the corner from where we live.

When we go to the park, my mother sits on a bench and does nothing. My sister sits in her stroller and does nothing. I play alone, bounce a ball, skip rope, hide behind trees. And I poke at the bodies of dead animals with a stick. I wonder whether if I poke them long enough, they'll start moving, come back to life.

On the day my grandfather dies, he's sitting at the kitchen table. He's adding columns of numbers, using a system he devised for counting, for he never went to school.

He wasn't working on the docks for the railroad anymore; he had retired. But he had been working, digging basements, because he needed the money. At the start of each day, they'd give the workers a bottle of wine to drink.

The people he worked for hadn't yet paid him for his labor. They owed him several weeks' wages. When he died, he was trying to figure out just how much money he was owed.

FOOD ON THE TABLE

I am nine years old, and I am standing on a pier in New York City, waving my white-gloved hand to my paternal grandfather (that no-good bastard, my father calls him), who is going back to Italy, again. My mother has dressed my sister and me in the Easter clothes she sewed for us this year. Although my sister and I are separated by four years, we are dressed identically. Pink dresses with starched lace collars; navy blue coats with decorative capes; natural straw hats; black patent-leather purses; black patent-leather shoes; white frilly anklets. And white gloves. Also gathered on the pier to see my grandfather off are my four aunts and uncles and my eight cousins, all also dressed in their best clothes.

Unlike anyone else, and against the rules, my grandfather has climbed onto the railing of the ship. He grips a pole for support, waves a large white handkerchief in a grand, sweeping gesture. My grandmother has washed and ironed it. She has washed, starched, and ironed the shirts he is taking, packed his clothes, cooked and packed a little snack—a frittata with onions—should he get hungry before it's time to eat on board.

There is no love between them, there has never been any love between them, but my grandmother does this every time my grandfather leaves because it is her duty. Theirs was an arranged marriage, not a love match, and although he has mistreated her for years, she takes care of him. This is her obligation.

My grandmother stands next to my father, her only son. He has his arm around her shoulders to support her. She waves a smaller version of my grandfather's handkerchief, and she is weeping. Why she is weeping, I don't understand, because even when he's home, he's never at home, he might as well be gone. My grandfather isn't weeping. And though I am waving at my grandfather, though we are all waving at my grandfather, my grandfather isn't waving at us. As always, he's putting on a show. He is acting the part of the Italian patriarch, reluctantly leaving his family in the United States because it is his duty to visit his relatives in Italy.

My grandfather plays to the crowd. We might as well not be there.

My grandfather leaves my grandmother to go to Italy for as long as he wants at least twice a year. And leaves her with no income to support her while he's gone.

(Years later, when I ask my father why he dragged us to New York to say good-bye to his father, when he didn't even like his father, my father says that we went not for my grandfather, but for my grandmother, and that my grandmother went because that is what a wife is supposed to do.)

I think I know why my grandfather is going away. I think he's going to see his girlfriend. I think he has another family back in Italy. What else can explain these frequent trips? And why he doesn't leave his wife any money? My grandfather doesn't know when he'll be coming back to the United States. When he's asked, he shrugs his shoulders. He'll stay there for a while, he tells the family, until he feels like coming back. Or until his money runs out. But no one knows how much money he has, so we can't guess how long that will be. When he answers his children's questions, he answers them like they have no right to ask them, like he's answering them so that they'll stop pestering him, not because he wants his family to know anything about his plans.

"But, Pa," one of my aunts says, "who's gonna put food on the table for Ma when you're gone?"

My grandfather rolls his eyes heavenward. He puts his palms together as if he's praying, and he shakes his hands up and down.

"How should I know?" my grandfather responds. "She's your mother, not mine."

When my grandfather says this, my father and my aunts walk out of whatever tiny kitchen the family has packed itself into. They look up at the ceiling. They mutter. They make little circles in the air with their upraised hands. This is a gesture that is Italian for "I don't believe this is happening. This can't be happening. Things like this don't happen, at least in our family," even though this has been happening in this family from when my father was a little boy.

My father looks angry; looks like he's trying to control himself. He looks like he wants to hit my grandfather. Years later I learn that, after my father came home from his first tour of duty in the navy, he saw my grandfather hit my grandmother. My father took his father, threw him against the wall, and said, "If you ever touch her again, I'll kill you."

My father loves his mother with a love that borders on adoration. "She was a saint," he tells me when I'm older, "to put up with that man." I don't think she was a saint; I think she was stupid.

My father tells me about how my grandmother always made do. How whatever she cooked—heart, tripe, lung—was good, nutritious, tasty. How she spent fifty cents a day on food, how he went to the market with her every day before she went to work and he went to school. How she shopped for the day, saw what was good, what was cheap. How she made pasta during the week, mostly with a red sauce, or with a vegetable sauce, or a sauce with a little prosciutto, or a handful of peas. How they ate lots of fruits and vegetables, especially broccoli rabe. And how on Sunday, she'd make a meat gravy, or, on special occasions, some beef or some pork, sometimes a stuffed veal pocket, or a casserole.

When my father was older, and working, she always cooked him a steak on Sunday, pan fried, with onions. She didn't make steak for anyone else, not her daughters, not herself, even though they all were working. "A man needs his strength," she'd say.

She had her little quirks about feeding herself, my father tells me. She'd cook for the family, but she wouldn't eat with them. After they finished eating, she'd cook something for herself, eat it alone, just like my other grandmother, something different from what she'd cooked for them. When she got older, she didn't feel like cooking anymore, and, though she'd fix herself a little something, she wouldn't cook for my grandfather. She was tired, she said, tired from cooking for all those people all those years.

When I ask my father why she never left him, he says, "Because the Catholic church didn't allow divorce. And besides, she wanted to keep up appearances, she wanted the family to stay together."

My paternal grandfather gives me more attention than I get from any other grown-up. I'm his favorite grandchild and I know it. He signals this when he offers me one of the eyeballs from the lamb's head my grandmother prepares for Easter Sunday.

I know it's a delicacy, given to special guests. I refuse it, very ungraciously, and, though my father is distressed, my refusal seems to give my grandfather as much pleasure as my acceptance would have. I am a child with a will of her own, like him. He respects this more than the dutiful attentions of my sister and cousins.

Once, my father tells me, "He treats you like a grandson, not like a granddaughter." Another time, he says, "He treats you like his eldest son. He's pinning the hopes of the family on you."

My grandfather has always stood outside the family. Always acted as if his family doesn't matter. He never lets them stop him from doing whatever he wants. He always indulges himself, even if there isn't enough money to pay the rent.

Even on ordinary days, my grandfather wears a solid gold watch chain; carries a hand-hemmed linen handkerchief in his pocket; douses himself with expensive cologne. He wears handmade Italian leather shoes. Tweed. Cashmere. Silk. Knee-length socks held up by elaborate and colorful garters. But not a hat. My grandfather thinks that if you're Italian and wear a hat, you look like a Mafioso.

CRAZY IN THE KITCHEN

Next to him, my grandmother looks like a drudge. She spends most of her life in work dresses, or house dresses, covered with neat aprons. Her few good dresses are black. She seems to be in perpetual mourning. And, of course, she is. For all the babies she's aborted. For the family she left behind. For the happy life that has eluded her.

"Grandpa is going back to Italy to see his girlfriend." We say this whenever our grandfather goes to Italy. We test these words far away from the grown-ups, who sit in strained silence on the sofa and folding chairs in our grandparents' living room.

"That no-good son of a bitch thought the world owed him a living," my father says. "That's why he married my mother. So that he could have a servant to work for him, to cook and clean for him, to raise his kids, while he took his trips to Italy, gallivanted around, wearing his fancy clothes, playing the big shot, always pretending he was something he wasn't. He was a real shithead, my father. The happiest day of my life was the day my father died."

My father and I are having lunch at Amarone's, our local Italian restaurant. Fried calamari for him; roasted vegetables and *battuta* for me. I have asked him to tell me about his father, about when he came to America, about his life here, about how he and his family moved back to Scafati, a town just down the road from Pompeii, when my father was a little boy. My father is nearly ninety now. These days, we meet weekly to share family stories. I want to find out as much as I can about my family before he dies. He's happy that, after years of indifference, I finally want to know about his past.

I am startled by the vehemence of my father's anger. I never knew that my father hated his father, wished him dead; never imagined that the congenial grandfather who handed me five-dollar bills whenever he saw me, who took me to the Metropolitan Opera and to Ebbets Field to watch the Brooklyn Dodgers play ball, wasn't as generous to his own children as he was to me.

*   *   *

"The first time he went back to Italy and left us to fend for ourselves, I was three, maybe four years old," my father says. "We're living on New York Avenue in Union City. He's supposed to be going to Scafati, to see his mother and father, but who the hell knows where he went or what he was doing over there. By that time there were three of us, my two older sisters and me. The other girls would come later.

"All I remember about the first time is my mother crying, my sisters grabbing onto my father's pants, him swatting them off, kicking them away as he left. 'But what will we do?' my mother cried. The neighbors open the doors a little to see what's going on.

"That son of a bitch turns around on the landing, looks back at my mother, and says, 'Don't worry. You'll manage.' Imagine saying that to a woman with three kids: 'You'll manage.' But I have to hand it to my mother. She stops crying, calls him a bastard, looks her neighbors in the eye, slams the door, goes inside.

"So my mother has to find work and fast. All that no-good father of mine has left her is fifty cents on the kitchen table. That's all. Fifty cents to tide her over until she can find work. Fifty cents was a lot more in those days than it is today, but with four mouths to feed, and the rent to pay, and everyone that we knew just scraping by so that we couldn't count on anyone else, fifty cents would last her maybe a day.

"My sisters are in school all day. But I'm too little to go. So my mother dresses me, takes me to one of the factories where she has relatives working, and gets a job.

"This one, thank goodness, is piecework. This one, she can do at home so she doesn't have to worry about what to do with me. It's an artificial-flower place. My mother has to make dogwood. There's this thin piece of metal; you wind some brown material around it; then you put on the petals. My mother teaches me how to do the stems. I'm not too good at it, and I'm not too fast, but it keeps me busy while she's working. Anyway, I have no toys, nothing else to do. I like being with her. Because no matter how bad things are, my mother is always good to me.

"When she's finished, she goes back to the factory, picks up some new materials, comes home. Naturally, I have to go with her; she doesn't have anyone to leave me with.

"All I remember is walking and walking and walking and wearing out one pair of shoes after another, and her not being able to carry me because she's either carrying all the stuff for the flowers or all the flowers she's made or she's gone shopping and has a couple of bags of groceries that she's carrying along with everything else. We don't have enough money for a carriage, and she can't hold my hand because she's always carrying something, so she tells me to hold onto her skirt when we cross the street.

"One time I don't listen to her, and I'm not holding on to her, and I take my sweet time crossing. Before I know it, I see this horse-drawn carriage bearing down on me and I get so scared I lie down right in the middle of the street. There are two horses; they're going at a nice clip and they pound along, one on each side of me. Then the wheels of the cart, the first set, then the second. I can see it all happening. In slow motion, like they say. I can hear my mother screaming. I can hear a whole bunch of people screaming. They thought I was dead.

"So I'm in the middle of the street. My mother drops her bundles, makes the Sign of the Cross, runs over to me. She thinks I'm dead. But I'm all right. Right in front of all these people, my mother starts slapping away at me as fast as she can. She calls me a *strunz*, asks me if I'm *stunod*. This is the only time she hits me, but I deserve it. From then on, I always hold onto her skirt, and I don't go anywhere near any horses.

"Every time she gets paid for her dogwood branches, my mother gives me a few cents because I help her. This is my first job. I'm about four years old. I keep a penny for myself, give the rest back to her because she needs it.

"When my mother shops at Mr. Romano's grocery store, I take whatever I've saved. We never get cookies; never get candy. Only *struffoli*, which my mother makes at Christmas. But me, I have a sweet tooth, even when I'm young. At Mr. Romano's store, they sell chocolate-covered graham crackers. There's a big tin of them. They're a penny apiece. You pay your penny, you take your cracker.

"I wait until Mr. Romano is waiting on my mother, until his back is turned. I put my penny on the counter. I take five or six crackers, whatever I can fit in my hand, and I shove them up under my shirt and run outside. In summer, by the time I get home, all the chocolate has melted onto my chest and my shirt's a real mess. But I want to give a cracker to each of my sisters, and one to my mother. This is when I start stealing."

My father laughs at the memory of himself as a four-year-old thief. He's told me before about how, when things got really bad, and his mother couldn't find work, he joined a gang that stole copper pipe and wiring from construction sites. Without her knowledge, of course.

He was still a kid, about nine or ten years old, and his father was away in Italy. His older sisters were working—they had to quit school to go to work when they were about thirteen or fourteen; they put on a lot of makeup and lied about their age to get work. But they were just starting out in the garment industry and weren't making much money. So my father had to do something. Only, he was far too young to work at a legitimate job.

The other gang members, all cousins of his, were older than he was. But they let him join because he was family, and because he was small enough to sneak through tiny openings at construction sites and hand out whatever materials he found. They also figured he'd be the one caught with the goods, and that the cops couldn't do anything to him because he was so young.

It was a good racket, for a while, my father said. But once they all got caught, got taken to jail. They lied to the cops; they gave them false names. One of his uncles found out and bailed them out. Probably paid someone off, my father said, because the case never came to trial.

His uncle told his mother. Which made her cry. She didn't want him to become a criminal. She told him that one good-for-nothing son of a bitch ("sonnamabitch" was the way she said it) in a family was enough. That made him stop.

"I had my first real job," my father tells me, "after my mother lost her job making artificial flowers. Soon after, she found work as a presser in a place that manufactures shirts. At this time, the garment industry is going strong in Hudson County, and everyone's finding work.

"I'm still too young for school. So when the whistle blows, and all the women crowd into work, my mother pushes me between her and a big fat friend of hers with huge bosoms, and they kind of push me along into the factory along with them. As soon as my mother and her friend get to her station, she pushes me under the counter where she does her ironing. That's where I spend my days, listening to the whoosh of the gas-fired iron, seeing the arms of the shirts dangling off the ironing board, watching my mother sidestep right, sidestep left, as she irons one shirt after another. Usually I fall asleep. And when I have to pee, there is a cup on the floor.

"For a long time, nobody notices. They're paying piecework, so whether you work fast or really fast doesn't concern them like the other sweatshops where women are paid by the hour. As long as you're doing your work, keeping your station clean, not fighting with anyone, my mother says, no one pays any attention.

"But one day, the floor manager sees me sitting on the floor. My mother thinks she's going to lose her job for bringing me to work. But instead, the guy pulls me onto my feet and tells me to make myself useful, buttoning the buttons of the shirts my mother irons.

" 'How much are you going to pay me?' I ask. I already know the value of a dollar. 'Five cents a dozen,' the floor manager says. From now on, I start helping my mother put food on the table. It doesn't really matter what my father does or doesn't do; I'm the man of the house now. I'm about five or six years old."

My father's father always wanted to be a big deal, always wanted to be a *uomo rispettato*, but without doing anything to deserve anyone's respect. He was a barber by trade in Italy and earned enough to get by. And when he came to America, he earned money cutting the hair of the people he knew. He saved some money; got married so he'd have someone to cook and clean for him; started having children because that's what men did, not because that's what he wanted; set himself up in a barbershop with the money he saved. Then he hired some barbers to work for him.

Because he really didn't want to be a barber. He wanted to be known as a man who had other men working for him as barbers. He wanted to be the barbershop kingpin of Hudson County, just like, back where he came from, there were tomato kingpins, fruit and vegetable kingpins, citrus kingpins, fish market kingpins, construction kingpins, waterworks kingpins, cattle kingpins. The way things were done there, he thought, was the way things should be done here.

Only, as soon as he found a shop, bought it, fixed it up, hired a few barbers, started to make a good living, started to save money, he'd either stop working or go back to Italy, leaving one of the barbers he'd hired in charge of collecting money, paying salaries, and giving the profits to his family. Which, of course, never happened. The business, my father said, would go to pot.

When my grandfather was away, my father went to the barbershop on his way home from school or work, to collect money from the day's work.

Every day, it was the same story.

"Business was bad," they'd say. "As soon as your father left, everyone stopped wanting to have their hair cut. They've all started going to Luigi's around the corner." The barbers would shrug their shoulders, raise their eyebrows, open their outraised hands. "What can you do?" It wasn't their fault. Meantime, my father says, they're stuffing their pockets full of money, giving him a few miserable dollars at the end of each day. But he doesn't blame them; he blames his father. "It's human nature," he says.

*   *   *

"And so," my father says, "there wouldn't be enough money to pay the rent. So we leave. My mother finds us another place to live. But she always finds something a little better. My God, in one of those places we left, you could see through the chinks in the bricks to the Meadowlands, and the wind would come roaring through the apartment. We'd pack up all our belongings in bedsheets and pillowcases, hire a cart to take us to our new apartment. Sometimes, we didn't even have the money for a cart, and we'd walk there, the six of us: my four sisters, my mother and me.

"We moved all the time. We lived on Fourth Street in Union City, on Ninth Street, we lived in North Bergen, and in West New York, in Brooklyn, and all over Hudson County. I went to so many schools, I stopped counting. I got left back so many times; I was always the oldest kid in the class. I was sixteen years old in grammar school when I decided to call it quits.

"Of course, my father, the big shot, was always telling his cronies and me that somebody he knew would pull strings and get me into West Point. West Point? I couldn't even add and subtract without using my fingers. I never got beyond the seventh grade. I was working all the time after school, before school, so I couldn't do my homework.

"My father's well fed, showing off. I'm skinny as a rail. I'm working for peddlers before and after school, making maybe fifty cents a day. I'd run up the stairs to the fifth floor of an apartment, take an order, run down, tell the peddler what the customer wanted, run up the stairs to deliver the fruits and vegetables, take the person's money, run down the stairs to get change, run up the stairs to give their customer change—those sons of bitches never trusted me with money to make change, so it was up and down, up and down all the time.

"If my father wanted me to go to West Point, wanted me to make something of myself, he should have stuck around.

"I left home when I couldn't take it anymore. During my first tour of duty, I saved some money, sent most of it home to your grandmother. Until I left home, I didn't have a bed to sleep in—I slept on the sofa, on two chairs pulled together. When I came back, my mother said I was too old to sleep on chairs. So she took some money she saved and bought me a folding cot. But I still didn't have a room. I slept in the living room.

"Just after you were born," my father tells me, "I happened to see your grandfather walking down the street with all his cronies. Me, I'm hustling back to work after checking on your grandmother during my lunch hour because she's been sick. He's walking down the street as if he doesn't have a care in the world.

"He waves at me, stops me, calls me over, introduces me to his cronies, none of whom I care to know, because they're all as worthless as he is, and he tells me, in front of all these men, that he is going to stop working and that, from now on, as a sign of respect to him, I will have to support him.

"He's at it again. Trying to make an impression.

" 'Support you?' " my father says. " 'I have a family to support. Why should I support you when you never supported me? I helped support Ma when I was a kid because I had to; I help her now.'

" 'You should support me,' your grandfather said, 'because that is the duty you owe your father as a sign of respect.'

" 'Respect, my ass,' " my father says. " 'I spit on your respect.' "

HOLY OIL

When my mother was seven or eight years old, my father told me, she had St. Vitus's Dance. When the symptoms first appeared, her father and stepmother didn't know what was wrong. My mother had had a bad sore throat some weeks before. After she was better, when she was walking up the stairs to their apartment after school, she collapsed and fell down the stairs. She wasn't seriously hurt. But after that, she collapsed a few times on the sidewalk on her way to school. Her parents, both superstitious, feared she was visited by the devil.

Soon after, her hands started shaking, her body started shaking. Eating became very dangerous for her. Once, she stabbed her hand with her fork. Another time, she cut herself instead of cutting the food.

Her father started to think she had St. Vitus's Dance, which was not good, but better than being visited by the devil. It was an affliction well known in the South of Italy.

My grandfather had heard stories of how people afflicted like my mother lost all reason. They stopped eating, and died. Or they threw themselves into rivers or off precipices. Some believed that the only cure was to dance and gyrate until you lost consciousness.

My grandfather did not want to lose his daughter. He was not a religious man, but he believed she could be cured if they made a pilgrimage to the shrine of St. Vitus in Eboli. That wasn't possible. Instead, he went to church and lit a candle to St. Vitus, patron saint of the afflicted, to save his daughter, the only person he loved, from this

117

terrible disease. It was the fourth time he had been in a church since coming to America, and he went reluctantly, from necessity. He hated the Church because the clergy in Italy helped the landlords quell rebellions of the poor. So, after his weddings, and the baptism of his daughter, he vowed never to enter a church again.

My mother's stepmother was more practical. She contacted a doctor who spoke Italian. Paid him with her savings. He prescribed complete bed rest for six months; there was no known cure for the disease. During this time, my mother was not permitted to walk or play or feed herself. My grandmother, who had no maternal feelings for my mother, had to watch her continuously, had to wait on her, feed her, massage her body with olive oil so she wouldn't get bedsores. Knowing my grandmother's attitude to my mother, I am sure that she performed her duties grudgingly, if not with outright hostility.

When she returned to school, my mother needed to use both hands to bring a glass of milk up to her mouth in the lunchroom. Careful as she was, she often spilled the liquid, and once she threw it over her shoulder, dousing another student. At her desk, she would try to shape her letters carefully. But she penned unrecognizable hieroglyphs, for which the teacher chided her. She was forbidden to run or play, and so the few friends she'd had before her illness abandoned her.

As a child, I wondered whether I could inherit St. Vitus's Dance. I wondered if my fainting spells meant that I had it. I wondered if I would begin to tremble like my mother, and need to stay home because I would never know when an attack was coming, never know when I might drop to the ground and bang my head against the sidewalk. Sometimes, alone in my bath, I would fill a plastic cup with water and practice trembling.

My mother's afflictions—her trembling, which made her drop things (the dropsies, she called it), her depression, her fits of weeping—made her the center of our attention. They gave her an unfair advantage over the rest of us. We, believed to be normal, resilient, and capable, were supposed to understand her needs, and care for her, although she seemed not to want our attention. And she was absolved of responsibility for our care. Given all she endured, how could we ask for help when a teacher berated us, a friend mistreated us, when our throats or our stomachs ached, when someone touched us where they shouldn't have?

I imagined the child who was not yet my mother spinning, whirling, falling to the ground, jerking like someone taken by the Holy Spirit. I saw her dancing before St. Vitus. I knew that my mother was marked, different from everyone else's mother, different from ordinary, competent mothers, who put food on the table at preordained times, who washed clothes without damage to themselves, who listened to children when they said they were sad.

"Leave your mother alone when she says she wants to be left alone": my father's first commandment. We dared not break it for fear of the consequences—banishment to our room, the loss of all privileges, bed without supper, a backhand to the face. But there was no time when my mother did not want to be left alone. "Your mother is a saint because of all she's suffered": the catechism of our childhood. But regardless of what my father said, I knew my mother was no saint.

Sometimes, my mother went crazy. Not just a little crazy. So crazy that we were sent off to relatives to be cared for. So crazy that she became a danger to herself.

Once, the day before my mother signed herself into the locked psychiatric ward of our local hospital, she made a menu plan and a shopping list for a whole month, and posted it on the bulletin board in the kitchen where one of us would find it.

I was married then. My sister had just finished having her latest nervous breakdown. She'd come back to live with my parents after the man she'd lived with left her.

It was my sister who called to tell me about the menu plan and the shopping list. It was full of stuff my mother never cooked, full of stuff we never ate.

Barbecued spareribs, roasted corn, green beans
Tacos, sour cream, guacamole, green salad
Roast beef, baked potatoes, peas
Chicken cacciatore, rice, asparagus
Macaroni and cheese, tomato salad

"She's not crazy," my sister says. "She's just pretending to be crazy. No one who's crazy makes out a menu and a shopping list."

"Oh," I say, noncommittal. I think the fact that my mother made a shopping list and a menu plan of meals my father and sister were supposed to prepare that she herself would never make, especially given all the crap she fed us while we were growing up, proves she's crazy. But I'm not going to get into this with my sister.

"It's nuts," my sister says. "What does she think? I'm going to shop for all this shit? Cook it? I think she went crazy just to spite me because I came back home."

I want to say, "First you say she's not crazy; then you say she is; which is it?," but I don't. I want all this to go away. My sister and her nervous breakdowns. My mother and her nervous breakdowns. I want to be left alone to raise my family. So I don't ask my sister why my mother might want to spite her. Instead of asking, I say, "What else did she put on the menu?"

When we were young, my mother never told us about her suffering. But she wore her life like a hair shirt. She lived as if she had joined a secret cult that practiced the mortification of the flesh, the annihilation of desire.

My mother's ascetic practice included many small, voluntary privations and punishments, ones that did not require a trek to a distant monastery. Ones she could tuck into the fabric of her ordinary life. Like not going out when it rained, because she never bought herself an umbrella or rain boots. Like scratching herself until she raised stigmatalike welts on her body. Like plunging her hands into scalding water while she did the laundry. Like touching the bottom of the iron with a fingertip to see if it was hot enough and burning herself. Like moving too quickly and bashing a leg into the corner of a chair. Like tasting boiling liquids without blowing on them and scorching her tongue.

Because my mother and grandmother were always fighting, my mother didn't pay attention when she cooked. And so. She'd slice a piece off her finger. Peel her hand instead of the vegetables. Stick her head too far into the oven and get a blast of steam on her face, and it would be red for days.

"Battle scars," my mother called her injuries. And they were.

My mother rarely spent money on herself for small luxuries, even though she could afford them, desired them. She would gaze into the window of a store, and look at something that captured her fancy—a filmy blouse, a slim skirt, a jaunty hat—knowing that she would never allow herself to buy it. Whatever she wanted, like the love of a devoted mother, was always beyond her reach.

She diluted dish detergent, laundry detergent, liquid soup, shampoo, with water until they were useless. Still, she used them, forced us to use them. "A penny saved is a penny earned," she would say. She rarely replaced anything she broke—a hand mirror, an electric mixer—but made do without it, as if she should be punished for the rest of her life for her transgression.

But mostly, my mother did without food.

She did not put anything on her plate until everyone else had eaten. She ate everyone's leftovers (and called herself "the garbage pail"). Ate stale bread instead of fresh. Drank cold coffee or coffee dregs instead of making a fresh pot. Ate foods she detested—fish, liver, eggs—because they were cheap. Didn't stop for lunch but made do with a leftover crust of toast from breakfast, which she ate standing by the counter.

When I was a girl, my mother never made enough food. It wasn't that we were poor, for she always managed to save money. It seemed like she wanted to starve us. Like she wanted to starve us because she wanted us dead, because she didn't know what to do with us, how to care for us.

When I was an infant, my father said, I'd cry, but my mother wouldn't nurse me. I'd cry so loud that the neighbors would knock on the apartment door to see if something was wrong. But still she wouldn't feed me.

If I started crying because I was hungry at four, my mother would wait until five to feed me. If I started crying at five, my mother would wait until six to feed me.

By the time I fed, I was so exhausted from crying that I would suckle for a few minutes, then fall asleep. My mother, assuming I'd had my fill, would put me back into my bassinet. But I would soon awaken, howling. By now, it was past feeding time, so my mother wouldn't feed me. And I would cry until she decided it was time for me to eat.

She was breast-feeding, so throughout this time she wasn't feeding me, she had my father yelling at her to feed me, and her breasts were leaking milk into the protective pads she put into her nursing bras, because her breasts would start to drip milk when I cried. (After my mother died, I found a supply of these pads and the nursing bras in her bureau. My mother never threw anything away.)

My father thought this was crazy. Me crying. My mother not feeding me. "Why don't you feed her, for Christ's sake?" my father would say.

"Why didn't you feed me yourself?" I ask my father.

"You know your mother," he says. "There was no arguing with her."

Still, my father insists that my mother was a good mother. She didn't throw us out the window, or against the wall, or drown us in a bathtub, or strap us into car seats and drive a car into a lake. My mother was too good a mother to do any of that.

When we were still children, my sister told me she had seen my mother naked, and that my mother had an extra set of nipples on her body. Maybe the extra set of nipples was the reason my mother was so uncomfortable feeding me. Maybe my mother couldn't figure out which nipple to use. Maybe my mother wanted to feed me; maybe she just didn't know how.

There we all were, in our dimly lit kitchen painted a garish shade of yellow, at the Formica table set with our "everyday" chipped dishes and mismatched glasses and flatware, waiting to see how big our portions would be, hoping that the food at this meal would be edible, and would be enough.

Breakfast. Burned toast, and watered down canned orange juice.

Lunch. A small plate of instant mashed potatoes and instant gravy. Or a can of Campbell's soup diluted with an extra can of water to "stretch" it. Or a hard-boiled egg sliced with a rusty egg slicer (an extravagance my mother bought on impulse at a garage sale).

Supper. Two burnt toasted cheeses for the four of us, or three sausages, or three pieces of chicken, or an omelet made with three eggs.

Sometimes my father doused his food with my grandmother's *olio santo*, holy oil, olive oil steeped with fiery chile peppers, to make my mother's food palatable. "Devil's oil," my mother called it.

My mother had absolute control over what was put on our plates. No bowls of food served family style for this family. No popping up out of your chair to look into the refrigerator for something else. No cooking your own food if you didn't like hers. No happy Italian family gathered around the table stuffing themselves with meatballs and spaghetti, sausage and peppers, everyone talking at the same time.

Our meals were like those in a badly run prison where someone is putting the food money in their pockets instead of on the table. My sister and I waited through meals like two inmates watching the guards through half-closed lids, to see whether they were dangerous.

But at the end of what passed for supper, my mother would go over to the cupboard and pull out one of her Dugan's desserts—seven-layer cake, pumpkin pie, lemon meringue. These kept my father from getting after her to make her own.

She always offered dessert to my father, never to me or my sister, though we knew that if we pestered her for something we could have it. Although my mother was abstemious, she indulged herself in a few bites of dessert.

During the meal, all I wanted was to head up to my room, bury my head in a book, and imagine I was someplace else. After supper, my father wanted us to stay at the table for some conversation, which really meant that he wanted to yell at us for everything my mother told him we'd done wrong that day. But I tried not to linger and left the table as fast as I could.

Although my mother wanted to eat like an American, her food habits recreated the privations experienced by her people in the South of Italy, though I am certain she did not realize this. For the families of many immigrants, living in America meant that you would no longer be hungry, that you could eat as much as the rich ate in the Old World. But in our house, there was no culture of abundance to erase our family's history: there had never been enough food to eat, and my people had never been able to control how much food was given to them.

Throughout my mother's life, her hands shook, causing dishes to fall and shatter on the floor, flour to spill all over the counter as she tried to shake some from a bag into a measuring cup, soap to enter my sister's eyes or mine when she washed our faces. But my mother's hands never shook so badly as after her stepmother died.

After my grandmother's death, my mother was alone in the house while my father was away at work. I had my family to take care of; my sister was living on the West Coast. Being completely alone never suited my mother. Yes, she loved to be by herself and not be bothered by anyone, but only so long as someone else was there.

Now that there was no one for my mother to fight with, she

became detached and depressed. Having an evil stepmother in the house for all those years was better than having no mother at all. While her stepmother was alive, at least my mother felt something, even if what she felt was hatred, rage, even if what she wanted was retribution.

Perhaps my mother really missed her stepmother. Yearned for her, as she had yearned for a mother's love. Or if she didn't miss her, missed the drama that having my grandmother in the house permitted her. But whatever the reason, unhappy as she had been before her stepmother died, afterwards my mother was unhappier still. And the affliction she'd lived with intensified.

After my grandmother's death, my mother had to grip a cup of coffee with both hands to bring it to her mouth. She had to make her hands into tight fists and rest them in her lap to still them. She had to steady her right hand with her left to put on lipstick, and often the effect she achieved was that of a raw wound rather than a cosmetic enhancement. Many pieces of her forget-me-not dishware fell to the floor as she wiped them.

Once, she was so distraught that she called me to come over and help her. She was clearing out my grandmother's room. I was married, busy with small children. Still, my mother's anguish was evident, and I couldn't forsake her.

She was packing things away, and she had dropped the glass bell that covered my grandmother's statue of the Blessed Virgin. It shattered on the floor. All morning, as she was cleaning up the glass, my mother was afraid she would slice herself with a piece because she couldn't keep her hands from shaking. And though she wasn't bleeding, I saw that there were little slivers of glass embedded in the palms of both her hands.

My mother believed that if she took up something that required using her hands, something that required concentration, it might retrain whatever was going wrong.

And so, she began to embroider.

She took little trips outside the house to a shop in the next town and bought what she needed—linen for a ground, silk and woolen threads, fine needles, a wooden frame, a tapestry bag to hold her equipment. Although all this was expensive, she indulged herself. She needed to. She believed that her life depended upon it.

At first, as she worked on scrap pieces of fabric to teach her hands their discipline, she pierced her fingers, and there were bloodstains on the cloth. But slowly, surely, she found she could insert a sharp needle into the material and pull it out without damage to herself or her work.

Her first successes were two pillows, a wheat-colored ground covered with flowers. Next were placemats and matching napkins that she would set atop her stepmother's crocheted tablecloths. (After my grandmother died, my mother used the tablecloths often, and not only on special occasions, but also for Sunday dinner in the dining room my grandmother no longer inhabited. She washed them by hand, starched them, and stretched them on a frame embedded with nails my father made).

Samplers came next. On one, my mother embroidered orchids, mimosa, almond blossoms, poppies, daisies, thistle, gorse, asphodel, iris, cyclamen, rockroses. On the other, parsley, thyme, sage, rosemary, dill. And although my mother didn't realize it, many of the flowers and herbs that she embroidered grew in or near Rodi Garganico, the village where her stepmother came from, on the Gargano peninsula in Puglia.

I didn't know this until recently, when I traveled to Puglia in search of my stepgrandmother's village, because I thought that going there would teach me something I needed to know about her, about my past, my family history.

One sun-drenched day, walking along a path on the edge of a hillside near the Adriatic, looking at the white houses of Rodi Garganico in the distance, I saw a very old woman dressed in black, sitting in the sunlight on a chair in the doorway of a small house by the sea. On her lap was an enormous white tablecloth (for her granddaughter's trousseau?). On it, she had sketched a wavering border and bouquets of flowers caught together by furls of ribbon. Many of the flowers she was embroidering were blooming on the hillside behind here, and they were the same as my mother's.

As my mother sat during those long winter days of sorrow after her stepmother died, her embroidery returned her to the old ways. And to the flowers on the hillsides of Puglia. All the way back to the village her stepmother had left so many years before.

Part Three

CHASING GHOSTS

HUNGER

My grandfather once told me that, when he was hungry, he used to walk past the priest's house in his village so that the aroma of the priest's dinner would season the moldy bread he would be having for his supper. My grandmother once told me that the fart of a bishop was more nourishing than the food she ate while she lived in Italy, and that her food didn't taste any better than the smell of the bishop's fart.

I knew, from my grandparents' stories, that they had come to America for a better life. But because they were proud people, they got on with their lives, did what they had to do, and didn't waste much talk describing the past. So although there was much that I knew, there was more that I didn't know.

I didn't know that the fields my grandfather worked were seven miles from where he lived. That *zappatori*—diggers—walked there with their tools on their backs. That they began work at sunrise and left their homes at three or four in the morning. I didn't know that they worked from sunrise until sunset. Then they walked back to their homes, where they'd eat something—bread, softened with water; in a good year, a few broad beans; some pasta; and whatever their wives or mothers could glean or steal without getting caught. I didn't know they would fall into their beds too tired to unlace their boots. A few hours later, they were awakened by their wives or mothers to leave for the fields. (If they got sick while they were working, they had to find their way home alone; their friends were forbidden to stop work to accompany them.)

I didn't know that farmworkers had to use the mattock, an archaic tool with a short handle. (Long-handled tools cost more.) It was not uncommon for workers' bodies to become deformed from years of using the mattock.

I didn't know that during harvest they were forbidden to go back home. They slept in the fields, without shelter or blankets. Those would have cost money, diminished profits. And besides, these people were used to living like animals.

I didn't know that while they lived in the fields, they were fed *acquasale*, a soup of hot water, salt, a little bread, and a tiny bit of olive oil. They were supposed to show their overseers that they were grateful for this food. While they lived in the fields, they were permitted to forage for wild plants and weeds. The overseers, on horseback, were amused by the spectacle of men and women crawling along the ground searching for wild onion, a shoot of *ruca*, to stuff into their mouths, amused by the spectacle of men and women fighting over a blade of dandelion.

I didn't know that farmworkers who ate every day were considered wealthy. I didn't know that there were frequent famines in Puglia. I didn't know that the landowners, *latifondisti*, used droughts to force workers into debt so they'd have to accept lower wages. I didn't know that workers paid 60 percent interest on loans, so their wages were taken to pay their debts, and they were forced to work only for an insufficient amount of food.

I knew that children started working at eight. But I didn't know they worked for half-wages. Didn't know how brutally they were treated. That they were beaten. Forced to run through the "blood line"—a line of overseers who lashed their backs with belts. Didn't know that if a boy shirked his labor, the overseer would tie a string to his penis and tie the other end to the stalk of wheat he'd missed, to shame him.

I didn't know that workers lived in what were called rabbit hutches, housing built by landowners. And that most lived underground, where there was no light, no air. That five to ten people lived in a room sixteen feet by sixteen feet. The average rent was one fourth of the worker's annual salary in a good year; workers paid a year's rent in advance. I didn't know that farm workers had no furniture, no changes of clothing, that they slept on the floor and ate on the floor, that each family owned one communal bowl.

I didn't know that taxes were levied on what the poor bought, that taxes could amount to a family's income for a year. (Landowners avoided paying taxes by buying wholesale in large quantities.)

I didn't know that parents with young children left them behind when they went to the fields. Older children cared for younger children. But no food was left for the children, because there was no food. I didn't know that parents had to hope someone would be merciful to their children and give them something to eat.

I didn't know that Puglia had the highest death rate and the shortest life expectancy of all the provinces in Italy. That there were virtually no doctors, no medicines, no medical equipment. (In Bari, only 180 people out of 120,000 had ever seen a doctor.)

I didn't know that a landowner had the right to have sex with—to rape—any peasant woman in his employ when she became engaged. This right was written into law. *Ius primae noctis.*

I didn't know that "good" laborers—submissive, obedient, respectful workers, who bowed when they encountered people of authority—were rewarded with a bonus at payday: one finger's worth of grease to rub into their shoes. Without the grease, shoes hardened, cracked, split, and were useless. Without shoes, you couldn't work. To buy new shoes, you had to go into debt. The cost to landowners of keeping their workers under control: one finger's worth of grease.

I didn't know that the land my people came from was colonized by Rome, France, Spain, by Garibaldi's army, by armies from the North.

I didn't know that the people of the South, my people, were considered by those people of the North (and are still so considered) to be primitive, barbarian, animalistic, racially inferior, ignorant, backward, superstitious, degraded, incapable of being civilized, lazy. That they were so regarded from the period of Spanish rule and that these beliefs justified the colonization of the South and the refusal of the North to fully integrate the South into the country after unification. A common saying, still used today: "Italy ends at Rome. . . . All the rest is Africa."

I didn't know that over 17,000 acres of land in Puglia had been held in common by the poor since before Roman times. That, after unification, this land was confiscated, sold to the rich. I didn't know that the poor tried to reclaim the land that had been seized from them, and that when they did, they were driven off, or were executed by armed gangs of thugs hired by landlords. Because they were poor, they could not afford lawyers, so they had no legal way to challenge the confiscation of land that had been their property for centuries.

I didn't know that my people were no longer allowed to enter this land, except to work it for the profit of the landowners (land confiscators). Wheat and grapes were planted on this confiscated land. The poor could no longer feed themselves, for they could no longer farm the land that was once theirs, could no longer forage on the land, could no longer graze their animals on the land, could not fish in the streams on the land, could not hunt small game on the land.

Instead, they were forced to farm the land that was once theirs for the landowners (land confiscators). The landowners knew that the poor could no longer raise their own food, and so knew they could be forced to work for very low wages; the workers had no choice but to accept whatever wages were offered them. (What they lost when they lost their land: their means of subsistence, their independence, their self-sufficiency.) They stopped being peasants and became day laborers. Entered a life that resembled indentured servitude, only worse, for there was no freedom to look forward to at the end of a number of years.

I didn't know that the diet of farmworkers consisted, mostly, of bread. Not pasta, not beans, not meat, not vegetables, not fruit. Just bread. And poor bread, made from flour that had been adulterated with clay, sand, chalk, that was infested with mites and contaminated with mite shit. Water was often not available; when it was, it had to be purchased; it cost more than wine. Many workers drank wine, not water, so many died from heatstroke. (This was no problem for the landowners; workers could be replaced more easily than farm animals.)

I didn't know that many people in Puglia died of thirst. The Romans, during the empire, brought water to Rome: eleven aqueducts served the city. But well into the twentieth century, no water was brought to the people of Puglia.

I didn't know that farmworkers were overseen by guards armed with whips and rifles. Didn't know that landowners hired gangs of outlaws, misfits, and thugs to terrorize farmworkers into submission. That these gangs assassinated leaders, threatened workers' families, stole their possessions, set fire to their homes. I didn't know that landowners collaborated with fascists to force the farmworkers into submission. Didn't know that the first third of the twentieth century (after my grandfather left Puglia, but while my mother's stepmother still lived there) was a reign of terror. I didn't know that armed gangs of thugs were granted immunity from the law for past crimes and future offenses in return for enforcing curfews, ensuring that farmworkers didn't vote, assassinating political candidates sympathetic to the workers, ransacking the homes of union organizers, ambushing groups of laborers and killing them.

I also didn't know that, throughout history, the people of the South mounted well-organized insurrections against the injustice of colonial rule. These movements were written into Italian history as criminal. During the uprisings against the inequities of Garibaldi's rule, ten thousand people died in the South in violent confrontations and executions; twenty thousand were imprisoned or exiled.

I didn't know that farmworkers launched a powerful revolutionary movement. Didn't know that women were among the most militant of strikers. That they were in the front ranks when crowds of strikers stormed public buildings. That they lay down with their babies in front of cavalry.

I didn't know that the epicenter of the labor movement was near where my people came from. Didn't know that the names of members of my family—Libera, Libero—were common only among anarchists, socialists, and union organizers. I didn't know that among the emigrants from Puglia were political exiles trying to escape reprisals. (I wonder whether my staunchly pro-union maternal grandfather, who joined the labor movement in the United States, belonged to the movement in Puglia.)

I didn't know that Puglia was called the land of chronic massacres. Government troops routinely fired into crowds of unarmed strikers. (Striking at harvest time was the only power farmworkers had, since landowners wouldn't bargain with them: they believed the workers had no right to make any demands. In 1907, about the time my grandfather emigrated, there were forty-five strikes, involving 109,000 workers.) This is what the workers wanted: union recognition; wage increases; contracts; shelters for sleeping in the fields; transportation to and from fields; payment for time lost for bad weather; better food; rest periods; broad-bean cultivation in winter to provide employment during this slack time; a holiday on May 1; the right to walk beside their employers during the Sunday *passeggiata*.

(Antonio Gramsci, on the South: "It was disciplined with two series of measures. The first was merciless police repression directed against every mass movement and involving the periodic slaughter of peasants." The filmmaker Pier Paolo Pasolini called this genocide. Booker T. Washington, when he visited the South of Italy, remarked that peasants and farm workers there lived in conditions worse than slavery.)

I didn't know that the emigration of Southern Italians—some

twenty-five million people from Italy emigrated between 1876 and 1976—was a form of rebellion against these harsh conditions and against the refusal of successive governments to build a more equitable society.

Without a history, there can be no present. Without a past, there can be no future.

I learn all this about my people not from the schools I attended, not from my grandparents, not from my parents, but from books written by Italian American and other historians. About the most painful truths of their lives, of my family's history, my grandparents were silent. Of my grandparents' lives in Italy, my parents only said, "It was hard for them."

Hard for them.

I take out my grandfather's wedding pictures, look at his face, his hands, his body, his eyes. Look for signs of what he's lived through. Look at my grandmothers' eyes for signs of what they've lived through.

And it is there in the eyes, the pain, the sorrow, the despair, the rage. But what is there, too, in the way my grandparents hold their bodies, is a dignity and a pride beyond imagination.

Without a history, there can be no present. Without a past, there can be no future.

I didn't know any of these things about my people. Nor did my mother, my father. But perhaps we knew them in our bodies. Perhaps my mother relived the life of her ancestors in the way she treated food. Perhaps my father's rage began there. Perhaps this is why I hoard food, treat it as if it's sacred, bless it, revere it, let it nourish me, let it excite me, calm me, placate me, spend as much time with it as I can. Perhaps I do this because my people could not.

As I learn all these things, I have many violent dreams. In them, I am the avatar of my ancestors. I fight, and defeat, all those who have disrespected my people, all those who have taken their land, who have forced them into submission, who have overworked them, starved them.

I ride on horseback, through the wheat fields of Puglia. I scale walls, flit across rooftops, drop down the sides of buildings, crawl into windows. I rout landowners from their beds, impale them on my lance. I find their stores of food. And I take everything that I find to feed my people.

PUGLIA DIARY

For my sixtieth birthday, Ernie takes me to the South of Italy, where my grandparents left early in the twentieth century, during the time of the great migration. We'll visit Rodi Garganico, my stepgrandmother's village (I don't know my mother's birth mother's village); Positano, my paternal grandmother's; Scafati, my paternal grandfather's. On this trip, we're not visiting Vieste, my maternal grandfather's.

I've never been to this part of Italy before, though I've been to many other places in Italy. Why wait this long to come? Lack of interest, yes, for many years. Though I was proud of my Italian American heritage, I felt little connection to my Southern Italian past. I buried my grandparents' stories deep in the crevices of memory. Shards of what I'd heard from them, I'd stumble upon now and again. But I went about my daily life, my American life, without thinking much about my ancestors.

When my father became ill, and I feared he would soon die, I wanted to learn whatever I could about what he remembered so that I could make a record. So my family's story would not vanish. I'd spent years writing about other people's lives, famous writers' lives. Why not about those of my family?

On our flight to Bari, I see the sweep of the Gargano peninsula. It is shaped like the bunion on my grandmother's toe. This is the second time I fly over land where my grandfather, my mother's father, labored—the first, when I fly over the train tracks he laid in Maine. Both times, tears. The same rush of feelings. The irony of my life: that I can afford to fly over the places where he labored.

Now I can see the fields where my grandfather worked the land. See him as a child, bent over, harvesting wheat.

We are staying in a converted *masseria*. It is exquisite. White stone. Moorish architecture. Wild poppies and wild daisies everywhere. An orange grove. A lemon grove. We lounge on a porch with arched windows and doors. Listen to birdsong. Watch a mother cat groom her kittens. Sip wine made from grapes grown nearby. Eat prosciutto and cheese *panini*. There are olive trees that are over a thousand years old here. They look like pieces of sculpture. It would take five, maybe six people holding hands to encompass one.

In my grandfather's time, a *masseria* like this one was inhabited by landowners, overseers—those who persecuted my people. Yet I am staying here as a guest.

At dinner, we sit in a vaulted stone room. Crisp white tablecloths, napkins. Waiters in black uniforms. Tables bedecked with flowers. Along the back wall, a collection of pottery from a nearby village.

Our menu:

First, an *amuse-bouche* of an asparagus frittata. The asparagus are thinner than pencils. The frittata is cut into circles; they are served with a little bit of parsley, and with a glass of white wine from the *masseria*.

A pasta in the shape of a large teardrop, dressed with a sauce of cauliflower, bread crumbs, a touch of onion, a touch of anchovy. *Cicatelli con cavolfiore e mollica fritta*. (The pasta chef is a woman; she recreates traditional pastas from a recipe book found in the *masseria*. These are pastas I do not know; these are pastas my family never tasted.)

Lamb brochettes with almond sauce and wild onions. *Spidino del massaro con salsa di mandorle*. The onions are the ones my grandmother talked about; the ones the workers foraged for, and were permitted to eat with their bread, if they were lucky.

A salad of shredded radicchio and sun-dried tomatoes.

Dessert: Crepes with ricotta cheese. It is spring, and the ricotta is sweet.

We eat too much.

All night, strange dreams. In one, there was a child I had to care for. But there was nothing I could do for this child; there was no way for me to care for this child. Another is the old not-being-able-to-find-my-way-home dream. In this version, I have to walk home, and, as usual, don't know which road I should take.

In our bedroom (from which you can see a sliver of the Adriatic), a painting of the shacks that peasants inhabited. Creamy white stone. Square. Little doors. No windows. I can't look at it.

Tomorrow we leave to find Rodi Garganico, my stepgrand-mother's village.

On the outskirts of Rodi, ugly cell-block apartments. In the center of the village, derelict, ancient buildings. The decoration over a church door—a seashell—the same as the one on my mother's gilt mirror ("I don't know why, I just had to have it," she said when she bought it.)

Tiny alleyways, so narrow you have to flatten yourself against a building to let someone pass by. The people, sullen; wary of strangers. I understand dialect, Italian; but Ernie speaks Italian better than I do, so, though he's reluctant to approach anyone to ask them about my grandmother, he's the one who will ask. A maze of alleyways, of stairways, leading towards the sea. You could get lost here if you didn't know your way. Heavy wooden door. Balconies overhanging the alleyways, protecting them from the hot sun. A village that seems uninhabited. Almost no windows. Small, grated holes in the walls to let in the air. A woman scrubbing her steps.

Sounds coming from a kitchen—pots and pans clanging; women arguing; they sound like my mother and grandmother.

The sea, cut off from the village, now, by the railroad. Was there a railroad when my grandmother lived here?

Outside the village, a strip of sand beach on the other side of the railroad tracks. A sole bather. Did my stepgrandmother ever swim in these waters? The smell of garbage burning in the air.

Rodi, at a distance, from the beach: Red-tiled roofs. White houses. A village tumbling down to the sea.

All the hotels in Rodi, except one, are closed until the season begins. This one has been ravaged, it seems, by holidaymakers. Flower boxes full of dead flowers. A rusty merry-go-round. The walls of our bedroom, inscribed with visitors' initials. Peeling paint. Garbage burning below the window of our room.

I dreamed we'd find a sweet little hotel in a perfumed orange grove (for that's how this one was advertised). There would be a little balcony where I could sit and look at Rodi. In my fantasy, I would have an immediate sense of connection to this place. And . . . And what?

For the village in the distance, though it is the village my grandmother came from, is not my grandmother's village. That one vanished from the earth the day my grandmother left. The village she inhabited survived only in her imagination. And in mine.

This village is not the one I came to see. But I did not know this until I came here. And though I try to think my way back through the years, to imagine what it was like when she lived here, I cannot.

I don't know what I thought I was going to find in Rodi Garganico. Someone who looked like my grandmother walking down an alley-way? Someone we'd stop and ask about my grandmother? Someone who knew her family? Relatives of hers who lived in Rodi still? People who knew whether my grandfather and stepgrandmother knew each other before he came to the United States? Whether he had ever passed through this village? Whether they were anarchists?

Did I believe I would find someone who could tell me about my stepgrandmother's life, what she was like as a girl? Yes, I think I did. These things happen, after all, in novels, in films. But not in real life. At least not in my life. But I want to know her history, not just imagine it. For although we are not related by blood, I consider her my ancestor.

No, I will never know my grandparents' histories. No matter how much I try to remember my grandparents' stories; how much I listen to my father's stories; how much I read; how much I study my grandparents' photos, their papers, the few artifacts that remain of their lives. No matter whether or not I visit the places they lived.

All I can do is conjecture, imagine, invent their lives. My story of their story, a distortion, a misrepresentation of what they lived. But my story of their story, now a respect I must accord them—though I cannot possibly get it right, though I cannot possibly understand who they were—so their lives do not pass into oblivion.

My story of their story gives me something I did not have before. It fixes me in time.

This place holds nothing for me, though I thought it would hold so much. Rodi Garganico is, for me, a place imagined, described to me in my grandmother's stories. But that imagined place is as real to me as if I had experienced it.

Even though I'm here, in Rodi, I'm in some in-between place. Trying to find a place that cannot be found on any map.

The memory of these places was all my grandparents had after they left. But places change, become someplace else. And the only real place I can visit is the Rodi Garganico in my memory. Horace Walpole: "Our memory sees more than our eyes in this country."

Standing on the beach, I realize the obvious: how far Rodi Garganico is from Hoboken, New Jersey. It has taken us a long time to get here even in the age of the airplane, the automobile. How much greater the distance between these places for my grandmother.

What could it have been like to leave this place she'd never left before, and leave its ways, for a man she didn't know, for a world she was unprepared to experience?

Everywhere in Puglia, round crocheted doilies, like the ones my grandmother crocheted. Placed between cup and saucer. Inside bread baskets. After my grandmother died, we found scores of them. My mother never used them; I didn't know what they were for. And so disposed of them.

On a walk, I see a woman, her back to the road, sitting outside her house, embroidering flowers like those that bloom on the hillside behind the village.

Deep sorrow. A yearning that will never be satisfied.

I know that what I wanted, what I needed, I will never find here, and that I will have to live with this knowledge, and that learning to live with it will be another kind of education.

If my people hadn't left, I would be: The woman washing her steps in Rodi. A woman in a field, bending to hoe the earth. A woman in black, walking along the side of the road, distrustful. A screaming woman in a kitchen—angry words; pots and pans smashing. The woman gathering snails by the side of the road after a rainstorm. The old woman embroidering a tablecloth for her granddaughter's trousseau, taking care that each flower is stitched perfectly. The woman cutting pasta on her guitar outside on a hot day. (Pasta, transubstantiation of water and flour.)

Ernie and I decide to leave. I am nothing but an invader here.

BIG SHOT

When my father is about seven or eight years old, my grandfather decides to move the family back to Italy, to Scafati, where his family and his wife's family live. He's sold his business. He has some money. And he has a plan.

My grandfather wants to go back home to show his relatives how well he's done in America. He has an older brother in Italy who has a Ph.D. in philosophy, and who's become a priest. The family doted upon this brother, gave him everything. They believed that if they used all their resources to put one son in a position of power, then he would help the other members of the family. Only it didn't turn out that way. For the older son did nothing for the family. He believed that if he entertained them with a lavish dinner once a year, they should be satisfied. Their pride in him should be enough.

Because his brother refused to use his influence to find him employment, and because jobs were scarce, my grandfather was forced to emigrate. He's returning home to show his family that, without their help, he's done well in America.

My grandfather's plan is to find a little rundown house in a good location, by the river in Scafati. He'll use cheap labor to fix it up. He and his family will live in one part of the house; he'll rent out the rest. He'll save the rent money from the first house, buy another, rent that one, save the rent money, buy another. In no time at all, he imagines, he will be one of the biggest landlords in Scafati. His family will respect him. Everyone will say how clever he is. He will live in an impressive house. He will give his mother expensive presents. He will take all his friends out for sumptuous meals.

"The reason he takes us back to Italy," my father says, "is because he says he's going to live there for the rest of his life. He has this plan that he's going to become a big-shot landlord, a big shot like all the other big shots he says he knows. This way, he won't have to work. He can live off all the rent money without working, without having to lift a finger.

"We last less than a year in Scafati before my father's money runs out. But my mother has saved money she's earned while we lived there, working in the canning factory, so we can move back to New Jersey.

"After we come back to the United States, my father never takes us to Italy again, although he goes back several times a year.

"By the time we come back to the States, he and my mother aren't getting along. That's when things get bad at home, and they stay that way until I join the navy to get out of the house."

I know some terrible things happened to my father in Scafati. There was a trumpet player in the local band who molested him and some of his friends. He lured boys up into his room, threatened them into submission, fondled them until they were aroused, then beat their erect penises because he was disgusted by them. My father was one of these boys. As he tells what happened, though, he laughs.

"We got the son of a bitch," my father says. "My friend tells his parents, and the trumpet player is driven out of town by a gang of angry parents. If they caught him, they would have killed him. And no one would have said a word."

Many times, my father was beaten by gangs of fascists. When they marched through town, he, a group of other children, and protestors, stood on a street corner singing the Communist anthem, "Bandera rosa." My father's resistance to fascism was visceral, not political: "I was just a kid," he says. "I didn't understand what was happening.

But I knew these people were dangerous, so that when I saw groups of Communists gathering to resist, I joined them." His mother was working; his father was with his cronies. So his parents never learned what happened. He told his mother his cuts and bruises had been dealt out by a local bully. He stopped taunting the fascists when his mother told him that if he was beaten up again, she'd beat him up.

Despite all this, my father remembers his time in Scafati as idyllic. He remembers a life filled with adventure—throwing stones into the river, playing with his friends, visiting his grandparents—and with wonderful meals and intimate family gatherings.

My father was considered a celebrity in the village, he says, because of the roller skates he brought to Italy with him. They were the first anyone in the village had ever seen. As my father glided through the village, over the blocks of granite paving the streets, people would point to him and call him *il diavolo che rulla*, the devil on wheels, the devil who rolls. He made money from those skates, he said, by renting them out to his friends.

There were days when he'd skate down the road to the ruins at Pompeii to beg money from travelers. Sometimes he'd take off his skates, wander about, look at what remained from this ancient city, imagine the past. My father's love of history, he says, dates from these excursions.

My father's maternal grandparents live close to his family. His grandfather is a conductor on the railroad, so they live well. They have a little patch of land behind their house to grow vegetables and raise chickens, turkeys, pigeons, and rabbits, which they share with my father's family. The family gets together several times a week and on weekends. Every time, they have good meals—pasta with vegetables from the garden; a roasted chicken, or stewed rabbit, or pigeon, on weekends.

My father becomes very attached to his grandparents. And they dote on him. He is the only boy in the family. They treat him well, unlike his father, who ignores him. They also lend help and emotional support to their daughter, his mother, which lessens the impact of her husband's indifference. (After the family moves back to New Jersey, my father never sees his grandparents again.)

Because his father wants to rent out all the other rooms in the derelict property he buys, the six members of the family (and later seven, when his mother gives birth to her last child, a girl) crowd into two rooms. There is no electricity, no heat, no stove, no icebox, no running water, no toilet.

When it gets cold, his mother lights a charcoal burner in the middle of the bedroom. Everyone sleeps in one room, on pallets on the floor. The air is smoky from the charcoal burner, but the windows stay closed. His mother is afraid of the night air.

His mother cautions the children each night to be careful: people's bedclothes often catch fire, and children are burned in their sleep. This never happens in his family. But my father has nightmares of rolling into the fire in his sleep. His screams wake the whole family; his sisters get mad at him, and his father calls him a sissy.

My father's mother sets up a charcoal grill on the balcony of their apartment. From the balcony, you can cast a line into the river and fish. Here, outside, his mother does all her cooking over a charcoal fire, even when it rains.

My father remembers the charcoal vendors coming through the streets, remembers the fires on the slopes of the Apennines when the woods were burned for charcoal, remembers the stench of smoke, and how the forests shrank, even in the short time that he is there. At this time in the South of Italy, charcoal is the only fuel used to heat homes and cook food.

All the family's water—for cooking, washing, cleaning—is hauled from the well near my father's grandmother's house. His grandmother is lucky because she doesn't have to haul her water far. The well makes her neighborhood very desirable. But my father's family lives a mile away.

"Who hauls the water?" I ask my father.

"Me, my mother, and my sisters, of course," my father answers.

"Not your father?"

"Not my father."

"Even after your mother has the baby?"

"Before she has the baby. And after."

"What's your father doing?"

"Who knows what my father does during the day? He's a man of leisure. He might have had a job in a barbershop, but I don't think so. My mother was working in the canning factory to make some money. I think he spent his days just hanging around."

"Didn't your mother complain?"

"Of course. But it didn't do any good. Besides, there were lots of men like my father who did nothing but hang around. How he behaved wasn't exceptional."

"Let me get this straight," I say. "Your mother gives birth to a baby, is raising five kids, one of them an infant, while she's also working in a canning factory, hauling water every day all the way to that miserable place where you live, and she's cooking outside even when it rains, and you don't remember your father helping her with anything?"

"No, he didn't help her with anything. Didn't I tell you before that my father was a shithead?"

My grandmother's work at the canning factory, and her relationship with her parents, keep her family going through this time. Like so many women of the South, though she complains, she accepts her fate. She resigns herself to the circumstances of her life and plows through the routine of her days, never stopping, never resting.

She awakens early in the morning, dresses the children, folds the bedding, starts the charcoal fire on the balcony, trails down to the well with my father and the three youngest girls. The oldest daughter stays behind to watch the baby.

After they haul the water back to their house, my grandmother heats it to wash the oldest children and dress them for school. She gives the children breakfast: some stale bread soaked in coffee, a piece of fruit; "We always had fruit," my father says—and sends them off.

She carries the baby to her mother's and goes to the factory. There, she cleans string beans, peels carrots, cuts plum tomatoes (the famed San Marzano tomatoes) in quarters to prepare them for canning. Sometimes, to make extra money, she takes a bushel of vegetables home to prepare them. My father and his older sisters help. Sometimes she keeps a handful of string beans, a couple of carrots, a few tomatoes, for herself. My father says she never gets in trouble; the owner of the factory expects the workers to take some food so they can be well-fed and work hard; besides, he is a relative.

When I tell my husband about my grandmother's life, he tells me a similar story about *his* grandmother's life.

His grandfather was a tailor, and after he established himself in America, he contacted someone in his village in the Abruzzi to arrange a marriage. Money was exchanged; my husband's grandmother was bought and paid for, more a possession than a person.

What his grandfather wants, my husband says, is not a wife, but a servant. When she comes to America, she knows no one. None of her relatives are here to give her support, to make sure she's well-treated. So she's at her husband's mercy.

He comes and goes as he pleases. Visits his friends whenever he chooses. Pays no attention to her except to have sex as often as he chooses, and to tell her what he wants to eat. After they have children, he pays no attention to them unless he's brutalizing them.

His eldest son is sent to college and graduate school: all the family's resources support this son. The three other sons—one of whom is my husband's father—and daughter are taken out of school and sent to work at unskilled or semiskilled jobs to help support the family and the eldest son, who becomes an engineer.

Through the years, a portion of their pay is handed over to this privileged son so he can indulge himself; he buys nice clothes, goes to the movies, to bars, to houses of prostitution. No one in the family complains about the injustice of this arrangement. Their father has terrified them into submission. He allows this son to take whatever he wants from his siblings.

Once, when my husband's father refuses to give his brother one of his shirts, his father tries to murder him. But he escapes, leaves home. He doesn't stop seeing his parents. He can't abandon his mother.

She spends her life cleaning and preparing food for the family and for all the friends her husband brings home. He is a tailor. He does well in America. He likes to show off by bringing his male friends home and having his wife cook for them.

He never takes her anywhere. She never visits anyone. Her domain is the household, her place is in the kitchen. Her only forays outside the house are to buy food. She never visits her children once they marry. They all come to see her.

I imagine my husband's grandmother as a young woman on the eve of her departure for America, knowing that she will probably never see her family again. Her family is happy that this marriage has been arranged, for it means that there will be one less mouth to feed in the harsh countryside of the Abruzzi, and the honor of one less daughter to worry about.

I can see her holding the photograph of her husband-to-be given to her by the intermediary. Imagine her wondering what this man is like, wondering what her life will be like with this man. If she is like many Southern Italian women, she probably doesn't hope for much from this alliance; it is wise not to hope, for if you do not hope, then you will not be disappointed. She would have known that they would not be intimate, that they would live parallel lives, as men and women do. She knew she would be responsible for the household and for the children, though he would make the rules. She knew that he would work and provide money and visit with his friends at the end of the day. And that, over this, she would have no control. He would come home whenever it pleased him. And if luck shined upon her, he would not come home drunk, and he would not come home wanting sex.

Still, she might have hoped for this much: That because there was so much money in America, her life as the wife of a well-respected tailor might have permitted her a few pleasures. A beautiful dress, say, to wear as they walked through their neighborhood. A trip to visit her family. Some money saved for her old age. And she might have hoped that this man would be loyal to her, and that he would treat her with respect and decency, if not with warmth, generosity, and kindness.

My husband's grandfather will eat only fresh-killed chickens, fresh-killed game, fresh-killed fish. So his wife buys them live, as he demands, and butchers them in the backyard. He will eat only homemade pasta and homemade bread, so she makes them daily for her large family. Nor can he abide store-bought tomatoes and vegetables, so she keeps a garden out back, and she hoes, weeds, harvests, without his help. He likes to eat alone, without conversation. So she feeds him first. Then she feeds her family. When all the others have taken their meal, she eats, alone, in the kitchen.

When he sits in the living room, and reads the paper, and smokes his pipe, and drinks his wine, he likes to be alone to think. So she cannot sit in the living room with him. Besides, at the end of the day, she has too much to do to sit down.

On holidays, when her grown children come to their parents' home for a festive meal, she cooks for days. She emerges from the kitchen halfway through the celebration, and sits at her place at the table for only a few moments before returning to the kitchen, the place where she spends most of her life. My husband says she never eats with the family. My husband says no one in the family thought this was strange or unjust.

She would stand in the kitchen, frying tiny meatballs to feed people as they came to visit, so they wouldn't spend even a moment in her home without having something to eat. As she stirred vats of tomato sauce, she wiped her brow with the handkerchief she concealed in her sleeve. She struggled up from the basement with trays of homemade pasta, often in intricate shapes that would take a long time to fashion.

After the family ate their antipasti, their pasta, their meats and *contorni*, their desserts, their nuts and figs, after they relaxed for a while at the table, after the children played, the old man would tell someone to go into the kitchen to tell his wife to make some *panini* from the leftovers in case someone was hungry.

My husband remembers that his grandfather never cleared a plate from the table, never entered the kitchen, never spoke to his wife.

"He never lifted a finger to help her," my husband said. "And no one objected. Sometimes the women tried to help. But she shooed them away. She didn't know how to let anyone help her."

After she died, my husband learned that his grandmother, who had given birth to five children, had become pregnant nearly every year. His mother once told him that the women in the family knew she had had more than twenty abortions. She had hidden these pregnancies from her husband because they were illegal and also against Church doctrine, and he would have forbidden her to terminate them.

Everyone in the family was terrified of my husband's grandfather. He had a murderous temper. That his sons were stronger than he was and could have defeated him didn't matter. His children were taught to respect their father, no matter what. In the name of respect, he abused them. In the name of respect, they were supposed to allow him to beat them. When the children objected, they were beaten even more severely. Their mother was too terrified, too worn out to protect her children.

And so, except for his favored son, he tyrannized his family, and treated its members as if he had the power of life and death over them. He allowed them no freedom, no dignity. He colonized them, even as his people in the South had been colonized.

She died years before her husband. She looked thirty years older than she was.

"She died from hard work," the women in the family said. "And all those abortions."

"She died because the old man was a bastard," my husband's father says.

"She died because she was despised and mistreated," my husband and I say to each other.

After his wife's death, his favorite son moves in with him. Now *his* wife (not Italian American but Irish American) takes on the responsibilities of the kitchen. She works almost as hard as her mother-in-law and she, too is mistreated. But she complains all the time. Her husband is always telling her to shut up. But after the old woman's death, there are no more freshly killed chickens, no more fresh pasta, and no more home-grown vegetables.

When the old man dies, although they all send flowers with ribboned bands that read "Farewell, Father," no one, except his favored son, mourns his passing. "Good riddance to bad rubbish," my mother says, when she finds out the old man has died. ("Good riddance to bad rubbish," she says when my father's father dies.)

At my husband's grandfather's wake, no one, except the favored son, sits in the chairs in the room with his body to welcome mourners. Everyone stands in the hallway where they cannot see him. They share stories about what a bastard he was. About how he would only eat fresh-killed chickens. About how their mother was a saint. About how he killed his wife. About how he almost killed each of them.

And during the wake, which lasts for three days, no one in the family, except his favored son, goes up to the coffin to pay their last respects.

After the wake, the family gathers in the Bronx at a local Italian restaurant. We eat the usual—antipasti, spaghetti with red sauce, chicken parm, Italian pastries or gelato.

The eldest son, the favored son, stands up to make a toast. "To the dearly departed," he says. "May he rest in peace."

"May he rest in peace," the family echoes. But no one stands.

NIGHTMARE (WITHOUT FOOD)

My mother and I shared very little. But we had the same recurring dream. Sometimes I thought that this dream traveled from her spirit to mine through the umbilicus connecting us while I was in utero, along with the fluids, nutrients, and antibodies that passed from her body to mine.

I wonder whether I began to dream this dream as my mother was dreaming it, while I was still safely inside her. When there was no decision she had to make about feeding me or not feeding me. When her body was generous with its gifts, generous in nourishing me. When feeding me was not accompanied (as it was after I was born) by anxiety, recrimination, regret.

My mother told me about her dream just once. We were drinking tea in my apartment. I was a new mother. She came to help me care for my newborn son in those difficult days after I came home from the hospital. Those days that no one can prepare you for, when you realize that your life, your old self, has vaporized. When you do not yet know what the word "mother" will mean for you, though you must do all the things that mothers are supposed to do.

During those weeks, we were closer than we ever were before, closer than we ever would be again. We were joined in a conspiracy of bottles, blankets, diapers.

My need permitted our closeness. We would sit at the kitchen table, stirring our tea, in those precious moments of silence when my baby was sleeping, those moments when new mothers understand, for the first time, the meaning of quiet, the necessity of solitude, and how the mere act of sitting down can be the most satisfying pleasure the world can provide. And during those moments, my mother spoke to me of her lost mother, of her loveless relationship with her stepmother, of her unrealized dreams, of how difficult it was to care for me as a child, of her nightmares.

In the past, I would have foreclosed this conversation, would not have wanted to hear what she had to say. But I was failing as miserably in satisfying this alien creature who, people told me, was my child, as she had as a young mother in satisfying me. I understood my mother's stories as an apologia for her difficult mothering. And an explanation for mine.

I said very little, because I was beyond expression, beyond language, almost beyond comprehension. All I wanted to do was sleep, for, like every new mother, I was sleeping almost not at all, and working harder than I ever worked before, at a job that I didn't understand, and one for which I had no training.

Everything was a shock; everything was a surprise. My fantasy of a baby clean, fed, diapered, sleeping peacefully in my arms while I rocked and read a book, was replaced by the piss-and-shit reality of new motherhood. "Why didn't anyone tell me what it would be like?" I screamed inside. "Why didn't she tell me?"—even though I knew I wouldn't have believed, even though I knew I would have thought it wouldn't be like that for me.

At a lull in the conversation, as we watch the snow accumulate on the street outside, I ask her why no one prepares women for the reality of motherhood. "Because," my mother said, "then there would be no more children."

I looked and felt ravaged. I couldn't figure out when my baby was hungry, when he was full, when he was tired, when he needed to be alone, when he needed me to comfort him. All his cries sounded the same, a wail of desperation in a code I could not decipher.

It was a brutal winter. I washed laundry. Hung it outside, where it froze. Took it inside to defrost. Draped it all over the apartment.

Walked through snowbanks clutching my baby to my chest to buy formula, once leaving him at home sleeping during a blizzard, terrified that when I came home, he'd be dead. I wished for spring. I wished for my old life.

My son was a tiny baby, premature, high-strung because I had smoked throughout my pregnancy. (This was before the harmful effects of smoking were publicized.)

He couldn't drink very much in one feeding. Soon after I finished feeding him, burping him, changing him, and putting him in his crib to sleep, he'd be ready to feed again. Whenever I fell into a sound sleep, he'd awaken.

Perhaps my mother believed that she could unravel whatever ill she had done to me as a child by helping me, by caring for my son. Whatever the reason, she was a model grandmother. Taught me how to be a grandmother. When she came to help, she ordered me to bed, took over, never told me whether she'd had any difficulty. My baby was fed and freshly diapered. My laundry was folded; my dishes were washed, dried, and replaced on their shelves. All this now seemed easy to my mother.

When my mother was around my children (in a few years there would be another son), she came alive. She played blocks with them on the floor; walked them in their carriages; took them on excursions to the beach; cooked with them; made them *zeppole* for breakfast when they slept over; let them bounce on her bed; laughed when they defaced her furniture, plopped their ice cream onto the sidewalk, unraveled rolls of toilet tissue. Caught the moment with a photo. And she always let them eat whatever they wanted—ice cream for supper; hot dogs for breakfast; donuts for lunch—whenever they wanted, though she would feign disapproval.

I was grateful for all this. But envious, too. Where was the mother I had known? When had she shape-shifted into this loving presence? If she could be so indulgent with my children, if she could enjoy them so much, I wondered, why couldn't she have indulged and enjoyed me?

*   *   *

Grateful for her help, I listened to my mother's stories during this miasmic time. Stories I would hear once, and not again. I was happy for them. They passed the time. They gave me explanations. They gave me more of her than I had ever had.

One of my mother's stories was about a dream she had every few days. A dream very like my own, although I never told her this.

Oh, the details diverged. Her dream might begin in a city; mine, in the country. She might find herself dressed poorly; I might be unaware of my clothing, or I might be wearing nothing at all. And the people she encountered were different from those I encountered. They had different faces, different ways of behaving, a different language. But stripped of all superficialities, our dreams were the same dream.

To begin. We are in a strange place, not an unpleasant place on the surface, but there is a disquiet we feel because we know we are not home. We want to be home, only we have forgotten where home is. We know we must leave this place soon, for otherwise something awful will happen to us.

We are, of course, alone. And we can recall what home is like, or rather, what we want home to be like—safe, secure, serene, beautiful. We know that there is a way to get there, if only we can find the right road, if only we can remember where home is, or, rather, was.

At some point in our dream, we look for a car, a bus, an airplane. We decide that it is absolutely necessary to find a way to hurry ourselves through a dark and unfamiliar landscape and if we just find the right conveyance, it will take us home. It will know where home is, even if we don't know.

So we look. And we think that we have found what we need. But it disappears. Or it isn't where someone told us it should be.

This is where the dream starts making us toss and turn in our sleep. This is when we each start moaning. This is when our sleeping partners try to wake us, when they ask us if we're dreaming, ask us if we're all right. They are used to this. This happens regularly—once every few days for her; once every other week for me.

We are moaning because we can't find where we left our car, where the bus station is, where the airport is located. So, now, not only do we not remember where home is, now we also cannot find a way to get there. Or, if not there, then anywhere but where we are. For where we are is not safe.

You will notice there is no food in our dreams. No place where we stop, sit, sip some water, eat something to nourish us for our journey.

At this point, we might encounter an earthquake, a mudslide, an invading army, a stampede of people running in our direction, a huge snowstorm, a scorching sun-baked plain—something that makes it even more difficult for us to find a way to be miraculously taken home. We never ask anyone to help us: we know that no one will or can.

Here, my mother becomes terrified of what confronts her. She freezes, like a deer caught in lightbeams. Sometimes, she finds herself falling into deep crevasses, sucked into oceanic whirlpools, licked by sheets of fire. She is sure, now, that she'll die trying to find her way home. This is when she awakens—screaming, thrashing, sweating, heart pounding. The next day will be a difficult one.

At overcoming impediments, I am better than my mother. I summon my courage. I move over, around, through whatever blocks my passage. I am not harmed, though what I am looking for still eludes me. And, by the end of my dream, when I awaken—thrashing, sweating, heart pounding—what I so desperately longed for is still missing.

Sometimes, though, I get distracted. Decide that some children I find along the way need my care. So I abandon my quest, but not without becoming enraged that I have put their needs before mine.

My dream. My mother's dream. A dream about losing a mother, a home, a country. Sometimes a dream about being a mother, too.

It is also a dream of exile. A dream about leaving, but not knowing what it is you have left. A dream of never being able to return home.

FOOD FIGHTS

There is something about watching another person rinsing the spinach in the sink, or chopping an onion, or tearing the lettuce that brings out the worst in people, that brings out the worst in you.

"There's still sand on those leaves," you say, the scorn in your voice perceptible. You imagine the sautéed spinach with garlic, gritty with dirt, the dinner ruined utterly, the day bankrupt thereby. You have convinced yourself that a good dinner is very important, the most important event in your day. More important, even—to judge by the way you behave—than the feelings of family members who partake of that dinner.

Still, you cannot control yourself.

"There's still sand on those leaves, I said. Will you please give them another rinse?"

And you think that if he doesn't realize the spinach needs another wash, he mustn't see anything truly important in this world—a beautiful flower on a spring morning; a sunset across a wide expanse of icy bay.

You remember the teachings of Zen Buddhism: the way you do one thing is the way you do everything. And so you are right to conclude that the way he washes spinach is the way he does everything else in the world. His way of washing spinach provides you with a window into his soul. (You remember the teachings of Zen Buddhism about acceptance. You tell yourself they do not apply here. For you cannot, no, you cannot accept the slipshod way he prepares food. Food must be respected, you tell yourself. That is the Zen Buddhist way.)

You reflect that your way of thinking that his way of washing the spinach provides you with a window into his soul also provides you with a window into yours. But you want to think about his soul, not yours. You think he should do something to change his soul, not that you must change yours.

But perhaps you can accept the way he is. Or accept the way you are. But then there would be no fighting in the kitchen, no drama. Then the kitchen would be a relaxed and serene place. Which you seem not to want it to be.

"The recipe says to mince the onions, not to chop them," you scold. You hate the sound of your voice. But you think, "That man is not a detail man; that man takes shortcuts. Which is why his Christmas packages look sloppy; which is why the kitchen faucet still drips; which is why the basement is still a mess; which is why the meals he cooks are good but not masterpieces." (You should be grateful, you know, that he cooks. Still, you want him to cook for you not the way he cooks for you, but the way you cook for him. Perfectly.)

When you think these things, and you cannot stop yourself from thinking these things, you hate yourself. You realize that beneath all that superficial niceness the people in your public life see—your students, the people who read your books—a truly evil person is lurking. A shadow self hides in the kitchen; she lunges after her prey like a wolverine. The people in your public life never see this self, would be shocked to know she existed. For this self lives at home. And her favorite place is the kitchen.

Often, when she appears, you blame your mother. You blame the way she fought with your grandmother in the kitchen. You tell yourself you have no role model for civilized kitchen behavior. And so you excuse yourself. You are, after all, your mother's daughter. Remembering the way your mother behaved in the kitchen makes you feel better, absolves you of responsibility for the diabolical person you are.

But this doesn't make you happy. You realize you can't blame her, you're too old. You realize that you're mean and petty, that your values suck, that you ruin everything, that you put what is not important—perfectly rinsed spinach, perfectly minced onion, perfectly torn lettuce leaves—before what *is* important—your marriage, your relationship with your husband, your capacity for tolerance, your serenity.

You remind yourself that you are lucky that you are married to someone who cooks and cleans. That you are married to someone who makes you dinner (sometimes, even, a spectacular dinner—a tiny rack of lamb on your birthday a few years before, crusted with champagne mustard and fresh bread crumbs in a Merlot sauce, yum, yum). That he always cooks for you on the nights you work late and come home too exhausted to cook (pumpkin ravioli with a sweetened butter-and-truffle-oil sauce, and strips of sage).

You vow that the next time you see your husband fucking up in the kitchen, assassinating the carrots, say, or massacring the eggplant, you won't utter a word. You'll find your center. Breathe in. Breathe out. You'll accept what he's doing. You'll prove to yourself that your meditation practice is helping, that your therapy is working, and the next time you go to your therapist, you'll thank her—they need that, therapists, some occasional positive feedback to balance all those hours of sitting there and listening to lunatics like you.

You think that if you can keep your mouth shut, if you can control yourself and not spring across the kitchen to pull the carrot out of his hand and tell him, "No, no, no, I said *mince*, not *dice*, and don't you know the difference after all these years?," then, one day, you can quit therapy. (And think of all the money you'd save, and all the great new kitchen equipment you could buy—an Italian gelato machine; a stainless steel espresso maker; a really gigantic pasta pot.)

On this particular evening, my husband and I are cooking a recipe of Marcella Hazan's. Nothing fancy. But splendid. Steaks (pan sautéed), finished in a sauce of sweet and dry vermouth, garlic, tomato paste, and red pepper flakes, reduced to a shining unctuous glaze; oven-roasted potatoes with rosemary; *insalata mista* with soft lettuces. The salad is his responsibility.

My husband is working with the Boston lettuce at the sink. It's organic. Hydroponic. We're careful about what we eat. And organic tastes better—not like a chemistry experiment.

We shop at Whole Foods. We spend a fortune. But we tell ourselves it's money well spent. Cooking is our hobby. We don't eat out. We don't go to the theater. We can justify how much we spend on food if we shift some food expenses over to entertainment.

The lettuce we've bought comes with a little tail of roots in case you want to plant it instead of eat it. (We don't.) It comes in its own little plastic house so that nothing can crush it as it makes its way from the farmer to your home. I am grateful for the care that is taken with this lettuce. At least someone cares about doing something well these day.

I am chopping garlic. And he is preparing the lettuce. Out of the corner of my eye, I see him take the little root clump in his fist to twist it free. But these roots must be cut away with a very sharp knife. And I know that if he continues, all those lovely little lettuce leaves will be crushed and mangled. And I must stop this. At once.

"Stop that!" I shout. "You're supposed to cut the roots of the lettuce away, not wring its goddamned neck!"

I bound across the kitchen, butcher knife in hand, as if I am ready for assassination. I pull the lettuce away, rescue it. I take it over to my work station to examine it. I am acting like the lettuce is one of our children, at risk from his father's brutality.

"Jesus Christ," he says. "You could have told me nicely. I would have listened. You don't have to shout." But otherwise, he says nothing. He is practicing self-control. And he is succeeding.

I am ashamed.

Ashamed, like the day I was cooking Brussels sprouts.

*   *   *

The Brussels sprouts.

I am the only person I know with a Brussels-sprout-shaped scar on my thigh. I will tell you how it happened, although it is not a pretty story.

One day, I am cooking Brussels sprouts for dinner. Why I am cooking Brussels sprouts, that piss-tasting vegetable preferred by the English, in an Italian American kitchen is because I am in my Anglomaniac period. (The Belgians believe that Roman legions brought the Brussels sprout to Brussels. But I don't believe it. Unless they brought them there, and left them. I've never found a recipe for Brussels sprouts in an Italian cookbook. And I've never seen one in Italy. Though I've been told that if they're very, very young, and if you sauté them in very hot oil till they go crisp, they're good. But I don't believe it.)

Anyway, when I'm cooking these Brussels sprouts, I'm writing about Virginia Woolf and going to England a lot. As I said, I'm in my Anglomaniac period, which lasts five years. I am cooking Brussels sprouts and other English things like trifle, and bangers and mash. To admit that I cooked bangers and mash is difficult. I persuaded myself that these were good things to eat, that Virginia Woolf ate these things, and that, in eating them, I was growing closer to her, understanding her.

I didn't consider that if Virginia Woolf knew me, knew where my people came from, knew what they had done for a living, knew how I had supported myself with strange odd-jobs throughout my adolescence, knew that we lived in a tenement, she certainly wouldn't have invited me to her parties, no matter how smart I was.

In 1908, Virginia Woolf travels to Italy and keeps a diary. She has nothing much to say about Italy—about Milan, Florence, Assisi, Perugia, Siena. She likes the colors of the houses. She remarks that in Italy you are constantly reminded of history. She writes a bit about a fresco she sees. She says that she thinks the priests in Siena are handsome. She says nothing about the food; she doesn't eat pasta.

(About this, I should have been suspicious. To travel to Italy, and not mention the food. And not eat pasta.) She compares everything she sees to England, and finds it wanting. The strangeness of this place, of the people's ways, disorients her. Except for the occasional walk, or a bit of sightseeing, she spends most of her time in her room, reading the novels of Thomas Hardy and George Meredith at a furious pace, to keep herself from realizing where she is, to remind herself of England, the superiority of its landscape, of its civilization.

In Florence, she meets an Anglo-Italian countess, a woman reputed to be extremely intelligent. After a brief meeting, Woolf decides that, no, this woman isn't intelligent; her reputation for learning is unfounded. She is a peasant in disguise, and therefore loathsome, as peasants are. She behaves like a child. Oh, the countess can feel, Woolf concedes. But the feelings of Italians always becloud their reason.

About the Brussels sprouts.

The night that I am cooking them, I plan on dressing them simply, with a little brown butter, caraway seeds, salt, and pepper. They will accompany the pork chops I'm sautéing and finishing in the oven.

But while they're boiling, my husband and I start fighting. We fought a lot in those days, though I can't remember what this fight was about. Probably about nothing important, because we agree about everything that is important—politics, and the importance of family, and what to eat for dinner.

On this night, I get so angry that I pick up the pot of Brussels sprouts, and fling the Brussels sprouts (boiling water and all) at him. I don't hit him, thank goodness. But one waterlogged sprout lands on my thigh and burns me.

The burn heals in time, of course. But the scar is still there. And it is shaped exactly like a Brussels sprout. So that each time I undress, each time I bathe, there it is, that Brussels sprout scar, to remind me that I am a dangerous woman, and that the kitchen is a hazardous place for me.

On the night I yell at my husband for how he desecrates the lettuce, I apologize. We are both trying (and usually, now, successfully) not to fight. We are married nearly forty years, and we should know how to get along, how to have a serene and joyful life together. (I don't say, but think, we should figure this out before one of us dies.)

My husband accepts my apology. "I'm used to it," he says. "You're always crazy in the kitchen." And then, because he's taking Italian lessons, is trying to be Italian Italian, he says "pazza nella cucina."

"Crazy in the kitchen." The words come back. I admit that, yes, I am crazy in the kitchen. And one day, I hope I will not be. I hope that I can become, in the kitchen, the person I am in other places. I can work on this, I know. Can work on it the way I work on perfecting my breads, my muffins, my minestrones, my pastas, my risotto. With care, attention, reverence, and discipline.

And though I know that the voice that derided him about the way he handled the lettuce was not my voice, but my mother's voice, I know that it is my voice too, and that it is too late in my life to use my mother as an excuse. I know I act this way, this crazy-in-the-kitchen way, because I want the food I make to be perfect. With each perfect meal I make, I can undo the past. Undo that my mother couldn't feed me, undo her fury at my grandmother. Undo my father's violence. Undo my ancestors' history.

I act as if, through this alchemy at the stove, I can erase my past instead of reliving it. But reliving it I am—all the fury of it, all the battles, all the despair. And must stop reliving it.

THE HOUSE BY THE RIVER

My father takes a little piece of cardboard, pulls a pencil from the pocket of his shirt, draws a diagram of the neighborhood in Italy where he lived for a year when he was a child: a little village called Scafati, in the province of Campania.

He shows the location of a road, the Via Nova, that passed through Pompeii on its way to Salerno; another road, perpendicular to the first, in Scafati. A piazza. A fountain. A church. A small river near the church. A house by the river. The canning factory down the second road, where his mother worked.

"This is where we lived," he tells me, pointing to a little square he's drawn to represent his family's home. "This is what I want you to find."

Scafati is not too far from Positano, where we're staying, the village where his mother lived when she was a girl. But before we go to Scafati, we want to see if we can find any members of my grandmother's family living in Positano.

We've asked the owner of the hotel, whose family has been here for generations, if he knows anyone with my grandmother's maiden name. He says he doesn't, says that it was common for entire families to leave the village at the same time. During the great emigration, people left in large numbers because it was difficult to grow food in Positano, for there is no arable land. The village is situated in a fault in the earth's crust; the houses, terraced into the limestone and limestone dolomite of the mountainside; its terrain is some of the most rugged in the region. To grow anything, even today, you must cart soil into the village from far away, and unless you own property elsewhere, you must buy the soil. If you are poor, the soil is too expensive to buy.

As I walk the alleyways and staircases of the village, I wonder whether every house I pass is the one she lived in; whether she went to school here—probably she didn't; wonder whether she played by the seaside; whether she helped her mother carry water from the well.

Positano is achingly beautiful. Still, this upscale resort was once so poor, so isolated, so incapable of sustaining its people, that in 1931, fewer than two thousand people remained. "The people move out, the tourists move in," the hotel owner says. I go to Santa Maria Assunta to light a candle in the Starry Chapel in memory of my paternal grand-mother, as I have lighted candles for my mother's mother and my stepmother in every church I visited in Puglia. This ancient church is where my grandmother worshipped as a child. But as I traverse the little alleyways and stairways leading to the sea, I see little girls in white dresses carrying lilies, little suited boys trailed by relatives moving slowly, reverentially along. Today is their First Holy Communion.

As the procession moves inside, the organ begins to play. Then there is a moment of silence.

A group of old women sitting together sing "Maria Madonna," their voices deep, guttural, dirgelike. This is church music unlike any I have heard before. It is not joyful; it instead honors life's inevitable sorrows, even in moments of celebration.

I light my candle and imagine my grandmother, more than a century ago, taking her First Communion here. I see her moving slowly, up the center aisle, surrounded by her family. My family.

I am connected to this place, although by a very fragile thread. Who I am, who I have become, is rooted in this beautiful place that my grandmother's family was forced to leave.

I want to stay in Positano. I don't want to go to Scafati. I've looked on a map, and it is a winding drive from Positano up the Amalfi coast, and around and through a confluence of highways leading to Naples. No matter how hard I stare at the map, I can't figure out how to get to Scafati, can't figure out how to find my father's home. When my father tells me about Scafati, he recites a well-known jingle about the place: "Scafati, scefeti, malacqua, malagente, pure erbe et malamenti." He writes the words down as best he can, probably incorrectly. Though he doesn't translate the saying, the meaning is clear. There is a lot of bad stuff in Scafati—water, people, and bad things that grow.

My father planned to come to Italy with us, but he's not well enough now to travel, might never again be well enough to travel. He says it's all right; if he dies today, he has no regrets, he's lived a good life.

But he wants me to find where he lived, take a picture, come home and tell him what it's like now.

Though I know our chances of finding my father's house are slim, I promise him I'll try. He's old now, and rarely asks me to do anything for him. "This is the least I can do," I think. And Scafati is a place with meaning for me too.

My father is old now, his memory imperfect. He can't remember which way is north, which is south, or, on second thought, whether the fountain is by the church or down the road. Whether his house was one or two blocks away from the church, or many.

I take his diagram, ask a few questions, scribble a few notes, hope for the best. In one corner of the diagram he's written a name: Joseph Bulari. A relative, he says. The man who owned the canning factory where my grandmother worked.

"Stop someone in the square," my father suggests. "Ask them if they know him. When we lived there, everybody knew him. He was a factory owner, a big shot. If you can find him, he'll show you where we lived, show you where my grandmother lived, show you the factory he owned, show you everything."

"But Dad," I say, "how old was he when you lived there?"

"A grown man," my father says. "A prosperous man. An important man."

"Then he's gotta be dead by now," I say.

"Oh yes," my father says. "Of course. But maybe you'll find someone who knew him."

"Why don't we tell him that we tried to find where he lived, but couldn't?" This is my husband talking, on the morning that we're supposed to find the house by the river in Scafati.

It's one of those mornings to cherish, when you want to abandon your plans to find the village where your father lived, and sit on a little patio looking at what you'll probably never see again, this village tucked into a bowl in a mountain, with colorful houses stacked like children's blocks, with its tile-roofed domed cathedral so near the sea, this improbable place where your grandmother once lived when it was a poor and desolate fishing village with people in astonishing numbers leaving for America and other parts of Italy. So that, by the time your grandmother left, there were hardly any people living there at all.

You want to go nowhere else this day. You want to look at the water, at the village, at the cathedral for hours, to imprint them in your memory, so you can revisit them to warm you on another day—a wet and rainy one in New Jersey in mid-October. You know that, though you may want to, you will never return here again.

On this day, the sky is cloudless. The sea, glistening. The breakfast, magnificent—little pastries, cappuccino, freshly squeezed orange juice.

There is the possibility of pizza for lunch, in a little restaurant above the water on the Via Positanesi d'America, that street named to honor emigrants who sent money back home from America so the lives of those who stayed behind would be less harsh.

Why leave this place on such a beautiful day to find a place where an old man lived more than eighty years before? Why drive many miles on a dangerous road that switchbacks up and down mountainsides? Why thread your way through a maze of highways, trying to find the right road? Why stop people and ask, in execrable Italian, if they can tell you how to get to the village, to a church by a river that has a fountain? Sorry, you don't know the name of the church. Sorry, you can't tell them the name of the river. Sorry, you have no idea, really, where this church or river is, except that it's in Scafati, and that your father lived there some eighty years ago.

"We won't find it," my husband says, "so we shouldn't go." But I say, "I gave my word."

I know that finding this place, if we find it at all, won't be fun. My husband will be driving because he can't read maps, can't navigate. He gets distracted, engrossed in the scenery, forgets to look at the map, turns the map around and around because he can't figure out whether we're heading north, south, east, or west, can't figure out whether we should turn right or left at the intersection where he's not absolutely sure we should turn at all. Which means that I navigate. He drives.

But although I read maps well—flawlessly, in fact, if I do say so myself—when I tell my husband to turn this way or that, he might not take the turn I indicate. Maybe he's drifting off and not listening to me. Maybe he's mesmerized by the road. Maybe, though he hasn't even looked at the map, he doubts I know which way to go, though I always do know which way to go.

And so I know we'll miss an important turn. I'll become exasperated. It will take three quarters of an hour for us to get back to the right turnoff. And I'll be pissed that he didn't listen to me.

I know that it will be a hellish day—him driving, me navigating. Or, as I tell people, him driving, me navigating and screaming.

I know I'll say something awful to him. He'll tell me to calm down, chill out. I'll tell him I won't calm down, chill out. When I travel, I like to know, at all times, where I am and where I'm going. I don't like to stumble upon places by chance. I plot routes carefully. Check and double-check directions.

(Once, a friend I'm traveling with tells me to put away my map, to enjoy the scenery. I say I can't put away the map, can't enjoy the ride unless I know exactly where I am. She tells me you always know

exactly where you are because you're always exactly where you are.
"Very Zen," I say, nasty. She laughs. I laugh. But I don't put away
the map.)

I know that at some point, and well before my husband and I get to
where we're going, he'll be hungry. He'll want a snack, a cup of
espresso, or a real meal. "What's the rush?" he'll ask, when I say we
shouldn't stop. "Why can't we enjoy the journey as well as the arrival?"

On this day, as always, I will insist we press on, though I know that
if he isn't fed, we're sure to start fighting. So I will concede and we'll
try to find a bar, a café, a trattoria. But not just any bar, any café, any
trattoria. We'll try to find one that's charming.

This will take a long time. This will take us out of our way. This
will require superior map-reading skills on my part to get us back on
track, to get us to where we're going.

(Once, years ago, my husband, our two sons, both young adults,
and I were driving from Rome to Florence on the Autostrada, and we
were hungry. It was well past noon. I suggested an autogrill on the
highway. I knew that you could get wonderful *panini*, a respectable
pizza, a lovely *tricolore* there.

But no, they decided they wanted a glorious picnic in a bucolic
setting overlooking Florence. And that we'd pick up fixings for the
picnic in Florence. "By the time we get to Florence," I say, "there'll
be no place open to buy food for a picnic."

"That's ridiculous," my elder son says, not knowing Italian ways.

"Trust me," I say. "It'll be siesta. Everything'll be closed."

"I'm absolutely sure," says my newly-graduated-from-business-
school son, "that there will be at least one enterprising Florentine
who'll keep his store open so we can buy food."

I say, "Fine."

So we drive and drive and drive and drive. And go into Florence.
And of course can't find a place to buy provisions. Can't find a
restaurant. So we go back on the Autostrada to find an autogrill,
which we know will be open. And get stuck in a traffic jam from hell
that lasts for hours.

I scream at them. They scream at me. Each of us screams at every other person in the car. They blame me for not sticking to my guns. I blame them for not listening to me. I say "I told you so" more than once. We hate one another; wonder what we're doing on this miserable road; wonder why we've come on this goddamned holiday. But in the cars surrounding us, also stuck in traffic, no one is screaming. Mothers are pulling out little treats and snacks for their families and handing them around. Biscotti and bottles for the babies. Panni and Orangina for the grown-ups. These mothers, Italian mothers, understand what happens to Italians when they're hungry. These mothers have come prepared.)

The drive to Scafati is as awful as I feared. The road we need is accessible, it seems, only by making a U-turn across four lanes of traffic. We get stuck in a traffic jam in Pompeii amidst a gaggle of tour buses. Policemen stop traffic so that tourists following leaders holding umbrellas aloft can cross the road from the parking lot to the ruins.

Finally, we find the road to Scafati. It looks like Union City. There are rundown stores selling cheap clothing, used auto parts, flimsy baby carriages, ugly furniture. We've driven miles and wasted a day to find a place that looks like the worst of New Jersey, looks like any poor neighborhood there, like the one my grandparents lived in after they came back to the States.

We expected to find a small road, meandering through farms, with a view of Mount Vesuvius, that will lead us from the ruins of Pompeii, where my father played as a boy, to a little village on a river where he was his happiest. For my father, this place is immutable.

We stop some old men who wear peaked hats like my father's. We figure we'll have better luck with old men with long memories. We ask them for directions. The old men speak dialect, which I under-stand. We go where they tell us. Find a church. Find, not a river, but a slimy green stream.

LOUISE DESALVO

We climb out of the car, shuffle through garbage to a tiny church.
But there are no houses nearby. Just derelict cars.

We find a woman, tell her what we're looking for, tell her my
father once lived here. Hope she'll see us not as intruders, but as
people who belong here. She's warm, friendly. Laughs. Says there are
many churches in Scafati, many rivers in Scafati, many churches on
rivers in Scafati, can't we be more specific? No, we're sorry, we can't.
Then I mention the fountain in front of the church.

Ah yes, she says, then it can be only one church, the church with
the fountain near the little river. And gives us directions, which we
bungle, so we wind up at the end of a tiny alleyway in the medieval
part of town, with me crying, sure we'll never get out. My husband
backs up slowly, annoying the people who live here, whose lives
we've disrupted.

Finally, finally, after a few more wrong turns, after stopping a few
more people for directions, we find the church. With the fountain.
On the river.

But it's shopping time and there's no place to park

My husband wants to park illegally. I'm against it. What if we're
towed?

"They don't tow in Italy," he says.

"They do," I say. It's like we're in third grade.

"They don't," my husband says. "Trust me." I never trust him
when he says to trust him. When he says to trust him, I'm sure he
doesn't know what he's talking about. He always thinks things are
the way he wants them to be, instead of the way they are.

He rests his head on the steering wheel, tired of all this. "Just tell
me what you want me to do."

"Leave the goddamned car here," I say, exasperated. Just in case, I
take all our documents, write down the license plate.

We go to the church. There's a wedding. "How nice," I say. "We'll
get to see a wedding." I figure if we go into the church, watch the
ceremony, see all the flowers, I'll snap out of my foul mood.

174

"You hate to go to weddings," my husband says.

"But this is an Italian wedding."

So, we go into the church. I tell myself it's the little Baroque church where my grandparents were married, persuade myself that seeing this wedding is deeply meaningful, that it makes up for the restful day I'm missing, makes up for the astonishing pizza I'm missing, even though I realize that this marriage might end up as miserably as my grandparents'.

But I don't feel any connection to this place, although I have imagined I might. Of course, there is no reason I *should* feel a connection to a place my family fled because they could not make a life here.

Mine, the dilemma of all the descendants of immigrants. To want to belong, yet to know that you do not.

I pull out the little piece of cardboard with my father's drawing. Turn it so that the drawing of the river is aligned with the actual river, so we can figure out where my father lived. Then I remember my father is dyslexic, and wonder whether he's drawn it right, or drawn it backwards.

We turn right, turn left, go around a construction site. (Villages in Italy are not supposed to have construction sites, not supposed to have ugly modern buildings that look like cell blocks, though they do.) My father has described a little house in the country, with a balcony on a river. This is not the country, and from these back streets I can't see the river. So I figure that we have to go back to the river and work from there.

We go back to the church. The wedding is over. There is rice all over the piazza. A man, older than my father, sweeps it away.

We go to the river, to the bridge over the river. I tell my husband we have to find any goddamned house with a balcony on the river, take a picture of it, take it home, tell my father we found his house. How will he know? How can he remember? It's more than eighty years ago, after all.

*   *   *

So we're standing on the little bridge over the river. But there's no sidewalk on the bridge. And the cars are zooming by. And because the cars are being driven by Italian drivers, Southern Italian drivers, I'm thinking that I'm going to die here, and that it would be very stupid to die here, playing lookout for my husband who's leaning over the railing of the bridge, using the zoom lens of his camera to find something, anything, that he can photograph.

"Do you see a house with a balcony?" I gasp. I'm choking from the exhaust fumes. I'm going to have an asthma attack.

"There are lots of houses past the bend in the river," my husband says. "And they all have balconies. Should I take a picture of all of them or just one?"

"Just one," I say. "If you take them all, he'll never think it's the one he lived in."

"Which one?" my husband asks.

"It doesn't matter," I say. I know the place we've been trying to find is one that exists only in my father's mind.

When we return home, my father and his wife come to dinner at our house. I make a simplified version of tiny potato gnocchi with smoked scamorza cheese, tomato, and basil, a dish from Alfonso Iaccarino's restaurant, where we've eaten.

The day after we go to Scafati, my husband and I decide that, after what we've been through, we should indulge ourselves. So we go to Don Alfonso's, the Michelin-starred restaurant in Sant'Agata sui Due Golfi.

It is a splendid meal. As I'm eating it, I think I will never forget it, although now I cannot remember what I ate that day, unless I consult my diary.

We had the tasting menu. There were—I know, for I have written it down—three kinds of bread: spinach; tomato; borage and nettles. A puréed-lentil soup with baby calamari, finished with olive oil infused with mint. Fusilli with a sauce with little chunks of bluefish finished with olive oil infused with basil. Amberjack with fried ginger, anointed with a special kind of salt and tiny Schezuan peppercorns, served with a pea purée. Duck breast with little peach fritters and fried peach slices, raspberry purée, and a sauce made with grapes grown by Don Alfonso, finished with an oil infused with star anise. For desert, a fantasy of espresso, served in a cookie cylinder and accompanied by cookies in the shape of spoons.

Throughout our meal, I imagine that it is a hundred years before, and that I am dining in a *masseria* in Puglia, or in a palazzo in Naples, and that all of my grandparents are young, and are standing outside, hungry, their faces pressed to the window. They watch others eat the bounty of their land. They wish they could be given the crust of bread left behind on a bread plate, the piece of fish or morsel of meat pushed to the side—"I can't eat any more; I'm too full"—the food other people are wasting, as they are starving.

Back in New Jersey, we finish our meal. My husband serves cups of espresso, chocolate hazelnut biscotti. My father looks at the pictures of Scafati my husband has taken. A church. A wedding. A river. A house with a balcony on the river.

"So?" I ask.

"I remember the river," my father says. "But I'm not sure about the house. It doesn't look the way I remember it."

"Shit," I think. "He knows." And can't continue with the charade.

"I'm not sure it's the right house," I say. "There were a few houses with balconies by the river."

My father puts the picture down. Sips his coffee. He's thoughtful. Tearful.

"Well, you know," he says, "it was a long time ago. And things do change."

"Yes," I say, relieved. "They do."

"But it was beautiful, wasn't it?" my father says. Remembering the clean river where he and his sisters swam. The farms that stretched to the flanks of Mount Vesuvius. The walks on the Via Nova to Pompeii, where he spent the day when he didn't want to go to school. Fishing from the little balcony where his mother cooked their food. His grandmother and her meals in the house by the fountain, and the whole family ranged around the table, complete, eating turkey, eating rabbit, eating pigeon, eating pasta with fresh vegetables. Remembering drinking the watered down wine given to young children in Italy. Remembering what it was like to have so much family around you, and being loved by a grandmother you will never see again, and being taught to pick vegetables by a grandfather you will never see again.

It was beautiful, wasn't it?

I want to tell my father that, no, Scafati wasn't beautiful. That it looked like Union City, that the houses looked like cell blocks, looked like the nightmare of ugly housing that has sprung up on the outskirts of the gems of cities everywhere in the South of Italy. And that, except for the church and the square in front of it and the fountain nearby, Scafati was the ugliest place I have ever seen in Italy.

I want to say that there were derelicts everywhere. And garbage. And rats swimming in the river. That Scafati was the Italy that people talk about when they talk about the problem of the Mezzogiorno. And that it had changed dramatically, and for the worse, in the eighty years since my father's family abandoned this place to return to America.

I want to say all these things. But I stop myself. For I have made this journey for him.

My father is very old now. He can never return to Scafati. Can never find the church with the fountain. Never find where his grandmother lived. Never again see the little house by the river. So he will never learn what has become of this place that he cherishes. Unless I tell him.

I pick up the picture. Give it to my father. And say, "Yes, it was very beautiful."

APPETITE

Once I saw an article in *The New York Times* about how you could cook a brisket if you packed it in heavy-duty tinfoil and put it on the hottest part of your engine while you took a long ride. Slow cooking, highway style.

I clipped it, started imagining a nice slow braise of veal with little pearl onions I would sneak into position under the hood of our car without my husband knowing what I was doing. I knew he'd be a spoilsport, that he would say no.

We were going to visit our gourmet pals in Connecticut. And I thought that cooking something along the way would be such fun. I saw us pulling up the long driveway to their house, saw me popping the hood, pulling out the packet. Opening it. "Surprise, surprise," I'd say. "Here's lunch!"

And the braise, of course, would be spectacular. The aromas, appetizing. We'd savor this perfect little lunchtime meal outside on their deck beneath the trees. Everything would be perfect.

But I make the mistake of leaving the article on the kitchen table. My husband finds it. "This is where I draw the line," he says. "There will be no slow cooking under the hood of my car. What if something goes wrong with your little scheme?"

"What if we take my car?" I ask. He ignores me and walks away.

Now, I am not the kind of woman who can be told what to do, and what not to do. Especially when it comes to food. My husband knows I'll do what I want to do anyway.

Still, I cave, because I am also the kind of woman who believes that if something can go wrong, it will. I imagine the juices leaking from the packet, the juices burning, smoking. Imagine a smoke screen preventing Ernie from seeing the road. Imagine an accident. Injuries. Ambulances. And the wonderful braise of veal scattered all along the roadway.

You see, I am obsessed with food. I'm always trying to find some new cooking technique to perfect, always trying to find something new to cook. I read cookbooks the way other people read pornography. And for many of the same reasons.

I think about food all the time. Once my husband and I go to the Armenian monastery in Venice where Byron studied. After the tour, when the guide asks if we have any questions, I don't ask about Byron, or about whether any of his manuscripts are archived here, or about his study of Armenian—all questions I would have raised ten years before. No. This time, I raise my hand and ask, "Do the monks who live here eat Italian food or Armenian food?"

My husband is in the front; I'm in the back. He knows it's me asking the question. And he knows, then, just how serious this food thing has become.

"To the loss of a fine mind," my husband says, lifting his glass of Prosecco as he toasts me during lunch a few hours later. And I have to admit that, yes, earlier in my life I would have pestered the monks to see manuscripts, to see precisely where Byron sat when he studied. But on this trip, whether the monks eat Italian or Armenian seems more important.

We are eating lunch on the roof on the Danieli, where we eat each day during our stay, watching the boats chaotically crisscrossing the San Marco Basin. That day, we have *spaghetti con vongole*, with clams as tiny as the nail on your pinky; and roasted vegetables dressed with an unfiltered olive oil. Tomorrow, we'll take the long boat ride to Burano, to find the restaurant in the central piazza where we ate *vongole* when we were here with our sons in 1989. We want to compare the *vongole* there with the *vongole* here. I say the *vongole* on Burano were better; Ernie says they're better here. Another one of our food fights.

I can find any restaurant where we've eaten in any place we've visited, no matter how many years have passed since we've been there. (Although I could not find my way without a map to the most important cathedral, ancient site, or museum.)

Once, driving through a remote village in the south of France, I tell my husband, "We've been here before; we've eaten here; we had a fantastic bowl of mussels here, the best mussels we've ever eaten." He tells me I'm crazy, we've never been here before. "A hundred thousand dollars says we have," I say. My husband and I bet like this a lot. The more I bet, the surer I am. Of course, neither of us pays up. But we keep a tally. So far, I'm winning.

So I tell him to turn right, and left, and right again, and right again, through an intricate system of one-way streets.

And there it is, the sweet little restaurant with the outside tables. With the flowers tumbling from the baskets along the railing. I've won my bet.

But they're closed. We can't have the mussels. Suddenly having those mussels becomes the priority of this holiday. So we come back for lunch the next day, even though we're staying at a hotel a hundred miles away.

When we're on vacation, a long ride to eat well, or to buy a special ingredient or a piece of kitchen equipment, trumps visiting churches and museums every time. In Liguria, for instance, we can tell you where to buy the very best dried mushrooms, where to eat the very best *farinata*, where to buy the hand-carved stamps for making *corzetti*, where to find the best truffle oil, which baker in Camogli makes the best bread, which the best focaccia.

But we couldn't tell you which palaces you should visit in Genoa, or which church is worth a stop in Portovenere, or whether the maritime museum or the aquarium in Camogli merits a visit.

In Camogli, we've spent too much time eating at one focacceria and then another; too much time figuring when the focaccia in each is piping hot; too much time sitting at a table at the Primula on the waterfront, savoring the best cappuccino we've ever had. (When we're away, whatever we're having is the best of whatever we're having that we've ever had.)

Our sons and our grandkids are the same. How could they not be?

When our sons are on vacation, they call us not to talk about what they've done but to tell us what they've eaten. Jay and Deb talk about the dessert with almonds at Chez Panisse, and how our grandson Steven ate his own dessert and his father's, and how Steven relished the fresh ravioli made with cod. Justin and Lynne describe the Italian restaurant they found in western New Jersey, headed by a woman chef, and tell us we absolutely have to go there.

Our daily morning conversations begin, "So, what did you have for dinner?" Both Justin and Jason are inventive cooks; both relish a good meal at the end of the day; both prepare wildly inventive meals without cookbooks. Justin: pan-seared tuna with a sauce of sautéed garlic, homemade mayonnaise, and lime juice; Jason: sautéed scallops with orange-ginger sauce on a bed of spinach.

When the family gathers for Thanksgiving this year, our grandkids, Julia and Steven, are watching the parade on TV. I think this will keep them occupied as I make our chestnut soup, finish our home-baked breads. After a few minutes, I check on them to see how they are.

"Nana," Steven says, as the twirlers are twirling and the marchers marching, "this is boring. Can we please watch TV Food?" This is our family name for the Food Network. The kids are mesmerized by Martha Stewart cooking turkey. And by Emeril Lagasse.

"This is so exciting," Steven says, when I check in on them again. "Let's kick it up another notch."

Another time, I'm taking care of Julia. She's playing dress-up. She puts on a scarf, pretends it's a shawl. Puts on my shoes, takes my pocketbook. Starts walking around.

"Where are you going?" I ask.

"To London to visit the Queen," she answers. Then reconsiders. "No," she says, "I won't go there. London is too scary. There are globlins in London. I think I'll go to Williams-Mamoma instead." Williams-Sonoma, my favorite store, not part of the lexicon of the average three-year-old girl, unless she has someone like me for a grandmother.

When I pick up either of the kids for some special time after school, we always have an activity—riding bikes, walking around the neighborhood, going for a ride, visiting a playground or a museum. And then we go shopping so Steven or Julia can choose a special treat that costs five dollars or less.

"Would you like to go to a toy store?" I ask Steven the last time we meet.

"No," he says, "I'd rather go to Whole Foods." He takes his time walking around; checks out the fruits; checks out the prepared foods; eats every sample of cheese; eats every sample of bread. I can tell this is going to take a very long time.

Finally, he chooses: a quesadilla, and a cheese-and-dill dip. Then Steven asks if we can afford to bring his sister and his parents a treat. He's gotten one; they should have one too.

"Of course," I say, proud of his generosity.

We walk through the store again. These choices take him just as long. Finally, Steven decides on a box of organic strawberries for Julia. And a bouquet of flowers and a six-pack of a premium beer for his parents.

I restrain my laughter. As we check out, he points to the beer. Tells the clerk, "This is for my parents; they like special beers. They drink it when we eat Indian food."

This past summer, my husband and I are going away for four days. At the other end of our two-hour drive is a kitchen, and we will arrive in time for lunch.

In the kitchen at home we have beautiful farmer's-market cherry tomatoes, a ball of homemade mozzarella swimming in its own milk, some fresh basil doing nicely on the windowsill, its roots in water. So I think, pizza Margherita, the queen of pizzas.

I figure that, before we leave, I'll make a pizza dough, real quick, in my Cuisinart, from a great recipe I found in one of Julia Child's cookbooks. It's not authentic, but it's easy to stretch, with a nice crunch. I'll put it in a bowl, stash it on the floor of the car. It'll rise while we're driving. When we're halfway there, we'll stop by the side of the road, I'll jump out, punch it down, re-form it into a ball, cover it again. Let it have a second rise. By the time we arrive, it'll be ready. In no time at all, we'll have pizza. But not just any pizza. My homemade pizza, one of the best we've had, even including those we've eaten in Italy.

So, we pack the car. A few bags of pasta we've brought home from Italy. Some Sicilian sea salt, gathered by hand. "They have stores there, you know," my husband says. "But they don't have these ingredients there," I reply.

I stash some of my kitchen equipment, which travels—my favorite skillet, my mezzaluna, my authentic Ligurian mortar and pestle carted home from our most recent trip, my Pugliese cookbook, my *panini* cookbook.

"We're going to stop, right, so I can punch down the dough," I say.

"You're not going to punch down the dough on the side of the road," Ernie says. "What if someone sees you?"

My husband cares about what people think about him, even what total strangers think about him. Me, I don't give a shit what other people think of me. But my husband thinks that the guy in the car on the Long Island Expressway will see me punch down my dough by the side of the highway and think less of him.

So I tell my husband that no one will know what I'm doing; no one will care. Frankly, I think it's kind of cool to be using your driving time to let a batch of dough rise. This is the kind of multitasking I approve of.

I tell him that when he eats the pizza I will make, he will think that it was worth all the trouble. "You're nuts," Ernie says, "but a wonderful kind of nuts."

On our last trip to Italy, to the South, to find my ancestors' villages, Ernie and I have eaten a lot of splendid pizza topped with the finest and freshest ingredients, cooked in wood-burning ovens. We have eaten pizza every day. Pizza marinara, with tomatoes, garlic, oregano—the original pizza; pizza *canzone del mare* (song-of-the-sea pizza), with cherry tomatoes, basil, garlic; pizza *verdi*, pizza with buffalo milk mozzarella, anchovy fillets, fresh parsley, capers, garlic, arugula; pizza *alla melanzana* (with eggplant); pizza *con carciofi* (with artichokes) and *con cipolle* (with onions). And, of course, pizza Margherita.

In a bookstore, I have discovered the cookbook *La Pizza: The True Story from Naples*. This is my fifth pizza cookbook. But it is definitive, because it relates the origin of pizza, tells how it is cooked in the finest pizzerias in Naples.

I have read it, underlined it, taken notes from it, especially on the chapter "Pizza Taboos," listing the rules for pizza laid out by the Associazione Vera Pizza Napoletana. Yes, there are rules for making an authentic pizza, and strict ones. You can't use any kind of fat in the dough, including olive oil; you must knead the dough by hand, although you can use a special pizza-kneading device approved by the Association; you can't use a rolling pin to flatten the dough; you can't use a baking tin; you can't use an electric oven—only a wood-fueled, bell-shaped oven.

The aim is to produce a pizza that will be "supple, perfectly cooked, fragrant and framed by a high, soft border."

Pizza is taken very seriously in the land of my ancestors. People argue about it. People come to blows about it. You would stand a chance of getting away with disrespecting someone's mother sooner than you would of getting away with disrespecting someone's favorite pizza. I take pizza very seriously too, and when we arrive home, I begin what my family calls my Pizza Period.

Before this, there have been the Risotto Period; the Tagine Period; the Paella Period; the High-Heat Roasting Period; the Slow Cooker Period; the Stir-fried Period; the Artisan Baker Period; the Homemade Pasta Period; the Lasagna Period; the Creative Salad Period; the Panini Period; the Homemade Yogurt Period, the Homemade Ricotta Period (a very short period, because making ricotta is such a pain in the ass and the result doesn't taste as good as the ricotta from my favorite Italian market); the Homemade Ice Cream and Homemade Waffle Cone Period; the *Minestra* Period; the Tuscan Period; the Ligurian Period; the Pugliese Period.

During each of these periods, I have purchased cookbooks, special ingredients, special equipment. I have so much kitchen equipment, so many cookbooks, so many special ingredients that any thief who comes to our house should avoid the jewelry box and head straight for the cupboards.

I *love* all my cooking equipment. I talk to my appliances. I praise them for jobs well done. And I don't yell at them if something doesn't go right; I just give them some time off. I don't want to get into a power struggle with my equipment.

I love my kitchen. It's not a gorgeously decorated, high-end, industrial-stove, giant refrigerator, handmade-tile-and-backsplashes kind of kitchen. It's an ordinary serviceable kitchen, with a small prep area, but it's a cheerful kitchen, and it's right next to my study, so I can run back and forth all day long, from writing to cooking, from cooking to writing. And I do. My kitchen is my refuge. My cooking makes my writing possible.

When we travel, we look for equipment and ingredients to lug home from wherever we've been—an authentic mortar and pestle (from Genoa, very heavy, carried by Ernie); salted capers (from Sicily, bought in Taormina); bottles of tuna (from Liguria, caught in the waters off Camogli); dried wild marjoram (from the area near San Rocco di Camogli in Liguria); dried wild mushrooms (from Varese Ligure); peperoncini and sun-dried tomatoes (from Alberobello, bought from an extraordinarily handsome young man who looks like one of my sons); wild honey and handmade pasta, estate-bottled olive oils and wine, and bottles of aged balsamic vinegar (from Don Alfonso's in Sant'Agata sui Due Golfi on the Sorrento peninsula). And whenever we visit Liguria, we always bring back dried wild herbs—marjoram, basil, and oregano (all from the forest on the Portofino peninsula; gathered and dried by monks).

Sometimes we return with food you're not supposed to bring into the country: fresh wild fennel, scamorza cheese, an amazing salami made on a farm we visit. With every excellent meal I make using my special ingredients, I drive away the phantom of my mother's kitchen, try to obliterate the want of my ancestors.

My husband and I don't go out to many restaurants; like many Italians, we prefer to eat at home. But when I order something in a restaurant, on the rare occasions when we go out, I am in an agony of waiting. I do not make good dinner table conversation. I am not a chit-chatter. I might be seated next to a Pulitzer Prize winner, and I don't give a shit about whether the book was hard to write. All I care about is *When will the food come? When will the food come? When will the fucking food come?*

I am not good company in a restaurant. I like to have complete control of my food. Which means cooking what I like just the way I like it, and serving it attractively, but certainly not in little piles or towers. At home, there's none of this waiting around for someone to bring you your food.

Restaurants. I don't understand them, don't understand giving a stranger control over what you eat. If my own mother fucked up my food, why should I trust a stranger?

But in Italy—first in Tuscany, then in Liguria, all over Sicily, and, most recently, in Puglia and Campania—I have learned to enter restaurants with joyful anticipation; learned to love eating in restaurants; learned to love choosing my food; learned to trust the chef and the staff; learned to trust the pace of the meal; learned to visit kitchens at the invitation of the chef with a feeling akin to the intense love you had for someone when you were in high school. (Though I still hate eating out in the United States.)

Why? Because in Italy, even in small, unprepossessing places, people care about food. Really care. They get teary eyed over little tomatoes grown close enough to the sea so their flavor intensifies. They caress eggplants the way a mother caresses a baby's bottom. They sniff melons before they buy them, the way an elegant woman chooses the finest perfume. They care about food in a way my mother never cared about food. And they want you to care, too. They want to please you, for they know that food is about pleasure. About appetite, and its satisfaction.

Once, while we are savoring wine and a small meal in an *enoteca* in Chiavari in Liguria, we see the owner at a table in the back, cleaning fresh porcini for the next day's service. He's doing this while we're eating our dinner.

On the table is a huge wicker basket containing the porcini. He has his tools—a knife for paring away imperfections, a brush for cleaning, some immaculate napkins for wiping off the dirt—lined up beside him. He cleans the porcini where we can see him work, to show the care he takes, to show how it should be done, to show the respect he accords this magnificent fungus, but also to show the respect he accords his patrons.

For all the time we're there, he scrapes and brushes and cleans and holds each mushroom close to his eyes to examine it. Each takes a long time to clean, and I watch in fascination, learning the meaning of patience and care. As he works, he smiles. His work is satisfying, and he's doing it as if there is nothing more important to do in all this world.

At La Cucina di Nonna Nina in San Rocco di Camogli in Liguria, for the first time in my life, I eat *corzetti*, a pasta made with wine, rolled out, cut into circles, then stamped between two pieces of hand-carved wood. At Nonna Nina, one side of the *corzetti* bears the restaurant's name; the other, the rays of the sun. The indentations and raised surfaces of the pasta introduce subtle differences in the texture of each bite. Tears come to my eyes as I taste. I am happy. I am in the moment. The owner's wife notices my pleasure. She introduces herself— Signora Rosalia Dalpian—and she invites me into the kitchen to meet her husband, the chef, Signore Paolo Dalpian. He shows me the *corzetti* stamp, which has been in his family for generations.

La Cucina di Nonna Nina specializes in traditional dishes made in the old way from heirloom family recipes. Over the years, my husband and I eat there a score of times. Each time, there is something new to savor; the menu changes with the seasons, and with available ingredients.

One spring, Signore Dalpian presents a ricotta torte he makes at the beginning of the season when the grass is at its sweetest, which means that the cheese will be at its sweetest. We travel back the following autumn, and there is no ricotta torte: ricotta torte is made only in spring, Signore Dalpian says. So we travel back the following spring to have it again. And yes, it's worth the journey.

In Recco, in Liguria, we eat at Da ö Vittorio because we want to savor their famed focaccia *col formaggio*, made with Crescenza or Invernizzina cheese made nearby. Only certain restaurants can advertise that they make this specialty; in Recco, famous for this focaccia, its production is scrutinized and regulated to make sure the approved restaurants serving it meet stringent standards. It is a huge focaccia, its dough is flaky and extremely thin, its melted cheese tangy and unctuous. The food writer Fred Plotkin calls it "the most addictive food on the planet." It is served in wedges, one huge focaccia shared among several diners. After our meal, we talk to the proprietors, the brothers Gianni and Vittorio Bisso, about how the focaccia is made. Back home, it is something we dream about. And when we return to Liguria, one of our first stops is to this restaurant.

On our second trip, after our meal, we talk to the brothers for over an hour. They remember us from our last visit; they're glad we've come back. During our conversation, we mention we would like to make our own *corzetti*. So Gianni gets a map, shows us a village—Varese Ligure—in the mountains, where we can buy a stamp for embossing *corzetti*. He takes the time to make sure we understand his directions. We travel there, buy two, make *corzetti* all year long.

On our most recent trip, when we arrive at Da ö Vittorio, we feel as if we've come home. After our focaccia, we're taken to see the special ovens; shown a model of the wagon that delivered focaccia through the streets of Recco during the Bisso brothers' grandfather's time; and on a tour through the restaurant's archive to see photos taken during the World War II bombardment of Recco, which nearly obliterated the village. The restaurant was one of the few buildings left standing.

In Sicily, in Aci Trezza, north of Catania, at a restaurant overlooking lemon groves and the Ionian Sea, I am eating pasta *ca Norma* (pasta *alla Norma*, in Italian)—pasta with sautéed eggplant, tomatoes, basil, and ricotta salata. This is the third time in a week we are dining here, the third time I've had this traditional Sicilian pasta.

The pasta is homemade; it is in the shape of an elongated tube pierced with a very small hole. I want to learn how it is made; I want to reproduce it back home.

I summon the courage to ask the owner. He obliges me by giving me his recipe for the dough, and telling me the strands are shaped by wrapping strips of dough around a knitting needle. No special tools are used; just the knitting needle any Sicilian household would have.

The owner tells me what kind of flour to use. I tell him I doubt I'll be able to find it back home. So he goes into the kitchen and comes out with a packet for me. And tells me if I can't find it, to write him, he'll send it. He wants me to make this at home; he's happy I care enough about this food to want to make it myself. When we leave, we say we'll come back the next time we come to Sicily, and we mean it.

In the Panificio Maccarini in San Rocco in Liguria, I am buying packages of pasta, ones I can't get in the United States—*troffiette, corzetti*, special small oblongs of lasagna—and, of course, Ligurian olive oil. (In the Milan airport, my husband will complain as he trundles fifteen pounds of pasta and several liters of olive oil, all too precious to be stowed, from one end of the airport to the other. But he's used to it. This is the way we always return home: our bags stuffed with delicacies.)

The owner of the *panificio*, Anna Maccarini, notices my excitement. Even though there are many people waiting for her to serve them, she stops and calls someone from the kitchen to help so she can teach me recipes for what I buy. She teaches me to use the lasagna noodles to make a recipe that's not baked: you use a low pan, she says, and you layer the pasta with a tomato sauce (with carrot, celery, and onion, the vegetables removed, macerated, and returned to the sauce). She teaches me her recipe for pesto. I complain about the basil in the United States.

She asks me what I'll do with the aniseed. I give her my recipe for a bread I make with orange rind, almonds, and ground aniseed, a family favorite. She writes down the ingredients.

I speak almost no Italian, but from years of living with my grandmother, I can understand everything Anna Maccarini says. Using gestures, helped along by my husband's meager Italian, we exchange a score of recipes before it's time to leave.

Signora Maccarini comes out from behind the counter. Hugs me. Kisses me. For a moment, though I am in my fifties, I want her to be my mother. I have found a food friend. A woman I return to each time we visit Liguria.

It is here, in a land that starved my grandparents until they were forced to leave for America, that I truly learn the pleasures of the Italian table.

Part Four

COMMUNION

COURTSHIP (WITH FOOD)

We—my new boyfriend, Ernie; my mother; my father; my sister; and I (but not my grandmother, who lurks in the kitchen)—are seated around our dark mahogany dining room table. It is beautifully set, with a hand-crocheted white tablecloth (my grandmother's); silver-plate (not silver; we don't own any); good glassware (not crystal); and Mikasa china (bought at an outlet store in South Jersey, the object of a day-long excursion I refused to join).

The china is white, with a fluted edge, decorated with forget-me-nots. My mother is proud of it. She never puts the pieces in the dishwasher, never permits anyone else to wash it, certainly never allows me to wash it. She suspects that I would drop a piece because I'm careless or simply to spite her, to destroy something she loves.

I disdain my mother's china, having, during college, acquired a taste for Danish modern stoneware (Danish modern everything), which I imagine I will buy when I set up house. (Because of my disdain, my father gives the Mikasa china to my son Jason the year after her death, knowing how much he loves the china, knowing how much he has loved my mother. I have come to love the china, not because it's beautiful, but because it was my mother's, and because, in the years since her death, I have learned to love her.)

I remember the day as warm. All my recollections of my mother's good meals include this warmth, which is, perhaps, my happiness at being well fed, and not the temperature outside or of the room.

On this day, as my mother brought the dishes to the table, she was smiling. As usual, she didn't want any help from me; she chased me out of the kitchen though I wanted to help (I wanted to impress Ernie). Now I wish that my mother and I had cooked this meal together so that we could have shared time in the kitchen, which we never did—a source of grief now; so that I could have this memory of us cooking together on the occasion when my parents entertained for the first time the young man who would become my husband.

This was the first time my mother had suggested I bring some-one—let alone a boyfriend—home for dinner.

"Why don't you call Ernie and invite him for dinner?" my mother asks. The night before, I had come home from a date later than I was supposed to, and very disheveled. And, though my mother had waited up for me, she didn't scold me, didn't say a word.

She wasn't the kind of mother who encouraged my friends to come to our house, to stay for dinner if they happened to be there at suppertime. She'd look at the clock, look at my friend, say, "Don't you think it's time to go home?"

I worried that, on the day of the dinner, my mother wouldn't be up to cooking, and that I would have to call the whole thing off. Or that something awful would happen at dinner—my mother would say something to show my new boyfriend I wasn't as nice as I seemed; she would insist that my grandmother sit at the table and the two of them would start arguing.

She was coquettish, my mother was, as she brought the meal to the table. Smiling at my new boyfriend, carrying a platter aloft as if it were a holy relic. This was an attitude I had never witnessed in her, this charm, this ebullience, this buoyancy of spirit. And it was because of this handsome Italian-American young man. He was going to be a doctor, after all, and this was important to her. She called it "having good prospects."

For the previous two years, since I'd been in college, I had been exasperating my mother by dating boys she considered unsuitable.

(They were; but I didn't want to hear that from my mother.) An aspiring actor (uncertain future; unreliable; saw me several days in a row, then nothing). The son of a famous and controversial scientist (not good, to be in the public eye, and probably his father had ignored him). A gorgeous blond charmer ("Beware of charming men," she said, "they always lack substance; people of character don't have to be charming"). And there was Roy, always Roy, my mad passion from high school, who appeared and disappeared and reappeared, and I was miserable with him, and miserable without him. (Roy, I never took home; Roy, my mother knew nothing about).

I would come home from dates with one or another of these boyfriends, reeking of alcohol and sex. My mother was sure that, before I graduated college, I would ruin my life forever. I would have to get married, have an abortion, give up a child for adoption. But there was nothing my mother could do to control me; nothing I could do to control myself. I knew that I wouldn't be happy with any of them. But I wanted to get married. Wanted to leave my house. And so I persuaded myself that I loved each of them, that marriage to any one of them would solve my problems.

I was sulky, sullen, distant, often drunk, always writing. Writing poems about these boys. About love and loss. About love and pain. Writing poems about good sex and awful sex. And poems about sex and food, the only poems I wrote that were cheerful.

My poetry, I am sure my mother read, because she always searched my belongings. But I didn't care what she learned about me. She couldn't be any more condemning of me than she already was. And besides, whatever she found would pay her back for her violation of my privacy by torturing her.

This one, I'm sure she found. Because, when I suggested we buy cannolis for dessert for that dinner because I knew that Ernie loved them, and because it would save her time, she said, "No, absolutely not; there will be no cannolis."

LOUISE DESALVO

In Search of the Ultimate Cannoli Experience

For those of you out there in poetryland
who don't know what a cannoli is
lend an ear for a minute or two
while I describe to you this incredible tasty delight
Brought to you by the same folks
who brought you the meatball
and the pizza pie.
(Better still, take yourself
to anyplace you can find that sells the little buggers
and buy yourself two—one won't do).

Picture
a tube, an edible brown tube,
crispy from having been wrapped around
a metal thing
(that in its off hours could serve as the support system for a limp dick)
and deep fried with sweet cream inside
oozing from an orifice on either side
and the way you eat the little bugger is to hold it
gently in the middle
and put it into your mouth, any other technique simply won't do—
it breaks in the presence of too strong a touch
spewing forth its insides
before the mouth can take the inside and the outside inside itself—
the ultimate cannoli experience.
It is fellatio, practiced publicly,
perfectly acceptable,
taught to thousands of little Italian girls
in little Italy, in Hoboken, and even in Ridgefield, New Jersey.

Is it any wonder that all grown up
we are
such incredible fucks?

Then Ernie came along.

The meal.

A platter of lobster tails, expertly broiled, a tinge of paprika on the white, burnished flesh: paprika, my mother declared when my future husband complimented her on their splendid appearance, assisted the browning. (How did she know?)

A platter of double-baked potatoes, a time-consuming effort, involving baking the potatoes, allowing them to cool, scooping out the flesh, mixing it with salt, pepper, cream, eggs, and freshly grated Parmesan cheese, then stuffing this mixture into the potato shells, decorating the tops with the tines of a fork, then baking them until a crunchy crust formed on the outside. (As opposed to the instant mashed potatoes, lumpy, that my mother usually made for supper, and proclaimed were better than homemade.)

A bowl of Le Sueur tender tiny peas. (A premium brand that my mother never bought before.) With tiny onions, fresh ones, because she thought the canned ones were inadequate (a new development). As she blanched them, popped off their skins, I ventured into the kitchen. "Leave me alone; I'm in control here," my mother said. This was something new. My mother had never been in control before.

For dessert, Indian pudding with vanilla ice cream, a premium brand. Somehow my mother has learned it's Ernie's favorite dessert and she's made it to please him. He thanks her; she smiles. A girlish, happy smile.

I want to learn how to cook well, though I know that, despite this meal, I will not learn from my mother.

And I do start to cook, and in my mother's kitchen, but not with my mother. With Ernie. Neither of us has cooked before, but we're eager to try.

We decide to throw a dinner party for two of our friends. We ask to use my mother's kitchen and our family's dining room. To my surprise, my mother agrees. (*She really wants me to marry this guy*, I think.)

Ernie and I develop our menu from a paperback international

cookbook that I buy. I persuade Ernie to make *boeuf en daube*, a dish mentioned in Virginia Woolf's *To the Lighthouse*, which I have read in college. We will also make my mother's double-baked potatoes and tiny peas with onions.

Ernie's mother is no cook, he's said. She serves the same menu every week—veal parmesan on Monday; meat loaf on Tuesday; sausage and peppers on Wednesday; spaghetti with red sauce on Thursday; fried fish on Friday; pot roast on Saturday; roast beef on Sunday. Every night, there is a salad of iceberg lettuce with oil and vinegar. Every night there is cherry Jell-O for dessert.

I tell Ernie the meal my mother made for him isn't what she usually cooks. I am one of those girls who just *love* the food at college, which tells you all you need to know about my mother's cooking—the homemade breakfast buns (coconut, walnut, both glazed); the lunchtime sloppy Joes; the dinnertime fried fish, served with lemon wedges and tartar sauce.

We are both eager to emigrate from our mothers' kitchens, to enter the world of good food. We vow that when we get married (though we haven't yet said "to each other"), we will eat magnificent food every night.

Poring over our little cookbook, shopping for food, we find, is more fun than most of our other excursions—to the Hudson Valley to see the leaves turn in autumn, to the Metropolitan Museum of Art, to the Modern. Reading recipes excites us. Sexually. And throughout our marriage the best sex we have is the sex we have after we've cruised our way through three or four cookbooks, reading aloud recipes that capture our imagination, that we'll soon try. Rustic free-form fruit tarts; blackberry crumble; Milanese-style scaloppini with peppery greens; baked penne with wild mushroom ragù and ricotta salata; coriander-crusted scallops in fennel broth. Food as foreplay.

Ernie is a superb, efficient shopper. He memorizes our list, decides to purchase an item without equivocation, isn't sidetracked, can shop for a meal (or, when we marry, for a week's food) quickly.

I am all indecision—"Should we choose this package of meat or that?" I get distracted by something I see that isn't on our list, a lovely plump chicken—"Maybe we should make *coq au vin* instead."

A few minutes into our first shopping trip, Ernie develops a strategy for dealing with me in food stores. (It's one of the reasons my emerging love for him deepens.) He suggests we shop separately and meet near the checkout counter when we're finished. He suggests I buy whatever I want. He tells me not to worry, he'll take care of what's on the list.

When I meet Ernie, my little basket contains

> one can of green peppercorns, because I like the decoration on the can (they are not in our recipe, but never mind)
> one bunch of parsley (I have examined each of the score of bunches in the store to find the best)
> a few parsnips (they intrigue me; I've never tasted them)
> Major Grey's chutney (I want to try a curry)

My progress has been slow because I am excited by what I see. I imagine all the wonderful things I can cook as soon as I have my own kitchen if I take up cooking in a serious way.

By the time we meet, Ernie has selected everything we need. He looks at what I've chosen, tells me to put back his parsley while he checks out—mine's better—and takes the little can of green peppercorns and the parsnips and the chutney without comment, putting them together with his selections. (The parsnips will rot in the vegetable bin of my mother's refrigerator, but the little can of green peppercorns and the chutney come with me to the apartment Ernie and I move into after our marriage. I use the peppercorns in a lovely sautéed steak with a green peppercorn cream sauce I make soon after we marry. The chutney, to accompany a chicken curry with onions and apples.)

My mother abandons her kitchen for the day of our dinner, and she bullies my grandmother into doing the same. She sets the table for us, then retreats to the TV room. *(She really wants me to marry this guy.)*

For two people who have never wielded a knife, skinned a garlic clove, or peeled or chopped an onion, the amount of preparation for one meal seems prodigious. But we proceed. Step by step. Magnificently. With one—major—glitch.

Our *boeuf en daube* calls for wine, a lot of wine. Which my father gives us from his supply because we're still too young to buy our own.

We pour the wine into the deep pot that has our beef, onions, carrots, and garlic, all nicely browned and glistening. Stand over it, looking at the magnificence we are creating, smiling with the glory of it all.

But we are novices; we don't know that wine throws off alcohol as it simmers. If you stand with your head over a pot of *boeuf en daube*, inhaling, for a while, you are going to get drunk. Shitfaced, in fact.

When our company arrives, we're staggering, in no shape to serve them. My mother, uncharacteristically, thinks this is funny. *(She must really want me to marry this guy.)* And makes excuses for us. My grandmother laughs. "'Mbriaghi," she says.

My mother takes over, serves our meal. Through the haze of alcohol, we see how much our guests are enjoying the food. We know that what we have created is magnificent.

We make it through the meal. Through dessert—cannoli, which we've bought at the Italian pastry shop. We're not yet up to scaling the dessert mountain of food preparation. Neither of us takes a bite.

We see our guests to the door, wave them away, rush to the bathroom, and vomit ourselves into oblivion.

Nonetheless, we are thrilled. We believe that we have joined a secret society of food lovers, and the pleasure we take in making food and eating it, sees us through many difficult times in our marriage.

For years, when I thought about the first time I ate lobster, the night my mother cooked for Ernie for the first time, I always became angry. I thought it was because what she cooked for him was better than anything she ever cooked for me. Which meant she knew what good food was. Which meant she could have cooked a good meal for me if she chose. Which meant that her not cooking a good meal for me was deliberate.

Now I see that I became angry because my mother was happy. I did not know my mother in this new manifestation. I had seen evidence of happiness, in photographs of her smiling, something she rarely did. But she only smiled in photos of her with other women (the women she called her girlfriends). Never in photos of her with my father, or with me, or my sister.

There they are, big-breasted women in bathing suits with little pleated skirts over sumptuous thighs, ranked together after what must have been an exhilarating plunge into a turbulent sea. *(My mother, swimming? Facing danger?)* Well-dressed women in tweed suits, stockings, pumps, long hair gathered into snoods, ranked together for the annual Kresge company portrait. *(My mother, working, talking with customers, selling shoes?)* Glassy-eyed women leaning into each other at parties while their husbands were away at war. *(My mother tipsy, enjoying herself, telling jokes?)*

With this young man seated across from her at the table (she had made sure of that), she seemed happier than I had ever seen her. That sinkhole of sorrow I knew had disappeared for this young man. My young man.

He had a wonderful, engaging smile. An *I'm so glad to see you!* kind of smile. An *Aren't we going to have fun together?* kind of smile. A *Seeing you just made my day* kind of smile. And so it was easy to smile back.

All that smiling had attracted me when we met while I was in college. But we had known each other since high school.

We despised each other. He rode a motorcycle (purple, with rusting wire wheels), wore a black leather jacket, hung out with hoods even though he wanted to become a doctor. He played the Italian American thug, which masqueraded his success in school, his quick and inquiring mind, his sweetness, his love of his mother—all liabilities where we came from.

He thought I was stuck up and collegiate, even though I had a bad reputation, spent most of my free time getting drunk at parties and sleeping with a boy I wasn't dating, who had a "real" girlfriend. And I was nasty. Whenever I saw him, I insulted him. He insulted me. Our banter was filled with mutual scorn and sexual innuendo.

We reconnect over a game of bridge at a mutual friend's, in the summer of my sophomore year in college. I'm surprised—and none too happy—to find him there. But since I've last seen him, he's turned (surprise, surprise) into someone nice, cute, smart, and funny, and he plays a mean game of bridge, finessing the ass off my partner. He's attracted to me (he tells me later) because of my wise-ass comments through the game (not, now, directed at him), my brains, my independence.

I wonder what's happened to the thug I used to hate. He wonders what's happened to the brat who used to give him such a hard time.

Later that evening, he comes to my house. We sit outside in his car and talk and listen to music. My grandmother shines a flashlight out the window at us, which is what she always does when I sit in a car, outside my house, with a boy. But he's not annoyed like my other boyfriends. He thinks it's funny. He knows the strange ways of Italian grandparents.

For the first month, we talk—about philosophy, existentialism, Sartre, Camus, psychology, religion. There is no sex.

We eat a lot of pizza (plain, extra cheese, well done) at Sano's Pizza Parlor. It sits on a plateau overlooking the Hackensack River Valley. And because we are besotted with each other, the sun setting over the industrialized wasteland built in the once pristine wilderness of the Meadowlands seems beautiful to us.

We talk about our future, our aspirations, our dreams. He's going to be a doctor. I'm going to be a high school teacher. Maybe teach college someday, write books. We both want to have children, travel, eat wonderful food. We believe our lives will intertwine.

When we start dating, Ernie's mother is as happy as mine, and for the same reason: he's never before dated someone she considers suitable. "Don't screw this one up," she says. "If you hurt her, I'll kill you."

Ernie's parents take us to Amerigo's, a restaurant in the Bronx serving what his family believes is the best pizza in America. On the drive there on the Cross Bronx Expressway, I sit in the back with Ernie. He puts his arm around me. His parents don't object.

And the pizza at Amerigo's is memorable. (Still the best I've ever eaten, including the pizza I've eaten in Italy.) It's made by the grandmother of the proprietor, baked in a wood-burning oven. Glorious crust. Chunks of tomato. Fresh mozzarella. Fresh basil.

It's the pizza at Amerigo's that makes me sure I want to marry this man.

When I see my mother so happy to be serving Ernie lobster, I realize how unhappy she has been with me.

There we are, gathered round a nicely set table. There is good food. Good wine. Conversation.

My mother leans forward, smiles at Ernie across the table, asks him if he'd like another helping.

"Don't mind if I do," he says, and fills his plate a second time.

"Be sure to save some room," she tells him, pleased that he likes her food. "We're having something special for dessert, something I know you'll like."

MATCHMAKING

Just before Ernie and I get married, we hatch a misbegotten plan to introduce his maternal grandfather, who has been living with Ernie's family since the death of his grandmother, to my grandmother, who has been living with my family since soon after the death of my grandfather.

Their spouses have died. They are lonely. They are unhappy living with their relatives. Ernie's grandfather didn't want to move away from his apartment in the Bronx when his wife died. But his daughters insisted he couldn't live alone; insisted he had to live with Ernie's mother so she could care for him. He refused; got sick; went into the hospital. When he was ready to leave, they told him they'd given up his apartment, moved his belongings. He cries about this still.

"Maybe they'll get along, become friends," Ernie says.

"Maybe they'll get married," I say, and not facetiously.

The fantasy of these two old people setting up house together makes me happy. Now that I am preparing to get married, I view marriage as the solution to every problem. It is certainly the solution to *my* problem—wanting to move out of my parents' house which, for the daughter of an Italian American family in the 1960s, isn't possible without getting married.

That they are both Italian, Ernie and I are certain, will be enough, we're sure, to kindle a friendship, if not spark a love match.

But what do Ernie and I know of the numerous dialects and

regional differences among Italian-born Italians? Of the loathing that people from one part of Italy have for people from other parts of Italy? What do we know of the fact that Italian-born Italians don't think of themselves as Italians, but as people from Sicily, or from Puglia? And not only as people from Sicily, but as people from Palermo (not Catania); not only from Puglia, but from Rodi Garganico (not Bari)? And not only as people from a particular town, but as people from a particular neighborhood in that town. And not only as people from a particular neighborhood, but as people with a certain set of affiliations within that that neighborhood. What do we know of the racism in the North towards people from the South (in Turin, for example, no one will rent to a Southerner)? We don't know that the South is called Africa, that Italians born in the North often believe Southern Italians are barbarians?

What do we know of the regional differences in Italian cooking? We don't know people from one part of Italy won't eat the food of people from another part of Italy. That people from one village cook different specialties from people in another village. That people from one family cook the village specialty differently from the people from another family. That each thinks the other's food is a travesty, inedible.

And what do we know of the profound divide of class in Italy? We don't know landowners do not mingle with their workers. People who are workers do not mingle with people who are artisans. People who are peasants do not mingle with shopowners.

About all of this, we understand very little. We were born and raised in the United States. Our families have taught us virtually nothing about the country our ancestors came from. We have learned nothing about the history of Italy, the history of the South of Italy, the reasons for the great emigration. Neither of us speaks Italian or dialect, though each of us understands the dialect spoken in our households.

Ernie and I see ourselves as similar because our grandparents were born in Italy. We think of ourselves as being more alike than different, although my grandparents are from Puglia and Campania, and Ernie's are from Sicily and the Abruzzi. Ernie and I have often heard disparaging remarks about our being Italian. And each of us has gotten into fights over it—at school, in our neighbourhoods.

However, we have also heard from our relatives the disparaging remarks that people from various parts of Italy make about people from other parts. We have heard our grandparents call people from Calabria hardheaded; people from Naples thieves; people from Liguria penny-pinching; people from certain parts of the North *polenta eaters* (which means they are bland, colorless, without passion or excitement). And we have heard everyone say that anyone from anyplace else in Italy is not to be trusted. So perhaps we should know that bringing our grandparents together is not as simple as it seems.

On the day that has been fixed for their meeting, Ernie's grandfather arrives punctually. Ernie's mother drives him, and she'll pick him up after she does a bit of shopping. My mother goes shopping with her; they are future in-laws; they are getting to know each other.

(The closer we get to my wedding day, the more congenial my mother becomes, the more time she spends with Ernie's mother. As much as I can't wait to move out of the house, so, too, it seems she can't wait for me to leave. "You are a thorn in my side" is what my mother says when she gets mad at me.)

The plan is that we will leave the two "old folks," as my mother calls them, alone together, so they can get to know each other. I am home, but I plan on staying upstairs, at my desk at the top of the stairs, from which I can hear what's going on but stay out of the way.

My grandmother has refused to change her clothes for the occasion, has refused, even, to wash up or tidy her hair, irritating my mother beyond measure. And she is a mess, her apron all stained with blood from the tripe she's been preparing. "Ma," my mother has pleaded, to no effect, "at least change your apron, for Christ's sake." Wearing her blood-stained, battle-stained apron, my grandmother chops her onion, her carrot, her celery stalks, her garlic, her tomatoes for the sauce for the tripe, doing all the things she would do on a normal day.

She puts the tripe into a pot of salted water to cook it until it's tender. She ignores the time. Ignores my mother, who follows her around, haranguing her. Ignores me, as I urge her to clean up. Ignores the fact that Ernie's grandfather will arrive shortly.

When Ernie and I planned this meeting, I had imagined my grandmother would welcome it as a change from her dull routine, which, I had hoped, would change her life. But no.

My grandmother, exasperated with my mother and me, shouts at us in dialect. Something that sounds like "Fatifatadoi," which I know means something like "Mind your own business." And continues stinking up the kitchen with the tripe for her supper. When she meets Ernie's grandfather at the front door, she's red-faced and sullen from her battle with my mother.

Ernie's grandfather has dressed nattily for the occasion. He wears his good brown tweed three-piece suit, a heavily starched white shirt with an old-fashioned rounded collar, and a cravat. He carries a small clutch of flowers from Ernie's mother's garden for my grandmother. And he has doused himself with the cologne he always wears, which Ernie's mother complains about because it gives her a headache.

Ernie's grandfather enters, bowing slightly. He is a very dapper dude. How can my grandmother not like him? But how could he ever like her?

My grandmother wipes her dirty hands on her blood-stained apron, pushes a few steel-gray strands of hair away from her eyes. Grunts a few syllables I can't understand. She takes one look at the flowers, makes a face, grabs them from his hand. She mutters under her breath that he smells like a whore, retreats to the kitchen, where she is cooking.

Ernie's grandfather bows to me, pinches my cheek, laughs. I've met him a number of times; we can't converse, but he shows me he likes me. He makes his way past me, and follows my grandmother into the kitchen.

As soon as he enters, she begins smashing the pots and pans down on the stove the way she does when she's furious at my mother, although my mother has already escaped out the front door.

I'm beginning to see that this wasn't a very good idea. I'm beginning to see how different they are.

Ernie's grandfather doesn't know what to do. He hesitates. Turns. Should he retreat to the porch? Stay in the kitchen? He hasn't even been offered a chair, and he's too much the gentleman to pull one out for himself. Should he continue standing? Should he sit?

I want to return upstairs. But I want to see what transpires. Want to make sure my grandmother behaves herself. I go over to her by the stove, gesture towards the refrigerator, suggest that she gives him something to eat, something to drink. But she ignores me. I turn to leave, but hover in the doorway to the kitchen. I don't know what to do, and I don't have enough Italian to speak to Ernie's grandfather myself.

Though my grandmother and Ernie's grandfather are both "Italian" in our eyes, neither is, of course, Italian. Ernie's grandfather is a highly skilled, cultivated man from the metropolis of Palermo, in Sicily. When my grandmother has been apprised of this, she raises an eyebrow, mutters "Siciliano," and shrugs. She knows everything she needs to know about him.

Ernie's grandfather is well-read and well-informed. He reads the newspaper *Il Progresso* from cover to cover every day. Though he doesn't understand English, he watches the news on television avidly. He has opinions about everything. He is loquacious even if the person he's with doesn't understand what he's saying. He holds forth at Ernie's family's supper table, which annoys Ernie's father, who insists upon silence at meals. But when he lived in the Bronx, his opinions were highly respected and he was regarded as an orator. He sat in coffee bars catering to Italians with his admiring cronies, and articulated his beliefs about politics, mores, and opera.

He likes President Kennedy, although he thinks he'll run into *biga trouble*; he wonders whether the Cuban missile crisis was really a showdown; he thinks the cost of medication is an obscenity; he believes rock and roll is nothing but noise.

He was a stone carver. He was invited to come to the United States to work on the adornments of St. Patrick's Cathedral, and never experienced the hardships my grandmother faced. He is proud of the work he did, and talks about it often. Now, though, he is ill with emphysema, a result of his lifelong profession, and can't live alone, though he would like to.

My grandmother ignores current events and she cares nothing about politics or world affairs, in spite of her anarchist family. She can write her name, and she knows how to read some Italian. But she never reads. She believes that no matter who is in charge, the people will get screwed—you have to look out for yourself, look out for your own. She is a farmworker from a very small village in Puglia, and is superstitious and a believer in the evil eye. She attends the local Catholic church for its ritual and to get away from our house, rather than for its system of belief.

My grandmother always earned her own living, though she never talks about her jobs. Her life with us consists of fighting with my mother, making bread and pizza, crocheting, knitting, cooking, protecting me from my father's rages. She is tough, spirited, and vulgar. Apart from the time she spends on Long Island with her sister, she prefers being alone, although she doesn't mind when I sit near her, and we sometimes bake bread, make pasta, or knit together. But what she thinks about when she sits in her chair by the window in her room, saying her rosary, staring at the New Jersey meadows, I don't know.

Ernie says everyone knows what his grandfather's thinking, what he's feeling, because he's always telling them—how much he misses his wife, how awful it is to have been taken away from his friends, how he'll never forgive his daughters for what they've done to him, how he loves Ernie's mother better than his other daughter with whom he fights all the time, how glad he is that

Ernie is getting married to me, how proud he is that Ernie is going to be a doctor.

I see them still. Ernie's grandfather, ever the gentleman, even in these peculiar circumstances, is politely standing in the kitchen, his hands clasped behind his back, at a safe distance from my grandmother's vengeful splashings and spatterings. She stands at the stove, stirring, ignoring him profoundly, looking at the wall, gazing into her pot, at her tripe, hoping she will not ruin it. She knows she will eat it alone. She knows she will not offer him any. She knows that soon his daughter will come to pick him up and that all she needs to do is ignore him until that time.

Ernie's grandfather edges closer to the stove, closer to the pot, closer to her, repelled by the aroma, or seduced by it, who can say, wanting to see what my grandmother is cooking, but not wanting to provoke her. He has never met anyone like her before, though he has seen women like her from afar. It is his job not to roil this old woman; he senses that she can become dangerous. It is his job to be as inconspicuous as possible until his daughter returns.

Sensing the old man's nearness, my grandmother stirs even more furiously than before. Splatters of tomato sauce fly from the pot. The tripe will take at least an hour to become tender. She will stand here and stir until it's finished. The time will pass. And he will leave.

Ernie's grandfather retreats, afraid that his best suit will be stained. He glances at his flowers, which my grandmother has unceremoniously thrown on the kitchen table. She has no time for such nonsense. She has work to do. Who does he think she is?

Ernie's grandfather stands there, not knowing what else to do. Stands there until an hour has passed and his favorite daughter comes back from doing her shopping, to rescue him. Stands there, as still and silent as the angels he has carved for St. Patrick's Cathedral.

I retreat to my desk. This is too painful to watch.

* * *

When, later, Ernie asks me what has happened, I tell him only that they seem to have had great difficulty understanding each other. They don't seem to speak the same language.

I don't say how ashamed I am for what we have done. I don't say I believe that, in our ignorance, we have done something harmful. I don't say that, during that hour, I am sure that my grandmother and Ernie's grandfather felt more alone than either of them felt before.

RESPECT

They were standing there, the two of them, the father and the son, the father, about my father's age (eighty-five or so), the son, about my age (late fifties), in front of a bin of cantaloupes on sale for a good price at the farmers' market in Hackensack where I shop sometimes. It was late autumn, not the season for cantaloupes. But I thought I could pick one for a salad I could make for my lunch with the prosciutto I had at home, and peperoncino, lemon, and olive oil. But the old man was looking for a cantaloupe, and their cart was blocking the way, and so I moved on.

I had gone to the market for vegetables for yet another recipe for minestrone, in my search for the quintessential minestrone. As if there were such a thing, the perfect minestrone, although at the time I thought there might be. I didn't yet realize—this would come later, at about the fiftieth minestrone—that each minestrone is different from every other minestrone, even if you use the same recipe, the same combination of vegetables, because the same vegetables taste different all the time, depending upon the weather, the soil, the season. That the pleasure in minestrone making, minestrone eating, comes from the appreciation of this particular minestrone before you, which never was before, which never will be again. And when I arrived at this insight, which I believed to be an important truth, I felt a remarkable sense of peace, for I knew that the searching could cease. That I could enjoy what is rather than searching for what might be.

I had been picking out the kale, the cabbage, the curly endive that I needed for my current minestrone with far less care than usual because I thought that I should be hurrying back to my house, back to my desk, back to my writing. Work that I sometimes believed was far more important than picking out vegetables (though I sometimes believe that there is nothing more important than picking out vegetables). The shopping trip on this day was a break from the day's work rather than an excursion in and of itself. And I was not taking my time; I was not "in the moment." I was preoccupied. I was rushing. I was in a hurry.

So. I was annoyed at not being able to get past them, the father and the son, who were standing in front of the bin of cantaloupes, blocking the way with their cart, but I was not annoyed at them. I had encountered them before, near the carrots (which I needed). And made up a little story about them, formed a very favorable opinion of them, and because of this, couldn't be mad at them even though they weren't moving, even though there was no way to get past them, even though they were blocking my way.

Near the carrots, I had observed that only the father was shopping, and surmised that the son (I knew he was the son, for they looked very much alike, large-nosed, flared-nostriled, full-lipped, and both dressed in lumberjack coats) had taken time out from his workday to help his father shop. And thought that this was a good thing, this taking care of the father, this taking of the father to the farmers' market to shop.

As I passed them, the son glanced at me, met my eyes, averted them (out of respect, I imagined, for to hold the gaze of a woman my age would have been discourteous), looked at my purchases, nodded slightly, as if he seemed to know from what I was buying—the cabbage, the kale, the curly endive, the carrots—that I would be cooking a vegetable soup, and to know, thereby, what kind of woman I was. Not a fancy woman who shunned work. But an ordinary woman who put a good meal on the table every evening. And he approved of me. Though I am not sure he would have approved of me if he knew I was a writer, a breaker of the silences, not a keeper of the secrets.

And I liked having his approval, though it was only imaginary, for during a writer's day, there is never a moment's approval, only a chronic, gnawing sense that this word, this sentence, this paragraph, this book, is not good enough, will never be good enough; that the puzzles will never work themselves out; that the problems will never be solved; and that if they are, the book will never be read anyway; and so the whole goddamned thing should be abandoned once and for all.

Abandoned. For what? To shop for vegetables, without the demon in the brain making up sentences, revising sentences, imagining situations, lopping the ends off paragraphs, writing nifty little segues, planning the next book, and the one after that, and the one after that. Even as the demon in the brain is making up stories about the people it sees while shopping—these two men, for example. One old; one, older.

But, of course, without the book, without a book, the demon in the brain wouldn't be quiet. *Why no book?* it would say. *When is there going to be another book?* it would harangue. *You need to be making up sentences. Without making up sentences, you don't know what to do. And unless you start making up sentences, I'm going to annoy the shit out of you. I'm not going to leave you alone.* And then the demon would begin its infernal list. *Why not a book on biscotti; you like to bake biscotti. Maybe one on minestrone, you've cooked thirty or forty of the suckers by now; what a fucking waste of time all that cooking is unless you get a book out of it. How about one about June Miller, Henry Miller's ex; you read all those books; there's all that sex, now that would be fun for a change. I know: how about a book about finding your inner something-or-other; those books sell, they make money, they make a lot of sense. You're wasting your time. You're not getting any younger. You should be writing. You should be writing. You should be writing.*

So whether you're writing or not writing, it's all the same. The demon won't leave you alone. Even if you say *Shut the fuck up.* So you may as well go home, may as well work, may as well write. And what you wish for is the day that the demon understands that there are moments when the writer would like to be the woman who simply shops for vegetables.

Anyway.

Because the son approved of my vegetables, and because of their looks, I thought these men had to be Italian, Southern Italian. The old man reminded me of my grandfather, so long dead. And in looking at this old man, I resurrected my grandfather, saw what he might have looked like at close to ninety, and he came back to me, embodied in this old man, and I thought that I might want to write about him, about my grandfather. Thought, too, that I might want to write about this old man and how he reminded me of my grandfather.

Then, the guilt: I was studying this old man to get material; I was turning him into a subject. I was using him, the way I use everything, for my work. I was feeding on human flesh.

Later, by the celery (which I also needed, having discovered that the celery I thought I could use had rotted unnoticed in the bottom bin of my refrigerator where, when I am writing, everything rots unnoticed), I heard the old man speak. Could the son get him another plastic bag?

He spoke in dialect that sounded like my grandfather's, and that's when I knew that they were Southern Italian. And I realized why I wanted them to be Southern Italian. Because they were normal people doing what normal people do, what I was doing. Buying fruits and vegetables. Being polite and civilized. Respecting each other. Being people worthy of respect.

The night before, while waiting for my husband to join me to watch a video, I was cruising through the channels, and I caught a few moments of an episode of *The Sopranos*.

When I first heard about the show, a few years before—that it was called *The Sopranos* and that it was about Italian Americans, I became excited. I thought it was going to be a TV series celebrating important Italian American women vocalists. *How nice*, I thought. *A celebration of our accomplishments.*

217

But when I heard what it was going to be about—the same old Mafia story, but, according to the publicity, with some dramatic new twists—I knew I wouldn't watch it. When I was small, my mother had inoculated me against having anything to do with anything that concerned the Mafia.

"If you hear the word 'Mafia,'" she said, "if you hear anyone talking about the subject, walk away, leave the room. Hearing anyone talk about those thugs is dangerous. Talking about those thugs is dangerous. Hearing stories about them will pollute your mind. We're not that kind of people. Always remember, there are a few of us who are like that, but this is not who we are."

Although my mother tried to control much about my life, she never censored anything I wanted to see or anything I wanted to read. She even checked The Kinsey Report out of the local library for me when I was a teenager because the librarian wouldn't let me do it. So it wasn't censorship that motivated her telling me not to listen to stories about the Mafia.

When I was older, I learned that my mother's attitude was shaped by the stories she heard at family gatherings about relatives of relatives who were, as they say, connected. And what she knew—about how the mob destroyed poor neighborhoods by selling drugs; how mobsters threatened and intimidated legitimate small business-men into paying protection money; how they corrupted politicians; how they got young kids in poor neighborhoods to act as drug runners; how they turned young kids into thugs, got them to think there was more money in crime than in getting an education; how she knew what the underworld had done to the poor in the old country, how they controlled the water, how they helped landowners squelch rebellions for better working conditions—made her sick. My mother was the most moral person I ever knew. She believed in justice; hated inequity; despised violence. Though she also believed that guilty people should be punished one way or another.

One time, my mother heard that the daughter of one of these thugs had become addicted to heroin, was in rehab, and my mother said,

"They got what they deserved. What did they think? That they could sell drugs in poor neighborhoods, black neighborhoods, build fancy houses for their families from the profits, and not pay for it?"

The daughter died of an overdose; left a few kids behind that the thug's wife had to raise. All my mother said was "Good riddance to bad rubbish."

I watched *The Sopranos* for a few moments, thinking I probably had some obligation to popular culture to take a look, to make a judgment, rather than dismissing it without ever watching it. I saw a man murdered. Decapitated. The bloodletting nauseated me. My mother's words came back to me. *This is not who we are. Hearing stories about them will pollute your mind.*

I started thinking about the hired thugs in Puglia who had ravaged my people. Who had protected the landowner's interests. Who had instituted a reign of terror where my ancestors came from.

The landowners in the South wouldn't even sit in the same room with farmworkers to listen to what they wanted: shelters for sleeping in the field; a living wage; transportation to their distant worksites. The landowners wouldn't sit in the same room with the farmworkers because they considered them animals. They believed they had the right to control their lives. And to hire criminals to destroy anyone who challenged them, to rule through fear.

And I thought that, yes, this is what criminal outlaw groups always are. Terrorists. And that's what the Mafia is: a terrorist organization. My mother used to say, "The only good thug is a dead thug, and, beyond that, the less said, the better."

So here they were, this old man and this older man, and the son was wearing a plaid jacket, the kind that workmen wear in the winter when they pour concrete, climb telephone poles, break up pavements with pneumatic drills—a jacket that will keep out the cold, but that won't make you uncomfortably warm while you're working. And the son also had on a tweed peaked cap, worn slightly off center, like the one my grandfather wore, like the one my father wears, like the one so many men from the South of Italy wore as they disembarked in New York from their ocean voyage, carrying a single suitcase or a bundle containing everything they owned in the world except their dreams.

And the son's hands were like my grandfather's hands, like my father's hands—big, muscled, reddened, callused, and always grimy from the work. The father was stooped, though not frail, and he wore a jacket like his son's, although the colors of his were more somber. And he wore a cap like his son's. And the father's hands were like the son's hands, too—big, muscled, reddened, callused, scarred, although the dirt in the creases of the knuckles had been worn away by time because he was no longer working, not even in his garden, if he had one.

His son pushed the cart around, following his father wherever he went, saying little, offering no opinions, and this was what I liked about him, that he was silent, that he made no suggestions, that he let the old man take the lead, that he let the old man go about his business in the way that he chose.

I stood, watching them, conjecturing, as they blocked my way. And I decided that, instead of asking them to move, I wouldn't disturb them, that I would go back down the aisle and around to the other side.

It took me a few minutes to accomplish this detour. (I got sidetracked by some very beautiful Sicilian eggplants that I could grill for dinner and garnish with garlic, mint, and olive oil.) But by the time I returned to the melons, they were still standing in the same place, the father and the son, and the old man was still taking his time, still choosing his melon. And his son was still silent, still waiting. (I imagined myself in the same situation, eager to move on, urging the old man to make a choice, selecting a melon for him.)

The old man picked up a melon, shook it, sniffed it, pressed the place where the melon had been attached to the vine to determine its ripeness, passed his hand over the skin to gauge its tautness, made a face, rejected it. This was not the kind of market where you could automatically be sure that what you were buying would be tasty. So he took another, shook it, sniffed it, pressed the place where it had been attached to the vine, felt it, made a face, rejected it. Took another, went through the whole process again, repeated it a few more times, and finally, was satisfied.

I stood across from them, miming an interest in the melons, but more interested in them than in the melons.

The son stood behind, waiting, watching his father choosing the melon, as if choosing the melon was all that mattered, as if choosing the melon was the most important thing in the world.

And I wondered if this son had always treated the father in this way, with such respect. (Respect. What my father said I never gave him. Respect. What my father said I never gave my mother. *All I ask of you is that you show us some respect.*) Or if it was not respect that I was seeing, but stony silence, born of years of enmity, of the son's learning that the less he said to this old man, the better. Had the strife of decades worn them into this placidity? Did the father tell the son, "You show me the respect I deserve"? Had the son shouted back, "You earn respect; you don't deserve it simply because you're my father"? But no, I thought, it couldn't be that. The son's face was too composed; too serene.

I wanted there to have been no strife between them, none of that intergenerational struggle born from the hardship of the past.

The father turned to his son and handed him the melon. The son placed it on the seat meant for babies. They were ready to move on.

I stood there, watching them go, wishing that I could have prolonged the moment. Imagined myself calling out to the old man, imagined him turning when he heard me. Imagined myself asking him to pick me a melon. Imagined him returning to the bin, choosing one for me with the same care he had devoted to choosing his own. But I knew that to demand his attention would have been a terrible imposition, given his age, given that we were not acquainted. And given the shopping he still had to do.

FEEDING THE DEAD

The last time my father and I talked, he told me that he is doing most of the cooking in his house. His wife (the woman he married not too long after my mother died) is now living her life behind a scrim of forgetfulness and often doesn't remember to cook their food, and when she does cook, she sometimes walks away from the stove, forgets she is making a meal, and burns it. So far, there hasn't been a fire because my father's always going into the kitchen, always vigilant, always checking. But still, it's a dangerous situation. And he wonders what will happen, who will take care of them, if he gets sick.

It's a shame, he tells me, because, when Milly cooks, when she remembers what she's cooking, she cooks well. She still makes a fabulous pot roast (he loves to soak up the gravy with a good, crusty bread) and a mean apple pie if she carries a timer around the house with her and if she remembers what the timer is timing. So it isn't as bad as all that. Then, too, her family helps by coming over with prepared foods and having supper several times a week. And there are "dinner and a movie" nights at our house, when we all have a simple meal—last night, some fresh figs and prosciutto; a pasta with vine ripened tomatoes, smoked mozzarella, garlic, and basil; some green beans with garlic oil—and then watch an Italian movie together.

These dinners occur once a week, usually on Mondays. And we have settled into a wonderful routine. My father goes to a local flower shop where the proprietor is Italian; he converses with her and buys some flowers to adorn our dinner table. Milly arranges the flowers for

222

a centerpiece while we cook. Me, I just take flowers and shove them into a vase, add water. But Milly takes each flower, clips the stem, arranges, rearranges. Her centerpieces are beautiful. She jokes that she can't forget what she's doing because what she's doing is right in front of her.

Milly mourns the loss of her recent memory. But she can laugh about it. "The advantage," she says, "is that I never remember the movies we watch. You could show me the same one a dozen times and I'd be happy."

Last night, we watched Carlo Carlei's *Flight of the Innocent*. It's one of my favorites, not only because it's gorgeously filmed but also because it describes the brutalizing effects of centuries of racism towards Southern Italians, shows how gangs in the South kidnap wealthy children in the North for ransom and also for retribution.

The hero of the film is the child of a family that has kidnapped and killed a boy from the North. A rival gang assassinates his family, but he escapes by hiding between the mattress and box spring of his bed.

He knows they want him dead, so he travels all the way to Rome to find a cousin to help him. Witnesses the cousin's murder. Finds the ransom money paid for the murdered child.

But he will not continue the legacy of his family. He decides that what they have done is wrong; he longs for life in a family untainted by criminality and bloodletting, and decides to return the ransom money to the murdered child's family. He saves the child's father's life—a rival gang, pretending his son is still alive, tries to murder him when he delivers more ransom money.

At the end of the film, the child is shot by the rival gang. While unconscious, he has a fantasy about a dinner. Everyone—Southerners and Northerners alike, he and his family, the murdered child and his parents, all the people who are alive and all the people who are dead—sit around a table in the sweet light of sunset, serving one another pasta. He imagines an end to vengeance, an end to racism, an end to injustice.

Earlier in the movie, the young hero enters the room of the

murdered child. He sees his desk, his toys. He sleeps in the child's comfortable bed. The difference between the hero's bedroom and this child's is staggering. Here, opulence. There, poverty.

At the end of the film, my father says, "That's the way it was when I lived in Italy. The people who had, had a lot. The people who didn't have, didn't have anything."

My father doesn't like to complain, so when he tells me that meals in his house are a problem I wonder whether things are worse than he says.

"I make out a menu every week," he tells me. "Tuesday, *aglia olio*; Wednesday, *pasta fagioli*; Thursday, some kind of pasta. Mostly Italian foods. All those things your grandmother and my mother used to cook. Nothing fancy, nothing that takes too long. This way I know what to buy."

My father tells me he likes to have a nice meal at the end of the day. If he doesn't, he's unhappy. The meal doesn't have to be fancy. He prefers something simple but wonderful to something elaborate. "All I need," he says, "is a hunk of cheese, some good Italian bread, a few grapes, and a glass of wine."

I tell him I like to have a good meal at the end of the day, too. "Life's too short," I say, "to have one bad meal." I think of all the bad meals we had when I lived at home, wonder how my father could have been satisfied by my mother's cooking.

I watch the Food Network on television more than I care to admit. Watching people I don't know cooking food I can't eat has become my drug of choice. I figure it's better than booze, better than cocaine. I think watching TV Food has something to do with repairing wounds from childhood, with seeing a kitchen where no one fights and every dish turns out perfectly, my antidote to everything imperfect in the world. There is nothing I like doing more at the end of my workday, before I step into my own kitchen to prepare a meal, than watching TV Food. It's where I learn easy recipes and arcane information—that male eggplants are far better than females, for example, and that you can tell a female by the little dimple at the bottom of the eggplant. Knowing this kind of thing makes me feel smug and superior to Mr. and Mrs. Ordinary Shopper.

But it also makes me a fussy, obsessive, extremely inefficient, take-an-hour-to-buy-a-few-items kind of food shopper. This is why shopping takes me so long, leaves me so exhausted, why I can only choose three or four items to my husband's thirty. He finishes our weekly shopping during the time it takes me to pick out a pineapple (surreptitiously pull out a frond and smell it), a pound of Portobello mushrooms (examine the gills on the underside of each), asparagus (check out the base of each stalk, see if it's dried out; check out each tip, see if it's dried out or mashed up or wet or missing); search out purple potatoes, Forbidden rice, truffle oil, faro (an ancient grain I don't know how to prepare, but, I assure myself, I can learn), aged balsamic vinegar. This is why I usually shop alone.

No one in my family wants to shop with me unless they have a lot of time, are in a good mood, or want to have a good laugh at my expense. "Hurry, tie a ribbon around those little jars, double the price," my son Jason quips as we enter a market, pretending he is the store manager. "That little lady's in the store again, and she's coming this way!"

As I approach my sixtieth birthday, I sometimes regret that there are only three meals a day I can prepare. When I say this to some of my friends, they look at me as if I need to be institutionalized, or as if I've become a homemaker, the kind of woman they don't admire. I sit on my sofa, surrounded by cookbooks, making lists of foods I want to cook.

Homemade pumpkin ravioli with crushed amaretti biscuits mixed into the filling.

Sweet potato gnocchi with Gorgonzola sauce.

Pasta with the little veal meatballs I learned how to make in Puglia.

This is my futile way of dealing with the fact that someday I am going to die. Making a bread, stirring a sauce, cutting a frittata into little wedges—the way I have chosen to shake my fist at mortality; the way I remind myself that I am still alive.

My husband once asks me, jokingly: if I had to give up cooking or writing, which would it be? I answer, "Writing, of course," which surprises him. He believes that I am a writer above all things.

But without cooking, there can be no writing. Maybe it's because books take years to write and a pesto is finished in a few minutes, so that if I couldn't make a pesto, the burden of making a book would be too onerous. Maybe it's because the rewards in cooking, if you know your way around the kitchen, are predictable and immediate, and they temper the reality that the rewards of writing are few, infrequent, and unpredictable, so that cooking is a wonderful antidote to the writing life. Cooking gets you out of your head. It's social. It makes you focus on the present. It's sensuous. Whatever the reasons, I know that I couldn't write if I didn't cook.

Though sometimes, it does get out of hand, like when I engage in cooking marathons, and sometimes I wonder what kind of a writer I would be if my writing time weren't interspersed with endless trips to the kitchen to check on something I'm cooking.

The urge to engage in a cooking marathon comes upon me when I least expect it, and usually when I have an enormous number of writing tasks to do—a muddle to clear up in my writing, an article to finish, proofs of a book to correct. At these times, the urge comes upon me to cook something incredibly complicated that will take me the better part of the workday and foreclose the possibility that I will unmuddle the muddle, finish the article, correct the proofs, that I will, in fact, do anything but cook all day.

Although this is very much a when-the-mood-strikes-me kind of thing, a few principles have become apparent over the years.

1. What I decide to cook must require an enormous amount of time and employ a cooking technique I have always wanted to perfect but have not yet mastered.

2. What I decide to cook must require a long list of ingredients and/
   or special equipment, and I must have none of the ingredients or
   equipment, so that I must travel to one or (preferably) several
   markets and also to Williams-Sonoma.

3. What I decide to cook must require that I use many pots and pans
   and that I make a gigantic mess, which I am not able to clean
   before my husband comes home from work.

4. What I decide to cook must require that I use every knife I own, so
   that my husband, when he walks in the door and sees them all
   neatly lined up, will say, "I see you've been practicing your knife
   throwing again."

5. What I decide to cook, when it is cooked, must not yield
   something that we would, under normal circumstances, really
   like to eat. In fact, it is essential that what I cook will be an
   enormous disappointment (the onion, escarole, and anchovy pie,
   for example; the *sformato di melanzane*—eggplant mold) and that,
   the day after, Ernie and I will both admit that it wasn't very good,
   and I will say that it was a foolish waste of time and vow that I will
   never make it again.

Like today. I'm supposed to be writing. But I am involved in what
has turned into a gigantic baking project even as I've promised myself
that I'll finish working on this piece about my father and me. It's not
yet noon, but the baking has already gotten completely out of
control.

Early this morning, I thought I'd make a simple little Italian
bread, an old favorite. I thought it would be nice to fill the house
with the smell of bread baking as I was writing about how the smell
of bread baking would make the words come more easily.

Then, I thought, Well, why not try a complicated recipe from my
new bread cookbook, a fig-walnut bread. I needed the figs, the
walnuts, a pan of a size I didn't own. If I'm making one loaf, I
reasoned, I might as well make two, and if l make two, I might as
well make four so I have a few loaves to give away. So here I am, on a

writing day, shopping for supplies, then making four loaves of fig-walnut bread, a leavened bread using a *biga*, an Italian starter, which I keep frozen and can easily defrost.

I cut up all the sticky little figs, which took half an hour and destroyed the edge of my good knife. So I took a little break in the baking (which was supposed to be a little break from the writing) for some knife sharpening.

I sit down at my desk; I want to begin writing a little scene about how I've been going shopping with my father. I also want to write about how I've gone to the cemetery with him because he's been pestering me to see where his parents are buried, where my mother and sister and other grandparents are buried, all crammed in death into one cemetery plot like we were all crammed in life into our tiny tenement apartments. I want to write about how freaked out I get when I see my father's name and birthdate are already carved on the gravestone, and yet how I don't feel any sense of loss while I'm there, how I don't feel very much of anything, though I like that you can see New York City from the gravesite, perhaps even catch a sliver of one of the buildings of Hunter College where I teach.

While I'm at the cemetery, I get pissed off at all the rules—no evergreens, no photos, no plastic flowers—so that there is a totalitarian sameness to all the graves, none of the lively eccentricity I have seen in foreign cemeteries—little strands of beads, locks of hair, braids of palm, gaudy plastic flowers, faded photographs of families adorning the graves. I decide that I will not be buried in a place like this, that I will be burned and have my ashes tossed across the waters of a nature reserve I love in Sag Harbor. I want to write about this dumb obvious insight I get about how we all die and how the dead outnumber the living and how the trees outside my house will be there after I'm dead, and this crazy idea that you shouldn't bring flowers to people's graves, you should bring food to the dead, that you should bring them the kinds of meals they liked to eat in life, that you should feed the dead, that you should have little picnics at their gravesites; and I want to describe how, when my father's not looking,

I plant a biscotti my husband's baked (I happen to have it in my bag in case I get hungry) deep into the soil of my family's grave for my mother and sister and grandparents. I want to write about this, even though I know that what I've done is crazy, that feeding the dead is a crazy idea.

And then I remember how, before my mother went into the hospital to die, sick as she was, she cooked meals for my father, packed them in little plastic containers, labeled each with its contents, froze them. She cooked a lot; she may not have known that she was dying, but she knew that she would be away for a very long time. I remember how, after my mother died, I called my father and invited him to dinner, but he tells me he's fine, he's going to have chicken scarpariello for supper.

"Chicken scarpariello," I say. "When did you learn to cook that?"

"I didn't cook it," he says. "Your mother did. You know, that chicken with sausage and peppers that she made that the kids liked so much."

I wonder whether my father is seeing ghosts. Whether his unexpressed grief is causing him to hallucinate.

"Mom?" I ask.

He hears the horror in my voice. Laughs. Tells me it's the food my mother cooked for him before she died.

I try to imagine what it's like for your wife to die; what it's like to eat the food she's cooked for you before she dies. It must be like inhaling the air trapped inside a balloon she's blown up and left behind.

Then I remember how, a couple of days after that, I call my father again, invite him to dinner again, how he says no again. I wonder whether my father is again eating what I've started calling my mother's death food.

But no. A neighbor, Milly the widow from down the block, my mother's old friend, has come to visit him, and she's brought over a casserole for them to share.

"Beware of widows bearing casseroles," I say, and he laughs. I already know he'll marry Milly, and that's fine with me. He'll have someone to take care of him, and I won't have to worry.

I want to write about all these things but I keep making trips to the kitchen to check the *biga*, the consistency of the dough (*I have to keep checking the dough or I'll fuck the whole thing up if the dough rises too much*, I tell myself for the thirtieth or fortieth time), to add the flour, yeast, figs, and nuts to the *biga*, to knead the bread and set it to rise, to heat the oven.

By now I realize that today it will be impossible to write about the trip to the cemetery, about my mother's death food, about Milly's widow casserole, and I really don't want to write about the cemetery anyway. I want to write about how my father and I have learned to get along. I've started out in the wrong place. But I have to write. I must keep my appointment with myself. I can't sabotage my writing. I must provide a good model for my students. I can't use my craziness about food to get in the way of my work because my craziness about food is supposed to help my work, not harm it.

So, I decide to write about how I'm making the fig nut bread on the day I want to write about going to the cemetery, about my mother's death food, about Milly's widow casserole. I tell myself that showing the process of writing the piece in the piece is a good thing. I tell myself I'm postmodern. I tell myself I'm full of shit.

By now, my hands are sticky; my keyboard is sticky; my desk has a little film of flour on it; my bread dough—which sits next to my computer so I can keep an eye on it while I write—keeps distracting me. And my brand-new cookbook has a grease stain trailing down the picture of the completed bread, which makes me sad because I've been doing two things at once (violating this week's primary personal development goal, to focus on one thing at a time), because I've been moving too fast (violating another personal development goal, to savor the moment and move slowly through life). But, I tell myself, the grease stain isn't such a bad thing. Because in years to come, it will remind me that there has been this bread, that there has been this day, and perhaps I will even remember that on the day that I baked this bread I also wrote these words.

I have asked my father if he needs any help, if I can do his shopping, bring over some food. But this resolutely independent father of mine always says no, he's managing fine, and he enjoys shopping and cooking.

Each week, my father goes to the senior citizens' center in his town and helps cook meals for the "seniors," most of whom are twenty years younger than he is. He has become known as the Spaghetti Man because no one else who works down there, he tells me, knows how to cook pasta al dente, the way it should be cooked. He knows his way around a kitchen, a big kitchen. And he's not afraid to experiment. "I throw in a little of this, a little of that," he says, "and *voilà*, we have a meal."

My father still shovels his own driveway, cleans his own house, fixes his own car, repairs his own appliances. Last year, he fell off a ladder when he was fixing the roof, lost consciousness, wound up in the hospital, pooh-poohed the whole experience, and was back climbing ladders again as soon as he returned home.

"You gotta present a moving target," he tells me when I ask him why he doesn't hire someone to help him. He believes that by keeping busy, he will continue to elude death.

Though he won't accept my help, I still feel guilty about my father having to cook for himself, so I show up at his house with plastic containers filled with food cooked especially for him and Milly. I cook without too much salt, without any saturated fat. He has a bad heart condition, and we're very grateful that he's lived this long. Still, he's a stubborn old bastard, refuses to change his diet, says that if he's lived this long eating anything he wants, it's stupid to change now.

"I should have died in the war, should have died in a fire, should have died from my first heart attack—they pronounced me dead, you know," he says, when I try to persuade him to watch his diet, "but I didn't. Don't worry about me. Only the good die young."

That he's not young anymore does not seem to cross my father's mind. He lives his life as if it's charmed. For what he says isn't exaggeration. Although he is not the kind of man who boasts of his past, who tells war stories, I know that he escaped death many times in the Pacific, that he watched his friends die, that he watched ships go down a few hundred yards from his ship. When he was a fireman, he eluded death by chance many times. But the closest he came to dying was when I was a teenager and he was a fire chief and men from his company were fighting a fire in a bowling alley in a nearby town.

The chief in charge of the fire ordered men from my father's company to go down an alley, break open a side door and direct water inside, an order, my father says, he never would have given.

There was no sign that this fire would be lethal—when they arrived on the scene the firemen saw only a few puffs of smoke, nothing more. Still, my father's instincts told him this was going to be a bad one. And he was right.

My father followed orders, went down the alley, stopped for a moment and turned to see what was going on behind him, to see where the rest of his men were. He saw a civilian, an elected official, far too near the alleyway, and he yelled at this man to move back, to get out of the way.

As soon as his men broke down the door, there was a tremendous explosion; the roof blew into the air; the walls blew out and collapsed. One wall came down just two feet from my father, crushing five of his men, the men he had been with until he turned away from them for what couldn't have been more than fifteen, twenty seconds. That pause saved his life. But left him grieving for a very long time.

I tell my father about Whole Foods, the great new market that has just opened. How it's spacious, with high ceilings and tile floors, and food so beautifully arranged that shopping becomes an aesthetic experience. How it's right on the Hudson River. How it sells prepared food: wonderful soups like Harvest Vegetable, beef barley, roasted tomato; roasted chickens; barbecued spareribs; grilled vegetables; sautéed chicken breasts; the works. And great bread. How you can buy your lunch there and eat it at a table overlooking the water.

My father agrees to meet me. Tells me he'll bring along his shopping list. We haven't been together alone in a while, although I see him every week with his wife, or with my sons and my daughters-in-law.

I suggest we meet, shop, then have lunch. I have vowed that I will protect him from my shopping habits. I will let him choose anything he wants without making a comment or suggesting that he choose something else, and I will not choose something else for him.

Still, I plan to show him all the prepared foods. I hope that if he sees what's available, he'll buy something already cooked and spare himself some work. He's looking very tired lately from doing so much of the household work. But he doesn't. He tells me he likes trying to replicate the foods his mother used to cook.

We enjoy our times alone together, talking about his past, about my mother, my sister, my grandparents. Until now, I have been reluctant to hear his stories. But lately I've realized that he won't be alive forever, and I want to know whatever he can tell me about his life, about the life of my grandparents, before he dies. I want to understand how my life continues theirs.

So we establish a ritual of having lunch together and revisiting the past. How two people who spent most of their lives fighting with each other have finally become friends is one of the great miracles of my life. And as we eat, my father tells me stories, and my father's stories of our family's past break the logjam in my feelings about him.

Recently, I have told him how, when I was a child, he terrified me, have told him how angry I am at how he treated me.

"I never meant to hurt you," he says.

"But how could I know that?" I ask. "I was just a child."

"I'm sorry," he says.

My father fiddles with what's left of his meal. "I'm learning to express my inner feelings," he says. "We're the only ones left now. We have to learn how to get along."

To end with this, I think, *that we have learned to get along.*

Today, he tells me how Milly's been forgetting things, how worried he is about her because she won't take her pills and she sleeps all the time.

"I have to wake her up every day," he says, shaking his head.

"What time does she get up if you don't wake her?" I ask.

"Oh, about nine o'clock," he says, as if this is a very bad thing.

I remember my father pulling the covers off me and my sister on weekends, yelling "Up and at 'em! The early bird gets the worm!"

"Nine o'clock," I say, "is a perfectly respectable hour for Milly to get up. She's worked hard all her life; she's entitled to rest whenever she wants to."

When my father was courting Milly, he would drop to one knee and serenade her—"Some Enchanted Evening," "Danny Boy," "Ave Maria"—until he broke down her resistance to remarrying after twenty years of living alone and doing things her way.

In the years they've lived together, she's asked me many times, "Was your father such a pain in the ass when he lived with your mother?" I tell her something, not everything, about our lives and ask how she deals with him when he gets nasty. "I love him. I ignore him. It's easier to be his wife than his daughter," she says.

A fog rises off the Hudson. We can see it through the windows as we eat. "At first," my father says, "I used to get mad about how Milly was always forgetting things—the food on the stove, the laundry in the dryer, her pills. Now it's better because I realize it's not her fault."

It has been hard for me to see my father today, though I am gladdened by our conversation. I have watched him walk toward the store slowly, and he looks as if he is in pain and short of breath; the old jauntiness in his step isn't there, and for the first time I see how very old he is and I realize that, one day, he is going to die. Still, as I tell him when he joins me at the table, for an old bastard he's plucky as hell.

My father looks away from me, looks at the Hudson, and his eyes tear. He reaches into his pocket, pulls out his wallet, fiddles with it, searches in one of its little compartments, retrieves something, and hands it to me across the table. It is my mother's wedding band.

"Her fingers were bigger than yours," he says, when I hold up my hand to show him how the ring looks. I wonder why my father is giving me this ring now, for he has cherished it since my mother's death, and I know that it will come to me when he dies. Is he sicker than he says?

His eyes tear. "You know," my father says, "the older you get, the more you look like your mother."

It's true. There are moments when I glance in the minor and see her face, not mine. When I first noticed this growing resemblance, I was disconcerted: I'd never wanted to be like my mother. Lately, I see the merging of our faces as a gift, this continuation of her in me.

My father reaches into his pocket, pulls out his shopping list. I wipe my eyes.

"So," I say, "what do you have to buy?"

He tells me he doesn't have to buy much—some celery, some provolone, a few cans of crushed tomatoes, some garlic, some parsley.

We clean up our places, find a cart, start making our way towards the produce department.

"Your mother," my father says, "now, she was a great cook,"

I want to say that, no, my mother was not a great cook, she was not even a good cook. That my mother, more often than not, was a really lousy cook. But I am grateful to him for giving me my mother's ring, and it seems important to him to remember my mother in this way. And so I say, "Yes, I liked her pumpkin pie."

WIPING THE BOWL

Just after my grandmother fell out of bed one morning, tore her nightdress off, and crawled around the floor naked (me, having come to watch her for a few hours so my mother could do some food shopping; her, refusing to let me help her back into bed; me, unable to control her or summon help; my small son Jason, witnessing this, terrified), my parents decided that it was time for my grandmother to be taken to a nursing home, that final stop on the railroad of life's journey.

She had been sick for months, but I was never told what her illness was. At first, she came downstairs each day, doubled over in pain, cooked a little something for herself, and retreated to her bedroom for the rest of the day. After a while, she couldn't get out of bed, and my mother took care of her—brought her food, changed her bedding, sponged her down, combed her hair, emptied her bedpan.

Through these few months, there was a silence in the house that had never been there before. My grandmother was too sick to fight. My mother was too exhausted. If my grandmother didn't want to eat something my mother had prepared, my mother shrugged her shoulders, took the food away, and went back downstairs.

So my grandmother was taken to a nursing home, where no one would understand her language, where what she needed would never be brought to her. She went unwillingly, the old fight resurfacing.

It took four men to subdue her, four men to hold her down, four men to wrestle her out of her bed, four men to strap her onto a stretcher, four men to take her down the stairs, four men to load her into an ambulance.

All the while she raved in dialect. Told the men that my mother was stealing her money. Sending her away so that she could take her money from her. Told the men that my mother wasn't her blood. Called for her mother to help her. Called for the saints to help her. Called for me to help her. But I wasn't there.

The nursing home she went to was not a fancy one with private rooms and a solarium and a music room and a beauty salon to get your hair done up for company. No. The nursing home my parents sent her to was a bare-bones, piss-smelling, short-staffed kind of nursing home, run by the county, where the very poor and the very unwanted came to end their lives in giant wards cared for as well as the overworked, exhausted, underpaid nurses could manage. Which is to say, they were not cared for very much at all.

My mother said that she did not have the money for that other kind of place. But I didn't believe her. And I was right. My mother *did* have the money. She had economized all her married life, had bought stocks, had saved thousands and thousands of dollars. She just didn't want to spend her money on my grandmother.

At the time, I did not have any money—I was in graduate school, with two kids, a husband in medical training, and lots of debt. Although whether I would have helped my grandmother if I had had the money, I don't really know.

After I went to college, left the house, got married, had children, she faded from my life. When I called home, I never asked to speak to her. When I returned home for holidays, we exchanged only greetings, never any conversation. Still, my presence, my family's presence in the house cheered her. She dandled my children on her knee, crooned to them in dialect, played cat's cradle with them, sat with them while they watched *Sesame Street* on television, kissed the tops of their heads, which she had never done to me or to my sister.

My mother went to see her stepmother almost every day that she was in the nursing home. And she always came home crying because

237

my grandmother wouldn't eat. She'd call me to tell me how my grandmother was faring, and would say she was upset because the food in the nursing home was unfamiliar to my grandmother but that there were rules against her bringing my grandmother food. After a while, my mother started to believe that my grandmother was refusing food to spite her. My mother couldn't let herself see that my grandmother couldn't eat because she was dying.

"Go see her," my mother said to me after a few months. She was terrified of my grandmother dying, perhaps because having even *this* mother now seemed better than having no mother at all.

And so I went to see my grandmother, carrying carnations for her, on a day when the maple outside the window of her ward blazed red, although she couldn't see it, because her bed was not near the window, and because she still could not get out of bed. And on that day, I gave my grandmother a few sips of water to drink, and I fed her applesauce, a food that, so far as I know, she had never eaten at home.

She didn't eat much, a teaspoon or two, from the small quantity I had dished out into a little bowl. Still, I told myself, a few teaspoons of something was better than nothing at all.

I could tell that she was near death. But I did not feel anything about this, because I was too busy with my life to let myself feel anything at all.

I could tell that she was near death because she could not pick her head up from the pillow, could barely lift her arms, and couldn't speak. Still, she looked at me, and I could tell that she recognized me, and her eyes teared. And I told myself that my coming here to feed her was a very good thing, and necessary; told myself that these few spoonfuls of nourishment would prolong her life. Told myself, who hadn't yet been to see her, who wouldn't see her alive again, that it was the least I could do for her, after all she had done for me. I remembered how she had taught me to bake bread, taught me how to knit. How she had acted like I was worthy. How she had told me not to pay attention to my mother's criticism. How she had interposed her body between me and my father.

I told myself that I would come to see my grandmother again, and again and again. That I could make the time for her. Should make the time for her. But didn't.

When my grandmother was finished eating, weak as she was, she reached for the bowl. It took much effort, this reaching, and I could not understand at first what she was reaching for, what she wanted, what she needed to do.

I gave her the bowl. She took it from my hand. Held it where she could see it.

And then she took the napkin that I had tucked under her chin to keep her clean. And she wiped the inside of the bowl. She cleaned the bowl as best she could.

In dying, as in living, she cleaned up after herself, this Southern Italian woman, who wanted no other woman to make tidy what she had messed.

It was, as I have said, the last time that I saw her. After that, my mother told me, she was in so much pain that she screamed all the time, disturbing the other women on the ward. So she was given morphine. And more morphine. Enough morphine to ease her pain. Enough to quiet her. Enough morphine to help her die in peace.

This is what I think about when I remember my grandmother. How she baked her bread. And how she cleaned her bowl. And how I never thanked her for all that she had done for me.

NO MORE COOKING, NO MORE FOOD

In the final autumn of her life, my mother could not move. Could not move her arms, could not move her hands or her fingers. Could not move her legs, her feet, her toes, her head. Could not speak, could not say anything. Could not move her jaw, could not chew, could not swallow. Hence could not cook, could not eat.

A tube inserted in her body was now her only means of sustenance. The tube, inserted against our will, against her desire, against the instructions that she had given us long before it came to this. For she knew, we all knew, that starving to death is not a terrible way to die if one has lived a sufficiently long life, if one is not starving to death before one's time, and that there is a euphoric delirium that precedes the dying, that eases it.

What my mother had said when she was still conscious, when she was having trouble swallowing, when she could no longer move her arms, when she was having trouble hearing, and seeing, was this: "Don't let them feed me through a tube. If it's my time to go, it's my time to go. And, please God, let me go quickly."

This, she said matter-of-factly, as if she were saying "Don't forget to take out the garbage; don't forget to unload the dishwasher; and make sure that someone takes the zucchini in the refrigerator and uses them so they won't go to waste."

The "please God" had astonished me, for my mother hadn't been to church, hadn't taken the sacraments, in a very long time, and I wondered whether, like so many others, she was turning to religion at the end of her life. But then I recalled that my mother had said "please God" frequently without intending to invoke any deity, as in "Please God, let these kids stop driving me crazy," as in "Please God, let Lou come home before this dinner is ruined," as in "Please God, let this old woman leave me alone."

We knew, and she knew, too, that providing nutrition through a tube prolongs the agony of dying, the final letting go, though of course we were not ready for that; at least, I was not—for this is not something that one can prepare for, this dying of the mother, this ceasing to be of the one who gave us life, this departing of the woman whose life is so entangled with our own, so that to lose her is to lose a part of ourselves that we never acknowledged belonged to her.

My mother, though, was ready. It had seemed to me that my mother had wanted to die ever since my sister killed herself. It had seemed to me that my mother had invited dying, had welcomed it: one day, a year after my sister killed herself, she told me that she had almost been hit by a car while crossing the street in front of her house to get to the mailbox to mail a letter to a friend; she said she didn't realize she was crossing directly in front of an oncoming car, but I wondered. And a little while before she entered the hospital, she deliberately stopped taking all the pills that were keeping her alive (without telling us; without telling her doctor, who had told her to stop only one; this we discovered later).

As my mother lay dying, I cleaned my refrigerator in a manner that would have pleased her, which is not something that I had ever done before. I drew up menu plans, made shopping lists, and spent a long time shopping for food at Fairway, my favorite food store at the time. Now that it was clear that my mother could not nourish me, it became important to learn how to care for myself. I focused on trying to make good meals, and in my journal I recorded everything I was cooking for my family, everything that I was eating, as if my cooking could feed her, as if my eating could be her eating, as if my cooking and eating could keep her alive.

*Steak, done rare; and ratatouille, and new potatoes boiled, then turned round
and round and browned with cumin butter, salt, and pepper
Pasta with caramelized garlic and onions, browned pignoli nuts and saffron
and nice golden raisins soaked in vermouth
Roast chicken, potato salad made with yogurt, sautéed pea pods
Italian burgers, pan fried with a vermouth sauce, tiny fresh carrots with lemon
and orange sauce; fresh corn
Scallops, pan seared, with fresh oregano, Parmesan cheese, green beans, a salad,
fresh strawberries with cannoli cream
Broiled lamb chops, lots of salad, fruit
Chicken and vegetable kabobs with brown rice*

The last meal I had prepared for my mother at my house before she
went into the hospital was nothing special, nothing fancy, nothing I
had spent time planning or preparing. A brunch with store-bought
bagels, smoked salmon from a local Jewish deli, freshly squeezed
orange juice. We talked about my love of Paris as we ate, about how
much I loved eating simple, perfectly prepared meals there in bistros
where you could sit outside. My mother seemed interested, which was
unusual for her, because very little had interested her since my sister
had died, so I suggested that all of us—her, me, my father, my
husband—should go to Paris together for her birthday, in August.
She didn't say yes, but she didn't say no either.

But by August, my mother was in the hospital. And on her
birthday, which she spent in the hospital, I made a party for her,
because I feared (and I was right) that it would be the last birthday of
her life. I bought the Carvel ice cream cake that she loved (made with
extra chocolate-cookie crunchies and extra chocolate syrup), her
favorite cream soda, party hats, party napkins, cups, and plates,
party balloons, party noisemakers.

No one else from the family was there. My father, husband, and
older son were working and would visit later that evening while I was
teaching; my younger son was away at college. But several nurses
(always on the lookout for sweets) wandered in. They all still believed

that my mother would survive, and that we should have a real party when she came home. Somehow, I sensed that she wouldn't come home. And I was right. So I am glad that I made her that party before she died.

The nurses and I sang for her. And, as I lighted the candles, I sang "Happy Birthday, dear Mommy, Happy Birthday to You," although I hadn't called my mother Mommy for a very long time.

My mother seemed pleased with our little celebration. And as she opened my gift of special hand cream in a flowered china dispenser, we talked about how much she had enjoyed baking, how much she had disliked cooking.

"The first cake I made your father for dessert," she told me, "was a refrigerator cake. I made it with chocolate wafers, chocolate pudding, and whipped cream. You made it in the morning; and it cooled in the refrigerator all day. It was a refrigerator cake.

"When your father came home from work that day, I was so excited. I told him, 'I baked you a cake for desert,' and showed him what it was. Instead of saying thank you, he said 'That's no baked cake,' and I cried. You know your father. He could be a real bastard."

I wanted to say "You don't have to tell me," but chose not to. I knew they loved each other still, for I had seen how my father dressed specially to visit her in the hospital, had seen her brighten as he entered the room, and so I didn't want, at this time, to speak of old wounds. Through it all—the depressions, the madness, the hospitalizations, the shock treatments, the suicide of my sister, my father loved my mother still.

Because she was awake, and still alert after her party, I read to my mother. Stories from Grace Paley's *Enormous Changes at the Last Minute*. I had chosen Grace's stories because I knew the working-class neighborhood she described would seem familiar to my mother, and because many of the stories were very short so that reading them to my mother wouldn't overtax her.

Through the next few days I read her "Wants," "Debts," "Gloomy

Tune," "Living," "The Burdened Man," "Enormous Changes at the Last Minute," "The Little Girl," "A Conversation with My Father."

The last story I read my mother before she stopped hearing was "The Immigrant Story." "Isn't it a terrible thing to grow up in the shadow of another person's sorrow?" one character asks. And I thought *Yes, it certainly is.*

"What if this sorrow is all due to history?" I read. "I thank God every day that I'm not in Europe. I thank God I'm American-born."

"Amen to that," my mother said. "Amen."

After I had finished reading the book, I told my mother I knew Grace Paley.

"Oh?" my mother replied, interested, and I wondered why I had never told her things like this before; why I shared so little of my life with her; why I hadn't told her before about my trip to Barcelona to a writers' conference, where I had seen Grace Paley; or about the marvelous sweet shrimp I'd had there, and the spinach with pine nuts, raisins, and Serrano ham. I surely could not tell her now, for she was having difficulty swallowing, and my telling her would have been unkind, and it seemed that soon she wouldn't be able to eat at all.

"Yes," I said, "I know Grace Paley," and nothing more. I remembered that I shared so little of my life with her because my mother disapproved of the life I lead, of the time I took away from my children to do my work.

Even when it was clear that my mother was dying, my father wouldn't believe it. Against doctor's orders and common sense, he would help her out of bed, and force her to try to walk, and when she collapsed on the floor, he would complain to the nurses that she wasn't getting enough physical therapy.

Once, I saw him trying to feed her pudding after she had stopped eating because she couldn't swallow. I saw him trying to force the spoon into her mouth, thinking, perhaps, that if he could get that small mouthful of food into her, he could keep her alive. My mother's eyes said, "I'm too weak to fight him; I can't resist; but I can't do what he wants."

The pudding dribbled off the spoon, down my mother's chin, onto her nightgown.

"Stop that," I said, rushing to the bed, pulling the spoon out of my father's hand, away from my mother's mouth. "Can't you see that she couldn't eat even if she wanted to?"

"But," my father said, "if she doesn't eat, she'll die."

Two years after my mother died, my father and Milly came to Paris with my husband and me to celebrate his seventy-eighth birthday. This was the trip that I had wanted my mother and father to take.

For my father's birthday dinner, we took him to the restaurant Jules Verne in the Eiffel Tower.

Morels were in season, and we each ordered them, prepared in a cream and cheese sauce, for an appetizer.

"How your mother would have loved this," my father said.

"Yes, she would have," I responded, although I was sure that my mother never would have come to Paris, never would have dined in this restaurant, for it was difficult for her to indulge in such sybaritic pleasures. She was always uncomfortable in restaurants, thought them a waste of money. Aside from eating at roadside stands when we went on vacations, my mother didn't go to a "proper" restaurant until after I was in college.

If, by some miracle, we had lured my mother to Paris, and to the Jules Verne, she never would have ordered the morels. She never would have permitted herself to spend so much money on food—$60 for an appetizer—even if she was being treated; especially if she was being treated.

She would have filled up on the bread. She would have studied the menu, rejected the possibility of an appetizer, asked about the prices of the entrees and picked out the least expensive item on the menu, even if it was something that she didn't like. She would been delighted at the *amuse-bouche*, for she would have felt that she was getting something free. She would have permitted herself coffee, even dessert—a chocolate mousse perhaps. But when the little sweets that are presented with coffee in French restaurants arrived, she would have been upset, realizing that she could have done without dessert and saved money.

She would have taken a box of matches as a memento of the evening. She would have been delighted at the little tongs for picking up the cubes of Demerara and white sugar served with coffee, and she would have taken several cubes, placed them in her handbag.

Taking sugar from restaurants was one of the many ways that my mother economized. When she and my father went on road trips, she always took four extra rolls and several packets of sugar from wherever she and my father ate their supper. If they had eaten at a buffet, she would take, too, some extra meat, some cheese, some fruit for the next day. When she got back to her table, she would pack it all into a plastic bag that she kept in her purse. Then she would take two tissues from her purse and shake some salt into one, some pepper into another, and fold the tissues into neat little packets and stow these as well. She would use the salt and pepper to season the tomatoes my father and she ate on the road.

Though stale, the rolls would form the basis of their breakfast the following morning, which they would eat in their motel room. They would drink coffee that my father would make in the small automatic coffeemaker that I had gotten them one Christmas. (The stolen sugar would sweeten my mother's.) For lunch, they would stop somewhere on the side of the road, and picnic on sandwiches made with the two other stale rolls and whatever my mother might have scavenged from the buffet table. They always traveled with a capacious Styrofoam hamper, into which they would pack cold cuts, fruit, and ground coffee (Eight O'Clock Coffee from the A & P) for the road. There would always be a package of Stella D'oro biscuits for my father to have with his coffee.

At the end of each day, my mother never recorded in her trip diary notes about where she and my father had traveled or notes about the sights they had seen. For she was uninterested in seeing new places; she went on vacations for my father's sake and because he insisted upon it. She never climbed to the tops of hills to see views, or mounted stairs to gaze down into the water of a canal, or clambered into a small boat to see a sight across the water. She lingered behind, and not grudgingly, while my father had his little adventures.

Staying behind gave her the opportunity to figure her accounts and to record what that they had spent for gas, food, and lodging.

"Monday, 16 July, Lexington MA. Breakfast, $0.00. Lunch $0.00. Dinner (Early Bird Special): $25.36 (with tip)."

She never recorded what she ate, just as she never recorded what she saw, for what she ate was immaterial, just as what she saw was immaterial. Because where my mother really wanted to be was in her own home, engaged in her daily routine. Habit was the way she warded off disintegration and chaos.

In the hospital where my mother died, they did not let their patients starve to death. It was inhumane, they said. And so, the tube. Against her wishes and ours. Inserted when none of us was there. While my father was having a greasy hamburger and fries in the hospital canteen. While I was shopping for the chicken, pea pods, and potatoes that I would cook for dinner.

And so the prolonged suffering. Hers. Ours (though ours was nothing like hers, of course). The prolonged dying. The prolonged life that would have ended sooner if it had ended naturally.

And the rage—my rage, chiefly, for my father was too spent to rage—that this had been done to my mother at the end of her life. That the choice she had made, a choice about which she was certain (and she had been uncertain much of her life, unsure of what to cook for supper, what to buy at the supermarket) was contravened.

*　　*　　*

I looked at my mother, through her long dying days, wanting conversation, wanting what she could not give, wanting what I would never have again, for she had long since ceased to speak. Wanting what I had never had with her, really: the sustenance of stories shared, embellished. I wanted normal talks, ordinary talks, talks like other people have, like other mothers and their daughters have—about what we did during the day, about what we cooked for dinner, about what we felt about our lives.

I wanted to know, too, what had happened to her when she was a child. What did she remember? What had my grandmother done to her? What did she know of my grandmother's life? Her father's life? Did she know about what life was like for them in Puglia before they came to America?

And I wanted to know how she made her pumpkin pie for Thanksgiving, the one thing, the only thing, she cooked that I would miss, that I wanted the recipe for. I wanted to know what her secret ingredient was, for that there *was* a secret ingredient, she told everyone who loved her pumpkin pie.

I wanted to talk to her about work, and love, and books, forgetting that, although intelligent, she was a woman who did not read much—*Reader's Digest*, or *Life* magazine, perhaps, at the end of her day, for there were far more important things for her to do, like cleaning her kitchen, doing the laundry, ironing my father's shirts, straightening her closets (though there was not very much to straighten, for she had few possessions).

"Come closer," I said to her, once, as she lay dying, hearing my voice come back to me through the ether air of the hospital. "Come closer," I said, and nothing more, though she couldn't respond to me, I know, couldn't move, couldn't come closer. I wanted to say, "I'll tell you something wonderful, something you've been waiting for me to tell you for a long, long time."

I wanted to speak to my mother one last time, though I knew she couldn't hear me, for there is a work in dying that excludes the living, work that requires concentration, work that precludes listening to, or caring about, the living. I have seen it, and so I know that dying is hard work, solitary work, work unlike any other, for it is the ultimate and most difficult work of one's life.

What my mother was doing must be done by each of us, alone.

I wanted to speak to my mother just one last time, for she was moving into the land of the dead, a place I didn't know about, didn't want to know about yet, though that place has beckoned me once, twice, three times, and that place had already claimed my sister, younger than me by four years. It is a place into which I will one day follow her, but not, I hope, too soon.

Would she remember me after she died? I wondered. Would she remember light? Music? The taste of oranges?

That my mother had loved me, I couldn't be certain. I sometimes thought that her not loving me was her greatest love. In not loving me, she could ensure that I would stay alive, for everyone whom she had really, truly loved—her mother, her father, my sister—had died. In not loving me, she ensured that I would not be like her, for I would despise her for not loving me, and so would not want to be like her, and so would not become mad. As she had become, often; as my sister had become. I would linger at the boundaries of madness, still, and often, though not recently.

What I wanted to say to my mother as she lay dying was "I love you," although I was not sure I did love her. But I thought that, perhaps, if I said the words "I love you," words that I had never managed to say to her before, words that she had never managed to say to me, then perhaps the feeling might follow. I wanted to love my mother before she died.

TEARING THE BREAD

My mother died in autumn, like my grandmother. Though these two could agree on nothing during their lives, they agreed that autumn, with its leaves all dry and sere and red and bronze and gold and falling to the ground, was a fitting time to die.

As my mother lay dying, I wanted to tell her this story. What I wanted to tell her, but could not, was a fantasy, a dream. I could not tell her because she could not hear. I could not tell her because we were beyond language, because whatever we should have said to each other before had not been said. Whatever we should have said to each other, we would not say. And so, this.

Imagine that we are together. And imagine that, just once, we aren't fighting, we aren't hating each other, you aren't disappointed in me, and I am not disappointed in you. Imagine that we know it will come to this; imagine that because we know it will come to this, we have learned to love each other.

Imagine that we are having a picnic. There is a cloth laid upon the ground (an embroidered cloth) and on it there are simple things: some cheese—the smoked mozzarella from Dante's that you liked so much, the fresh mozzarella from Fairway that I liked so much—and roasted peppers (I might have made them myself if I had the time that day); some mortadella, because neither of us likes the taste of prosciutto. And bread, yes, bread. Not my homemade bread, because today I was too busy to bake the bread. But good bread, nevertheless, a sturdy Italian bread, like the one your stepmother used to make.

I had asked you whether we should take your stepmother with us to our picnic. But you hesitated, not wanting to introduce any discord into this day that we were planning. And then said, "Not this time; maybe next time," and so I knew that you were not yet ready, that you might never be ready to join her in celebration. But that we were together in this way was miracle enough for me for now.

About the bread, there would have been some disagreement. You would have argued for a fat crusty Italian loaf without sesame seeds. (You had, by now, given up your taste for what we used to call American bread.) I would have wanted them—the seeds, that is—for the complex, nutty flavor they gave the loaf. But we decided that at this time in our lives, we could buy two breads and enjoy them both: the one that you wanted, without the seeds, and the one that I wanted, with.

Today, we sit together on the cloth under the shade of an almond tree in a sacred grove of almond trees in full blossom, this place that we return to where we have never been before, and we eat. And because there are almond trees, we must be in the South of Italy, in Puglia, perhaps, where I have been, but where you have never been. The South of Italy, the place I return to often, as if, in returning, I might find what was there when our people left, and what was left behind.

It is a place that I inhabit in my imagination, though I have never lived there, and it has marked me, for it is the place of our people. Italy, a place that we never visited together, although such a journey might have helped us understand what neither of us understood during your lifetime: how we were shaped by the past, how all that was good, and all that was not good, had its origins in a place that we never experienced together, but that we experienced always.

I take us there in this imagining although we lived our story in suburban New Jersey, a place where I have never seen an almond tree, a place where we never picnicked together alone, a place where we carved the initials of our unhappiness into the gnarled tree trunks of our lives.

Today, though, we are content—blissful, even. How beautiful the trees are, you say, their flowers, so silver-pink, the searing eyes of the individual blossoms seeing that we are together. They are, I say, a transfiguration, a predilection, and a blessing, and I tell you that I am so happy that we are here in this place together.

We eat, and we drink the milk of almonds. And we talk. We have an ordinary, normal talk, about what we did during our day. Mine was filled with writing, reading. (Books about the South of Italy and the life your parents and stepmother left there and, yes, they are helping me at last understand you, understand myself. Understand how you were between two worlds, which both despised who you were, so that you had to become "American," had to bury the Southern Italian in you, had to hate your stepmother for what she was so that you would not hate yourself for who you were. Understand that our people were hungry, always hungry. Understand that they came here so that they could eat enough to fill their bellies.).

Your day, you told me, was full. You had changed the lining in all the cupboards in the kitchen, made a soup for dinner—a nice minestra *(so strange, so wonderful, to me, that you were now cooking the foods your stepmother cooked, as I now cook the foods that she cooked, the foods you despised for their foreignness)—and you sat down in the afternoon to embroider: primulas, roses, poppies on a beige linen ground for the pillows that now decorate my bed.*

Today we do not cut the bread, for we have forgotten to bring our knives. Today we tear the bread with our hands. It is hard, this tearing of the bread, this partaking of it. It is hard because the loaves have a thick, nearly impenetrable crust. Yes, it is hard, we both agree, to break the bread, to tear into it, to get at the tenderness inside. It is hard to break the bread. But it is not impossible.

EPILOGUE: PLAYING THE BOWL

One Friday, I take my granddaughter, Julia, to her toddler music class. She calls the class "Oh my" because these are the first words of her favorite song, "Oh my, no more pie." Whenever she knows she's going to "Oh my" she sings the first line of the song "Oh my, no more pie," over and over again.

When Julia sings, I hear a young voice, but there is something old about the voice, just as there is something old about the child. She is one of those children who look like they are older people locked in childish bodies, one of those children who understand.

On this particular day, the teacher shows the grown-ups how to improvise musical instruments at home: how measuring spoons can be jangled; how measuring cups can be smacked against each other to produce percussive sound.

"See," the teacher says, picking up a cheese grater and playing it with a spoon, "use your imaginations; you don't need to buy musical instruments to make music." The teacher is smiling; she's making music seem like so much fun.

On this day, preoccupied with a piece of writing that has not been very much fun in the making, I am cranky. I think, *This is one message*—that music is fun—*but not the most important message*. The arts, I think, aren't just fun. They're essential. They're bone, flesh, blood, sinew, soul, spirit. And art can be hard, goddamned hard. To make; to witness.

But these are kids, after all.

The teacher dumps little plastic bowls and wooden spoons onto the floor in the center of the room. "Just watch the chidren and see what they do," she says. "Plastic bowls, turned upside down, make perfect drums. You can let them do this at home."

She turns on a recording of African drums, the rhythms insistent, intricate, energizing. The children start moving to the rhythm. They sway and stomp and jump and run. Even I start moving.

One little boy dashes into the center of the circle, picks up a bowl and a spoon, turns the bowl over, starts beating it. Soon, all the children are beating on their improvised instruments.

All, that is, but Julia.

Julia sits in the center of the circle, flips her bowl, takes her spoon, starts stirring. She's stirring clockwise; she's stirring counterclockwise; she's stirring as quickly as the other children are drumming. She's shaking her head and stirring. She's throwing her head back and stirring. She's stirring and tasting and stirring and tasting some more. She's closing her eyes, lost in the stirring. She's pretending to cook as if cooking were all that mattered in this world, as if her life depended upon her cooking, as if the gods cared.

And she's making waffles, sauce, matzo balls, biscotti, scones, she's making pudding, she's making pie, and she's calling out the names of what she's making, and she's tasting what she's making.

So here is this little girl, this little child with a wise face, who seems to have seen all things, to remember all things, this child with her mother's face, and my face, and her mother's mother's face, and my grandmother's face, and her mother's grandmother's face, and the face of every woman in the world. And this child is stirring and cooking and singing through the celebrations, through the pogroms, invasions, bombings, evacuations, emigrations. She's stirring in Russia, in Austria-Hungary, in Puglia, in the Abruzzi, in Campania, and in Sicily. And she's stirring and singing, this child who sees the future, who knows the past, who sees sorrow, sees joy, this wise, wise child, who looks to the future, but who brings back the ancestors.

She stirs and tastes and cooks and tastes and sings, and she sings, "Oh my, no more pie; oh my, no more pie. No more pie. No more pie."

ACKNOWLEDGMENTS

Although this work depends in large measure upon my memories of my grandparents' stories, and upon the recollections of surviving members of my family, most notably my father, the following sources were essential in understanding my family's background and its food history: Nikko Amandonico, *La Pizza*; Luigi Barzini, *The Italians*; Robert J. Casey and W. A. S. Douglas, *The Lackawanna Story*; Dominic T. Ciolli, "The 'Wop' in the Track Gang," *The Immigrants in America Review*, July 1916; Nzula Angelina Ciatu, Domenica DiLeo, and Gabriella Micallef, eds., *Curaggia: Writing by Women of Italian Descent*; Ann Cornelisen, *Women of the Shadows*; Alfred W. Crosby, *America's Forgotten Pandemic*; Hasia R. Diner, *Hungering for America*; Norman Douglas, *Old Calabria*; Barbara A. Driscoll, *The Railroad Bracero*; Donna Gabaccia and Franca Iacovetta, *Women, Gender, and Transnational Lives*; Donna R. Gabaccia, *We Are What We Eat*; Richard Gambino, *Blood of My Blood*; Patience Gray, *Honey from a Weed*; Edvige Giunta and Samuel J. Patti, eds., *A Tavola*; Edvige Giunta, *Writing with an Accent*; Fred L. Gardaphe, *Italian Signs, American Streets*; Jennifer Guglielmo, *Negotiating Gender, Race, and Coalition*; Nancy Harmon Jenkins, *Flavors of Puglia*; Ian F. Haney Lopez, *White by Law*; Dorothy and Thomas Hoobler, *The Italian American Family Album*; Matthew Frye Jacobson, *Whiteness of a Different Color*; Gina Kolata, *Flu*; Maria Laurino, *Were You Always an Italian?*; Frances M. Malpezzi and William M. Clements, *Italian American Folklore*; Jerre Mangione and Ben Morreale, *La Storia*;

Michael J. Meyer, ed., *Literature and Ethnic Discrimination*; H. V. Morton, *A Traveller in Southern Italy*; Michael A. Musmanno, *The Story of the Italians in America*; Bruce Nelson, *Workers on the Waterfront*; Nunzio Pernicone, *Italian Anarchism*; Antonia Pola, *Who Can Buy the Stars*; Katherine Anne Porter, *Pale Horse, Pale Rider*; David A. J. Richards, *Italian American*; Mary Taylor Simeti, *On Persephone's Island*; Pasquale Verdicchio, *Bound by Distance*.

For understanding the history of Puglia before, during, and after my grandparents' emigration, the treatment of farmworkers, and their revolt against landowners, Frank M. Snowden's *Violence and Great Estates in the South of Italy, Apulia 1900–1922* was essential. The facts presented in "Hunger" were largely drawn from this account.

The day I discovered that my stepgrandmother's village had a Web site—www.rodigarganico.com—I most fully realized the distance between her world and mine. 1 journeyed to Rodi Garganico first in cyberspace—and also to my paternal grandmother's village via www.positano.com—before the trip I describe in these pages.

I want to thank the many people who inspired the ideas in this book, and the many people who helped me refine them. Edvige Giunta insisted that I write about my stepgrandmother. And, at a time in my life when I was ill, and uncertain that I could recover sufficiently to write again, Jennifer Guglielmo asked me to write an essay that sparked my interest in my grandparents' past. Suzanne Branchiforte organized an important conference on emigration in Genoa, and invited me to participate. Kym Ragusa shared important insights about the complex nature of ethnicity.

This book was imagined and begun while I was Visiting Distinguished Writer-in-Residence at the University of South Carolina in Columbia, South Carolina. There, many conversations with members of the Department of English (among them, especially Kwame Dawes), the faculty at the College of Education (in particular Alan Weider), and my graduate seminar in memoir helped me believe this book could be written. Robert Newman, past chair of the Department of English, made my visit to USC possible; he listened to my plans for this book, encouraged me to write it, and sponsored readings of my work in progress. Distinguished Writer-in-Residence Janette Turner Hospital, organizer of the series "Caught in the Creative Act," generously invited me to participate in classes, radio broadcasts, and public events, where I refined my ideas.

Vicky Newman may not remember a dinner table conversation in which she helped me untangle a conundrum at the heart of this book, but I do, and am grateful for her insights. Mary Bull's sensitivity to this story, her friendship, and her response to my past work, helped me keep writing. Kimberly Angle, Pamala Barnett, Cassie Premo Steele, Ed Madden, and Anna Moore—all members of a memoir group I belonged to while at USC—listened to a very early stage of the work, and their enthusiastic response indicated that yes, I should keep writing this book. In Columbia, conversations with Allison Askins, Rick Black, Jean Bohner, and Claudia Smith Brinson were also helpful.

This book was finished while I was teaching at Hunter College. I would like to thank, especially, Hunter's president, Jennifer J. Raab, for her enthusiastic support of my work and for the M.F.A. program in creative writing. Sylvia Tomasch, chairperson of the Department of English; Donna Masini, acting director of the M.F.A. program, and my colleagues Harriet Luria, Vita Rabinowitz, Jenefer Shute, and Trudy Smoke all urged me to complete this work. As always, conversations with the students in my seminars in writing at Hunter helped me refine my vision for this book.

My agent Geri Thoma believed in this book from its inception. For this, and for our fourteen-year relationship, I am immensely grateful.

Karen Rinaldi, publisher at Bloomsbury, understood the design of this book and its meaning. I thank her for bringing this book to life and for her perspicacity in editing it into the form in which it now appears. During the revision process, Amanda Katz helped shape the manuscript, refine its meaning, and eliminate its opacities, and for this, I am grateful. Greg Villepique, managing editor at Bloomsbury, led the team that brought this book into being. Julie Metz, designer, took the time to find what I did not believe existed: the perfect picture for the cover. Jolanta Benal read the revised manuscript with care and sensitivity.

Brooke Kroeger and Alex Goren's positive response at a significant stage of the writing helped me continue. Kate Probst, my friend of forty years, has seen me, once again, through the writing of another work; she understands the ups and downs of the stages of my writing process better than I do, and knows just when to gently chide me into returning to my desk. Joshua Fausty's support has been invaluable.

My family—Deborah, Jason, Justin, Julia, Lynn, and Steven De-Salvo—have been a constant source of support and pleasure throughout the years this book was in progress. My grandchildren, Julia and Steven, delight me with their presence, their creative spirits, and their understanding of the power of story to shape our lives.

And, to those to whom I dedicate this book, thanks beyond my powers of expression:

To Edvige Giunta, my writing partner and friend, who has helped me bring it to completion. Without our daily talks throughout the years, our conversations about the writing process, and the essentiality of good cooking to the fully realized life, without her support of Italian American writing and of my previous work, without her understanding of the significance of my family's history, without her insisting that I write about my stepgrandmother, this book would not have been written.

To Craig Kridel, for our Thursday morning breakfasts—which were the heart and soul of my time at USC, and the place where I hammered out the shape and substance of this book—and for so much more. During our conversations at our corner table (over very bad coffee and very good pastries), he helped me refine and shape the meaning of this work, helped me imagine my grandfather's role in it, helped me understand its potential significance when I could not, helped me see that it could, and should, be written.

To Ernie DeSalvo, my husband, the perfect partner for one committed to the writing life; he knows when to ask how the work is proceeding, knows when to avoid the issue entirely, knows when a dish of his specialty—stir-fried spareribs with five-spice powder—is just what this writer needs. Without his urging that I must write, no matter how feebly, while recovering from an illness I believed would sideline me, I would not now be writing.

And to my father, Louis Sciacchetano, for giving me the gift of his recollections of our family's past. Through them, we drew closer, and as I listened to him tell me about the lives of my grandparents, I began to understand my family's past as I have never before. Virginia Woolf once said that it is essential to write the lives of the obscure. Without my father's stories, I could not have written these people's lives. Without him, there would be no book.

A NOTE ON THE AUTHOR

Louise DeSalvo is the Jenny Hunter Endowed Scholar for
Creative Writing and Literature at Hunter College in New York City.
She is the author of numerous critical works and the controversial
*Virginia Woolf: The Impact of Childhood Sexual Abuse on Her Life
and Work*, named one of the most important books of the twentieth
century by *The Women's Review of Books*. Her memoir, *Vertigo*, won the
Gay Talese Award for the best Italian American book published
between 1993 and 1997. Most recently, she has published *Writing as
a Way of Healing: How Telling Our Stories Transforms Our Lives*, and
has coedited *The Milk of Almonds: Italian American Women Writers
on Food and Culture*. She lives in Upper Montclair, New Jersey, and
in Sag Harbor, New York.

A NOTE ON THE TYPE

Linotype Garamond Three is based on seventeenth-century copies
of Claude Garamond's types, cut by Jean Jannon. This version
was designed for American Type Founders in 1917, by Morris
Fuller Benton and Thomas Maitland Cleland, and adapted for
mechanical composition by Linotype in 1936.